LOURDES LIBRARY
GWYNEDD-MERCY COLLEGE
GWYNEDD VALLEY, PA 19437
YO-FBF-885

THE LORD'S PRAYER

22.00-20.71
BV
230
.A966
1991

THE LORD'S PRAYER

A Survey Theological and Literary

Nicholas Ayo, C.S.C.

LOURDES LIBRARY
GWYNEDD-MERCY COLLEGE
GWYNEDD VALLEY, PA 19437

University of Notre Dame Press
Notre Dame London

92752

Copyright © 1992 by
University of Notre Dame Press
Notre Dame, Indiana 46556
All Rights Reserved

Library of Congress Cataloging-in-Publication Data

Ayo, Nicholas.
The Lord's prayer : a survey theological and literary / Nicholas Ayo.
p. cm.
Includes bibliographical references.
ISBN 0-268-01291-1
1. Lord's prayer. I. Title.
BV230.A86 1991
226.9'606—dc20 90-50929
CIP

Manufactured in the United States of America

The book is dedicated to
my grandfather, DR. JACKSON JOSEPH AYO;
and to my father, JACKSON, JR.;
and to my brother, JACKSON, III

CONTENTS

FOREWORD

It is difficult to name another short prayer or piece of devotional writing in the Christian tradition that has inspired more comment than the Lord's Prayer. From Origen and Tertullian in the third century down to writers in our own day as diverse as Leonardo Boff, Simone Weil, and Karl Barth, there has been an undiminished tradition of commentary and paraphrase from all periods of the church's life. The reason for this torrent is not hard to fathom. The Lord's Prayer is, as Saint Thomas Aquinas noted in his own day, the perfect prayer since it comes from the lips of Jesus in response to the apostolic request "Lord, teach us to pray" (Lk 11:1).

But, it might be urged, why yet another book on this prayer? Can even a writer as gifted as Nicholas Ayo add to the insights of—to name a few—John Cassian, Francis of Assisi, Dante, and Teresa of Avila? Distinguished company, indeed. It does not fall to me to speak for the author but my guess would be that he would insist that the significance of a classic is never fully realized; that the classic, as contemporary hermeneutical critics note, always bears a "surplus of meaning." Some of that surplus, further, is only gathered at particular times and from particular points of view. Like the householder of the gospel, each age seeks the *nova et vetera*—old things and new. The conclusion, then, is clear: each age must look again at the classic. This book invites us to join into a meditation on the Lord's Prayer that began in Christian antiquity and continues down to the present day.

There is a further point. The Lord's Prayer is one of those formulaic compositions which the average Christian can repeat, as it were, on automatic pilot. At the liturgy, for example, we all must restrain speed of recitation since the words come to us so easily and with such familiarity. A book like this forces us to stop for a moment to inquire: what do these words mean and—more importantly—what do they mean for *us*?

This work proposes answers to both of those questions. Readers will soon learn under Father Ayo's tutelage that the seemingly familiar words bristle with ambiguities and invite multiple interpretations; indeed, there is at least one interpretive crux that has exercised biblical commentators since the time of Origen. Those vexatious issues get a full ventilation in these pages.

Beyond those questions are the perennial ones that every person of prayer confronts: the origin of the impulse to praise; the tug of the future; the plea for bread; the need for wholeness in the face of temptation; deliverance from the specter of evil. The questions may be perennial but the answers are peculiar to every age which asks them. Like every great classic, the Lord's Prayer both sums up inherited wisdom and urges us forward to further insight and discovery.

It is the conviction of every person of prayer (a conviction ordinarily called *faith*) that the answers are there even when they are provisional or faintly heard if we are ready to speak the words of Jesus and, simultaneously, *listen* to them. Prayer, after all, is as much listening as it is speaking. To that simple but profound challenge Father Ayo's book should come as a welcome companion.

Lawrence S. Cunningham
Department of Theology
University of Notre Dame

ACKNOWLEDGMENTS

The author would like to thank the many people who made this work possible. I am grateful to my immediate family, to my religious family, the Congregation of Holy Cross, and to the University of Notre Dame, and especially the Program of Liberal Studies. The Notre Dame Press and in particular John Ehmann deserve special mention. Barbara Martin, Hao Tran, and Ann Mariani helped me as my student assistants. Sherry Reichold and the several computer operators in the Stenopool gave many hours in preparing the typescript, but I am particularly indebted to Margaret Jasiewicz for her labor and helpful suggestions. I would thank so many people who befriended me in this task: my colleagues Michael Crowe, Stephen Fallon, Philip Sloan, and Michael Waldstein, as well as others such as Berard Marthaler, Daniel Sheerin, and John Quinn. No one gave me more encouragement and useful advice than Carole Roos, whose editorial acumen rescued this book from an obscure style. Lawrence S. Cunningham, who wrote the Foreword, has always been supportive to me.

THE LORD'S PRAYER IN MATTHEW 6:9–13

Our Father who art in heaven

Hallowed be thy name

Thy kingdom come

Thy will be done

On earth as it is in heaven

Give us this day our daily bread

And forgive us our trespasses

  As we forgive those who trespass against us

And lead us not into temptation
(And do not bring us to the test)

But deliver us from evil

(*Roman Liturgy*)

Our Father in heaven,

  hallowed be your name,

  your kingdom come,

  your will be done,

  on earth as in heaven.

Give us today our daily bread;
and forgive us our debts,
as we forgive our debtors;
and do not subject us to the final test,
but deliver us from the evil one.

(*New American Bible*)

THE LORD'S PRAYER IN LUKE 11:2b–4

Father

Hallowed be thy name

Thy kingdom come

Give us every day our journey bread

And forgive us our sins

Even as we forgive everyone who is indebted to us

And lead us to enter not into temptation
(And do not put us to the test)

(*Author's translation*)

Father, hallowed be your name,

Your kingdom come.

Give us each day our daily bread

and forgive us our sins

for we ourselves forgive everyone in debt to us,

and do not subject us to the final test.

(*New American Bible*)

INTRODUCTION

Christians are all familiar with the Lord's Prayer from childhood in most instances and surely from the prayer practice itself, whether in public liturgy or in private piety. Rarely does one stop to study and to study thoroughly the text word by word and line by line as it has been given us in two somewhat different versions by Matthew and by Luke. One often assumes that the Lord's Prayer was well learned once upon a time. After all, the Christian prays the Our Father frequently throughout a lifetime. A deep understanding of the Lord's Prayer, however, may never have been achieved. With the hope that such a study will enrich the believer's appropriation of the Lord's Prayer I have written this book. Precisely because this prayer is so central to our daily Christian life it deserves to be known with the same depth that we wish to know whatever and whomever we deeply love.

My hope is to say something about the fundamentals that pertain in an important way to an intelligent appreciation of the Lord's Prayer. Each line of the prayer, both in Matthew and in Luke, is examined word by word. Each petition is analyzed in itself and in its relation to the other petitions in the prayer. The Lord's Prayer has traditionally been divided into the thou-petitions that address God as such: *Thy* name, *Thy* kingdom, and *Thy* will, and the we-petitions that address God with regard to our need: give *us* bread, forgive *us*, and deliver *us* from every evil. These two groupings, and the introductory invocation of the "Father who art in heaven," are studied both separately and in their inter-relationship. The entire Lord's Prayer, furthermore, is situated in the context of the gospel. The overall review of the Lord's Prayer leads to the conclusion that these few words of Jesus sum up the principal concerns and hopes of Christian faith. Using the resources of the biblical exegete, the church historian, the theologian, the literary critic, and the person of interior devotion and prayerful spirit, I try to write whatever might be said succinctly about the Lord's Prayer that would be helpful to know for an educated Christian of today. In short, this book is an omnibus study of the paradigm gospel prayer.

In addition to my own commentary, in Part Three I offer the commentary of others, ancient and contemporary, from East and West. Then in the last part, I look at the place of the Lord's Prayer in the liturgy and conclude with an overall review of the various readings of the prayer.

From the widespread and fruitful biblical scholarship about the text of the Lord's Prayer I have borrowed heavily. The reader is introduced to the Greek text itself, without needing to have a prior knowledge of Greek. The translation of the Greek is followed through the Latin and into the vernacular, from early English to later English, with care given to the liturgical English with which we pray to this day. A long and elaborate exegesis of the gospel text is offered to the reader. Even the analogues of the Lord's Prayer in the New Testament are noted, so that in every way the Bible itself is used as the first commentary upon the prayer that Jesus taught his disciples how to pray.

Beginning with the Patristic commentaries, which are many, I have borrowed heavily from the ancient commentaries on the Lord's Prayer. Quite possibly no other text is examined so frequently by the early sacred authors of Christian tradition. How the Lord's Prayer has been read through the centuries and how it has been used in the liturgy are part of the history of the prayer itself. I try to do some justice to the various readings of this prayer. To this end I have included an anthology of readings from authors both old and new who have written classic commentaries upon this prayer of prayers.

This study borrows heavily from the theological investigations of the Lord's Prayer that have followed upon the Patristic and Medieval commentaries. Using biblical exegesis, Patristic studies, and theological resources as a guide, I have tried to make some critical distinctions in the reading of the Lord's Prayer that bring out the more defensible meanings of that text. It is not a text without many ambiguities, nor a text which lacks profundity. Hence, there remains room for disagreement, and room for various interpretations of each line and indeed, of almost every word. I try to write a comprehensive commentary that would situate, insofar as this can be done, the Lord's Prayer as a synopsis of the Gospel, as a model of what Christian prayer always centers upon, as a summary of basic religious education, and as a call to active Christian love and service in the world.

I also offer meditative reflections on the spiritual meaning of the Lord's Prayer. These insights emerge from my own research and most of all from my own contemplative prayer experience with the Lord's Prayer. Authors ancient and new have lauded the Our Father as the school of Christian prayer, and they have spoken of it as the perfect prayer. I have tried in my limited and less than perfect way to echo some of that estimation of the Lord's Prayer by my own account of its profound meaning in relation to the general human predicament and in particular to the "good news" in its most essential elements.

I

The prayer that Jesus taught his disciples, and which is given in the gospels of Matthew and of Luke, has been called the Lord's Prayer since the Patristic period when the early Fathers of the church began to study it. The first reference to this title that I would note is in the third-century commentary by Cyprian of Carthage, who was indebted to Tertullian. In Latin the prayer is referred to as the *oratio Dominica*, the Lord's Prayer. Often church documents such as encyclicals are named by quoting the first words of their text. Employing its opening words, the Lord's Prayer is frequently referred to as the Our Father, or in Latin the *Pater Noster*, which is also sometimes written as one word, *Paternoster*, or abbreviated as the *Pater*. One also finds a rare reference to the Lord's Prayer as the "Abba" or the "Abba, Father," a title which follows the wording of the texts in the gospels and in St. Paul (Rom 8:13 and Gal 4:6).

Throughout the history of Christendom, the Lord's Prayer has enjoyed a special place of honor both in the church liturgy and in devotional prayer of every kind. In the literature of the Patristic period it was frequently commented upon and has been the subject of poetry and music through the centuries. Descriptions of the Lord's Prayer abound, but none of them are more penetrating than the very early remark of Tertullian in his third-century commentary on the Pater: "a compendium [breviary] of the whole gospel" (*breviarium totius evangelii*). In perhaps the single most helpful contemporary commentary on the Lord's Prayer, Ernst Lohmeyer takes Tertullian one step further by declaring that the opening words, "Our Father," are "a breviary of the breviary" (*breviarium breviarii*).[1] Schurmann echoes the same insight by noting that the gospel is the context for understanding the Lord's Prayer, and the Paternoster is the context for understanding the gospels.[2] Palmer calls the Pater the "love-song of the Christian world."[3] Marty insists that the Lord's Prayer is "a battle cry, a shout for the end time."[4] Carmignac declares that the Our Father, "despite its severe conciseness, constitutes a perfectly structured poem."[5] Joachim Jeremias calls Matthew's sixth chapter (vv. 5–15) where the Lord's Prayer is given "a catechism on prayer."[6] La Verdiere declares that the Our Father is the "number one prayer for Christians of every age, time and culture."[7] Thirtle speaks of the Our Father as the pearl of prayers and the fountain-prayer, from whence flow all other Christian prayers.[8] Atherton Lowry calls the Pater the prayer of prayers. Thomas Aquinas in the *Summa Theologica* (II, II, 83, 9) refers to the Paternoster as the perfect prayer.

Peter Chrysologus declares that the Our Father gives "the theme of praying, the subject matter to ask for, and the norm of making petitions."[9] Augustine writes to Lady Proba about how personal prayer is related to the Pater Noster: "Whatever be the other words we may prefer to say . . . we say nothing that is not contained in the Lord's Prayer, provided of course we are praying in a correct and proper way. But if anyone say something which is incompatible with this prayer of the Gospel, he is praying in the flesh, even if he is not praying sinfully."[10]

This succinct prayer of some thirty-eight words in the Greek of Luke's gospel gives the believer the mind of Jesus and the soul of the gospels. It is a prayer to be learned by heart, and its impact as a total prayer is more than the sum of its several parts. While in the early church the prayer was memorized in order to be publicly recited before the congregation of the faithful at the moment of baptism, the prayer is not properly speaking a rote prayer. The words cannot contain the fullness of the reality. The Lord's prayer is Jesus Christ as a living prayer, and the Christian in imitation of him. It is more of an ideal of all prayer, a pattern of praying, an outline for many prayers, a paradigm of every prayer, the archetype of the heavenly prayer, guaranteed to be heard because it is the prayer of the Lord Jesus to the Lord God of Jesus, who is Abba, Father. In the divine office of morning and of evening prayer, when all of the petitions of the faithful have been expressed aloud, the Our Father is recited by the congregation as an overall "collect," which gathers, includes, and summarizes any and every supplication for the goods that lead to salvation in God. Every prayer is enfolded in this unique prayer that is the essence of all prayer, and which Jesus gave us in answer to his disciples' request: "teach us how to pray." Indeed, the whole gospel might be imparted in its substance "by merely explaining, in their completeness and life, the terms of the Lord's Prayer—the first words taught to children all over the Christian world."[11]

We read in the gospel that we should love the Lord God "with all our mind, and all our heart, and all our strength." We have suggested that the Lord's Prayer is a précis of the whole gospel, the distillation of the substance of the good news. Before we pray this seminal Christian prayer we must listen to it. Most of us learned the words long ago, and no longer ask of them any questions. Gregory of Nyssa wrote that the Lord's Prayer did not "yield a meaning that can easily be understood at first sight."[12] Schurmann calls the Our Father a "school of prayer" and a "school of life." It remains the task and the privilege of the reader to embody this unique prayer of Jesus in his or her own way of life. Every Christian is invited to live their prayer, and to pray their life. We are to be both Martha and Mary, both watching and praying. We are to cry the gospel with our lives; we are to proclaim the Lord's Prayer with our very way of being. The Paternoster gives us the challenge of Christian faith, and not just of an ancient sacred text. Jesus is prayer incarnate. The imitation of Christ is not in words alone, but in lives that acknowledge the Lord Jesus as a living person with whom we love our brothers and sisters in this world. Manson writes that "the best exposition of the Lord's prayer is the life, death, and resurrection of him who taught it."[13] Thus in this commentary I hope to instruct the heart as well as the mind.

II

The Our Father is known to most people through their life of prayer. The liturgy in particular has kept alive the gospel text as a prayer widely recited and deeply loved. The version in public prayer and customarily known by heart takes its text from Matthew's gospel (6:9–13) although it has come to us by a different chain of translations. In the prayer life of the church, the Pater Noster in Matthew has prevailed over the shorter version in Luke. It is often recited with the addition of the doxology, "For Thine is the kingdom and the power and the glory," long familiar to Protestants and more recently also to Catholics. The doxology itself is not found in the oldest and best gospel manuscripts. It is thought to be a liturgical practice of ancient tradition, which is found in later gospel manuscripts because the scribes were already so familiar with the Our Father as spoken in liturgical worship that they unthinkingly added the doxology to the text they were copying. That text with its particular English translation, "forgive us our trespasses," for example, was established with the *Book of Common Prayer* in 1549 by Henry VIII, who wished to establish a useful standardization of the liturgical texts.

There are variations in the Lord's Prayer as it is found in Matthew and in Luke. One need not think of these two versions as either authentic or inauthentic. They give us two portraits of the same prayer, just as the gospels offer four portraits of the same Jesus. Although our liturgical prayer is derived from Matthew's gospel, the Lucan text sheds light on what might have been the substance of the prayer in its original oral form before either gospel was written.

Those original words, whether in Hebrew or an Aramaic, remain lost to us, although attempts have been made to reconstruct a probable text. Public prayers at the time of Christ were usually said in Hebrew, but it seems even more likely that Jesus prayed the Our Father in Aramaic. The eighteen benedictions and the Qaddish of the Jewish synagogue liturgy may be influential in the eventual wording of the Lord's Prayer. The search for the historical Lord's Prayer is reminiscent of the search for the historical Jesus. That there was a historical Jesus we know; that the canonical gospels give the substance of his words and true portraits of his person we believe. That we can discover the very words of Jesus and the exact biographical details of his activity when he walked the roads of Palestine is far more problematical.

Whether or not Jesus ever spoke the Lord's Prayer as concisely as we have received it from the evangelists is debated. Some commentators think that the Lord's Prayer is the very composition of Jesus, translated, adapted somewhat, and edited in minor ways and for pastoral reasons by the Christian community and its evangelists. Joachim Jeremias argues that the Abba Pater gives us the very words of Jesus.[14] Abba is found in every major source of the New Testament—the four gospels, the lost Q source, and two of Paul's principal letters. Other commentators think that Jesus left his disciples an outline for prayer in his various teachings, and that this outline took on the form of the topical sentences we recognize as the petitions of the Lord's Prayer. The written text was not made to be the last word. The argument is made that the beatitudes were constructed in just this way from more ample moral instruction given by Jesus on many occasions. The evangelist then concentrated the teachings of Jesus and gave them a dramatic setting in the story of the sermon on the mount, or that of the disciples receiving the Lord's Prayer as a finished composition in answer to their specific request, "teach us to pray." One theory argues that the evangelists distilled the teachings of Jesus into a compact form more easily memorized. In actual practice Christian prayer would expand upon the outline given in the Our Father. A similar theory has been argued with regard to the writings of Homer and of Moses. An elaborate and disparate tradition of stories existed originally in an oral tradition, which later was written down and edited in a more concise and fixed way.

In a similar vein, we wonder whether the Lord's Prayer is the prayer of Jesus himself which he shared with the disciples or the teaching of Jesus about how the disciples should pray. Did Jesus who is without sin and who knew the Father in an unique, intimate, and consummate way pray in yet a different manner? Whether or not we have an actual prayer composition by Jesus or only a distillation of his various actual prayers and teachings, and whether or not Jesus made this particular prayer the essence of his own prayer or primarily instruction for the disciples may be questions for which we have no definitive answer. If Jesus did not compose the prayer, however, it remains unlikely that he prayed the Lord's Prayer as we now know it. If he composed it, and if he also used it, we have an astonishing treasure beyond description. If he neither composed it nor used it, we still have given in these words the mind and heart of Jesus, the soul of his prayer life, and his express will and direction for how we are to pray. Of course, Jesus surely prayed "Abba" (Father) with a poignant awareness of the living God, and that one word of his remains shorthand for the entire prayer of Jesus, what Christians understand finally by the "Lord's Prayer."

As the result of these reflections one might conclude there are multiple versions of the Lord's Prayer. Perhaps this is the prayer Jesus dictated, either as a polished composition or a rough outline. Perhaps this is the prayer Jesus prayed aloud, or at least taught. Perhaps the Lord's Prayer is the prayer of the early Christians, as the community of Matthew prayed, and yet again differently as the community of Luke prayed it. There is indication of some liturgical adaptation and of a particular formulation of the Lord's Prayer, and its use in the sacraments of baptism and eucharist is noteworthy. One commentator writes, "To pretend to recall stages of change and revision which were bound up with the manifold life of the Church of the First Days, liturgical custom among Christian Hebrews and Christian Hellenists, the influence of oral tradition and written memoranda both in Aramaic and Greek, catechetical instruction, the teaching of Missionaries and other converts leaving the Mother Church at different times, the influence of usage and of translation in the Churches which they founded, would be a palpable absurdity. An approximation to such a work is all we can hope for."[15]

The Lord's Prayer we say today is based on the gospel versions and descends from the liturgical usage of our predecessors. It need not exclude the accommodation of that prayer to the situation that we live in today. After all, it is the risen Jesus who taught the disciples how truly to pray, and it is the gift of the Holy Spirit whom Jesus ever sends into our midst that teaches us today how to pray. Prayer is not merely the repetition of an ancient formula and a meaning exhausted long ago; it is ever new while showing no discontinuity with the instructions of the Lord and the abiding essence of the gospels.

III

Mark's gospel includes what may be a truncated version of the Lord's Prayer: "When you stand to pray, forgive anyone against whom you have a grievance, so that your heavenly Father may in turn forgive you your transgressions" (11:25).[16] One might also cite in the first gospel the account in the garden of Gethsemani, where Jesus prays to the Father (Abba) and asks only to do his Father's will (Mk 13:32–42). The gospel of John surely has all the elements of the Lord's Prayer without giving one complete rendition. The seventeenth chapter of his gospel is often cited as his equivalent of the Pater Noster. The Lord's Prayer in Matthew and in Luke, however, remains normative. A comparison of the Lord's Prayer in Matthew with the one in Luke should enable us to comprehend more amply the prayer in its biblical richness. As in the exegesis of any biblical text, the reader should keep the context uppermost in mind. Thus the Lord's Prayer must be seen against the background of the entire gospel of which it is a part, and in particular the reader must take the passages immediately before and after as a commentary upon the prayer text by the evangelist himself.

There is widespread agreement that Matthew's gospel has a Jewish audience and Hebrew context, whereas Luke wrote for a gentile audience and within a Greek context. Matthew positioned the Lord's Prayer in the sermon on the mount, that reconstruction of the teaching of the Law from Mt. Sinai by the one greater than Moses. Matthew would have been familiar with a Galilean dialect, and he sets his sermon on the hillside in Galilee. Luke would have known the Aramaic and Greek of the world beyond Israel, and he sets his text at the outset of the journey of Jesus to Jerusalem. That journey toward the holy city of God takes up more than half of Luke's gospel, and the pilgrimage motif would be understood by all peoples with religious sensitivity.

The immediate context in Matthew's version of the Lord's Prayer is Jesus delivering his lengthy sermon on the mount. Within that sermon which touches on many moral concerns of the new Moses teaching the new Israel, there is a section (6:1–21) concerned with religious practice: almsgiving (vv. 1–6), prayer (vv. 7–15), and fasting (vv. 16–21). The Lord's Prayer is inserted as an example and model of prayer immediately after two preliminary remarks: (1) the prayer of the disciple of Jesus is not a display for the approval of this world as the hypocrites do, and (2) it is not to be a babble of repetition of divine names in hope of gaining a hearing with the divinity as the pagans do. Rather, "This is how you are to pray," and the Lord's Prayer immediately follows (vv. 9–13). By way of commentary upon the prayer itself, Matthew adds the postscript, "If you forgive others their transgressions, your heavenly Father will forgive you. But if you do not forgive others, neither will your Father forgive your transgressions" (v. 14). Later on in the sermon on the mount there are comments relevant to the petition "Give us this day our daily bread." Thus, "Ask and it will be given to you; seek and you will find; knock and the door will be open to you. . . . Which of you would hand his son a stone when he asks for a loaf of bread, or a snake when he asks for a fish?" (7:7–11), and, "seek first the kingdom [of God]. . . . Do not worry about tomorrow; tomorrow will take care of itself. Sufficient for a day is its own evil" (6:33–34). Similarly, the petition of the Lord's Prayer that asks forgiveness as we forgive receives some elaboration in texts such as: "For as you judge, so will you be judged, and the measure with which you measure will be measured out to you" (7:2), and "Do to others whatever you would have them do to you" (6:12).

The immediate context in Luke's version of the Lord's Prayer is Jesus' response to a request from the disciples who speak to him right after he has finished his own prayer. They wish themselves to learn how to pray, and to have Jesus teach them as John taught his disciples. The implication may well be that they sought a distinctive prayer that would characterize the disciples of Jesus as particular in their way of praying. Jesus says, "When you pray," and the Lord's Prayer immediately follows (11:2b–4). This episode devoted to the Lord's Prayer follows the story of Martha and Mary, in which Mary who sat at the feet of Jesus and listened to his words is praised for "she has chosen the better part and it will not be taken from her" (10:42). The story of the listening Mary and her serving sister, Martha, is immediately preceded by the parable of the Good Samaritan, when Jesus clearly praises the active mercy of the Samaritan and urges his listeners to "Go and do likewise" (10:37). Clearly, the Lord's Prayer is not a refuge from service to one's neighbor, nor is active service to the needs of even Jesus himself an exemption from the necessity to enter a prayerful quiet and to hear the word of God. The Lord's Prayer itself receives some implicit and subsequent commentary that immediately follows in Luke's story of the persistent knocking on the door for the loaves of bread (11:5–8) and the further outcome that ends with: "If you then, who are wicked, know how to give good gifts to your children, how much more will the Father in Heaven give the holy Spirit to those who ask him?" (11:23). Later in the eighteenth chapter of Luke, there is another long commentary on prayer that contains the example of the persistent widow (vv. 1–8) and the tender story of the Pharisee and the Publican, whose prayer concludes: "O God, be merciful to me a sinner" (vv. 9–14).

In Luke's gospel, Jesus himself is frequently portrayed at prayer before all the important events of his life. He prays at his baptism (3:21), during his ministry (5:16), during the night before choosing the twelve apostles (6:12), before asking his disciples to profess their faith (9:18), before his transfiguration (9:28), before teaching his disciples to pray (11:1), for Peter not to lose faith (22:32), during his agony in the garden of Gethsemani (22:41), for forgiveness for those who crucified him (23:34), and finally at his death on the cross (23:46).[17]

The question arises in the comparison of Matthew and Luke about which version of the Lord's Prayer is the closest to the words of Jesus, and hence most authentic. Matthew makes several additions which Luke lacks. The consensus among scripture scholars favors the addition by Matthew of phrases not found in Luke, rather than subtraction by Luke. Few commentators think that either evangelist would be willing to subtract from the tradition of the Lord's Prayer in any substantial way. Adding to it might be acceptable insofar as it provides a liturgical setting and a commentary upon the prayer. Redaction or editing might also be acceptable because it provides an emphasis and clears away misunderstanding. Matthew seems to take themes from elsewhere in his gospel and insert them in the Lord's Prayer to adapt its meaning to a Jewish audience. Thus Matthew can be seen as adding to his source, rather than adding to the independent Lucan tradition.[18] Rabbinic prayers of this period frequently began with the liturgical phrase: "Our Father in heaven." Matthew adds to the opening invocation, the third of the thou-petitions, and to the last of the we-petitions. While he added, he also preserved the original formulations of the text. In Matthew the old and the new exist side by side, much as the two creation stories in Genesis are preserved rather than one story made from them both. Luke, on the other hand, seems willing to adapt the formulation of the Lord's Prayer in a few places where the needs and circumstances of the Christian Greek community in their liturgy might be served. Matthew would seem to be more poetic and more Semitic in his phrasing; his Lord's Prayer is not edited so much as it is amplified for liturgical use. Consequently, Luke may be closer to the original Aramaic of the Lord's Prayer in his spare phrasing, despite the fact that in a few places Luke was willing to reword the tradition for his own time and place. More details of the text of Matthew and of Luke are given in the appendix.

THE LORD'S PRAYER IN MATTHEW

(additions not found in Luke in italics)

Our Father *who art in heaven*

Hallowed be thy name

Thy kingdom come

Thy will be done

On earth as it is in heaven

Give us this day our daily bread

And forgive us our trespasses

As we forgive those who trespass against us

And lead us not into temptation
(And do not bring us to the test)

But deliver us from evil

THE LORD'S PRAYER IN LUKE

(with Lucan words or phrases in italics)

Father, hallowed be your name,

Your kingdom come.

Give us *each day* our daily bread

and forgive us our *sins*

for we ourselves forgive *everyone* in debt to us,

and do not subject us to the final test.

(*New American Bible*)

IV

Unless one understands the *eschatological* approach, and what that word means in theology, one will have difficulty praying the Lord's Prayer as a specifically Christian prayer. Eschatology overshadows the whole New Testament; it is imperative to grasp its role in order to see distinctively how the Our Father is more than an Old Testament prayer. The *eschaton* in Greek refers to the last things or the last days. An eschatological approach suggests the final times, the resurrection of the dead, the fulfillment which God has already begun on earth in Jesus Christ who is Lord and who will judge the world. In that sense, eschatology means *realized* eschatology, or Christian eschatology. Christians do not await the coming of the savior, nor do they await salvation. Christ has come; our hopes are now fulfilled, even though Christ will come again. Thus, Christians await the *second* coming of Christ, and they pray the Our Father in the light of the first coming of the Lord. One biblical scholar summarizes the eschatological reading of the Lord's Prayer:

> The Christian community of the first century, anxiously expecting the Second Coming, prays that God will completely

> glorify His name by establishing His kingdom, which represents the fulfillment of the plan He has willed for both earth and heaven. For its portion in this consummation of time, the community asks a place at the heavenly banquet table to break bread with Christ, and a forgiveness of its sins. A titanic struggle with Satan stands between the community and the realization of its prayer, and from this it asks to be delivered.[19]

Because it is so important to understand the eschatological approach to the New Testament in any consideration of the Lord's Prayer as the paradigmatic Christian prayer, some examples may be in order. If someone has won a cash lottery and yet awaits the actual delivery of the money, her poverty has been taken away. She is now rich, though she has not fully appropriated that richness until a future day. But it would be inappropriate not to rejoice now in her salvation. The impossible has happened; the outcome is no longer in jeopardy; the good fortune is an event that cannot be undone. Or to take another example, if the sun comes out after a deluge and a rainbow is hung in the sky, then the rains are finished. God has promised. It will take time for the flood waters to drain, and in the meantime one may know misery, but the sun is shining, hope has come, and there is an end to the deluge. A promise has been given; a new day dawns; the promise has been fulfilled. When the magi come to adore the infant Jesus in Bethlehem, they do not see a baby only, but a king. People of faith do not see this tired and sinful earth only, but the kingdom of God in their midst. People of faith do not see only their bodies which are moral, vulnerable, and sinful, but transfigured and whole human beings in a state of grace and with the expectation of glory. Thus Christians are a eucharistic people, always and everywhere giving thanks to God, because Jesus Christ has been given to us, and in him God has given us everything. We are rich. The sun is shining. The only Son and King of kings has come to us. And we Christians in our eucharist hold in our hands, not only a piece of bread, but also the body and blood of the Lord Jesus, present to us here and now in this great sacrament. An eschatological reading of the Lord's Prayer is a sacramental reading; it sees in the words not only signs of what we pray to happen, but the reality that we celebrate of what has already happened and because of which and in which we now pray.

The gospel of Matthew throughout shows a concern with the eschatological kingdom of God. Eschatology deals with the final times and the ultimate triumph of God. While it is disputed how much Jesus himself anticipated these final times in his own lifetime, it does seem clear that the early Christians reflected in Matthew's gospel did emphasize the coming of the Lord in glory. The end was thought to be near, and ultimate concerns pressed. The kingdom had come in Jesus who was Lord, and who would come again, and soon. In the Lord's Prayer, Matthew prefers a particular Greek verb tense that lends support to the theory that this prayer was read in the light of the once-and-for-all coming of the kingdom. Accordingly his concern for bread may be read as a concern for the bread of the heavenly banquet, the bread of tomorrow given to us this day. Matthew's call for forgiveness centers on the reconciliation that prepares for the final judgment. Matthew's conclusion of "deliver us from evil" (more likely, "the evil one") speaks to this concern with the endtime and the final and terrible struggle between Satan, the seeming lord of this world, and Jesus Christ, the almighty king of the universe.

In Matthew's Greek text of the Pater, he consistently puts the verbs in the aorist tense, which was reserved for events that happen once and for all. We do not have such a distinction in English. In Greek, the aorist tense would be used appropriately to say: "she *lost* her eyesight." What happened in the past cannot be undone and perdures in the present. The aorist tense would not be used appropriately to say: "she *lost* her fortune," since she may regain her wealth someday. Thus Jesus Christ has come once and for all; the world is saved once and for all, even though the effects of salvation must be realized more fully in the unfolding of history until the end of time. That is why the Lord's Prayer as said by Christians is not just a petition for future blessings; it is a praise for the blessings already given and even now being given as one prays. Because the Son has come we know that the Father (Abba) is even now, before our prayer begins, engaged to love us in Jesus Christ, to give us life, to provide our every bread, and to deliver us from the final evil which is separation from the infinite God whose life is our only life. The Our Father is not just a theological prayer that acknowledges a God to be worshiped and human beings in need of life support. It is a historical prayer rooted in a historical event that happened once and for all. In that moment heaven and earth were united, the divine and the human were commingled without loss of the integrity of either; the mystery of One and the Many was manifested in the child born of the virgin Mary. The Lord's Prayer rises and falls with the gospels, and Christianity rises and falls with the historical event that is the Lord Jesus Christ who suffered under

Pontius Pilate, was crucified, died, and on the third day rose again to judge the living and the dead.

The gospel of Luke throughout shows a concern with the present-day kingdom of God and long-term human history. For example, Luke adds the word *daily* to this important text in the synoptic gospels: "If anyone wishes to come after me, he must deny himself and take up his cross *daily* and follow me" (9:23). Action in progress or a state of affairs that continues indefinitely was usually indicated by the present imperative in Greek. In the Lord's Prayer, Luke uses this tense in several verbs, lending support to the theory that his Lord's prayer was read in the light of the ongoing kingdom of God that is within us here and now. As the history of the church lengthened and the endtime did not arrive, Christians had to adapt more rootedly to a lifetime of prayer and service. As one commentator put it: the faithful "were the called, but not yet the elect." Admittedly, the kingdom in its finality was given even now in faith, yet the concerns for daily bread were necessary for the building up of the final coming of the kingdom of God. Luke's concern for bread may be read as a concern for the bread of our everyday life, given to us not only *this day* but also *everyday*. Similarly, Luke's call for forgiveness of *everyone* centers on the reconciliation that is required for brothers and sisters to live together, even when we sin against each other every day.

In the comparison of the Lord's Prayer in Matthew and Luke, we might conclude that Matthew emphasizes the final-times perspective, and Luke the ongoing point of view of sacred history. Thus, Matthew emphasizes the lordship of the infinite God, who makes the world from nothing and whose will is sovereign to bring about all events. In the mystery of God all time is but a moment. Matthew represents the eternal point of view. Luke emphasizes Immanuel, the God-with-us, the Lord who became flesh in our history, and for whom the unfolding of creation must be given time and space. This *Many* of creation belongs also to the sovereignty of the *One* and infinite God who mysteriously sustains eternal life in this world. We cannot understand how anything outside of God should exist at all. Yet creation does exist, and we know we cannot act outside the providence of the almighty God. Matthew more readily represents the eternal point of view—the One. Luke represents the temporal point of view—the Many. Together Matthew and Luke represent eschatology and everyday, tomorrow and now, transcendence and immanence, the mystery of the *One and the Many*.

PART ONE
The Thou-Petitions

OUR FATHER

LUKE'S LORD'S PRAYER begins simply with "Father." Matthew adds "Our" Father, "who art in heaven." One might ask what is added to our understanding by the word "our," explicit in Matthew, and no doubt understood in Luke, who introduces the Lord's Prayer to the community of disciples with "Lord, teach *us* to pray." How is the Father *our* Father? Matthew's version is given during the sermon on the mount, when the new Israel is being instructed by the new Moses, who is Jesus Christ. The context surely reminds us of the ancient people of God, now gathered together under the leadership of the Lord God, and related by spiritual and social bonds of the most extensive kind. The Lord's Prayer is thus the prayer of the Christian *people,* the people of God and the fulfillment of Israel. Christians emerging from a Jewish background would have no problem in saying *our* Father, God of *our* people. Were Father read as an address to the one God similarly understood by Jews as well as Christians and other religious people, it would make it easier to open the prayer to all of humanity. However, only Jesus knew the Father intimately as the only Son. While Father read exclusively does indicate this unique relationship of the incarnate Son of God for Christians who acknowledge him Lord, all human beings remain the beloved children of this same Father, who "so loved the world that he gave his only Son, so that everyone who believes in him might not perish but might have eternal life" (Jn 3:16). The Father is known especially in the Son, but the Father knows and loves every human being. "See what love the Father has bestowed on us that we may be called the children of God" (1 Jn 3:1).

An argument could also be made that *our* (Father) establishes not only a vertical relationship with God, but also a horizontal bond among the members of the praying community. Since they have in common a Father in heaven, they are brothers and sisters to each other on earth. The sisterhood of man is based upon the fatherhood of God. Consider this text of John: "If any one says, 'I love

God,' but hates his brother, he is a liar; for whoever does not love a brother whom he has seen cannot love God whom he has not seen" (I Jn 4:20). The disciples said to Jesus: "Teach *us* to pray" (Lk 11:1). St. Cyprian points out the communal prayer character of the Christian community at Pentecost when "All these devoted themselves with one accord to prayer, together with some women, and Mary the mother of Jesus, and his brothers" (Acts 1:14).[1] When the Lord's Prayer was used in baptism ceremonies in the early church, the new member who claimed God as Father by reciting the Lord's Prayer by heart also claimed the Christian community as new brothers and sisters. Thus *our* Father included both a vertical claim from this rebirth by holy mother the church from a common Father in heaven, as well as a horizontal claim to a spiritual family bond among Christians. The communion of saints is based on the fatherhood of God in which we all share and the brotherhood with Jesus, which is particularly realized when we are gathered as one to pray the Our Father. The later use of the Lord's Prayer before the communion in the Roman mass lends support to the contention that this prayer functions in the Eucharist as the verbal equivalent to the kiss of peace. Here is the kingdom of God now and yet to come—one faith, one bread, one body. Here and now Christians in prayer are profoundly united in the one mystical body of Christ, and yet still waiting for the fulfillment when they shall fully "be one, as you, Father, are in me and I in you, that they also may be in us, that the world may believe that you sent me" (Jn 17:21).

Both Matthew and Luke begin the Lord's Prayer by addressing the *Father*. Luke does so without any qualifier. Since it is more acceptable to add to a sacred text by way of elaboration than to subtract, one might conclude that Luke's form of address is the more original. Another explanation, however, could be given. Luke is less Jewish in writing style than Matthew and thus less ornate in his prayer language which is addressed primarily to gentiles. Jesus himself simply addresses his Father with the Aramaic word, "Abba." That word was the common speech of a son to his father. Although how exceptional this address may have been is disputed, "Abba" implies some informality and intimacy, just as the English word "dad." The evangelists use both the Aramaic, "Abba" and the Greek "Pater," which probably reflects how Jewish and non-Jewish Christians were side by side in prayer. Thus Mark writes in the Gethsemani account: "*Abba, Father*, all things are possible to you. Take this cup away from me but not what I will but what you will" (14:36). And Paul writes: "For you did not receive a spirit of slavery to fall back into fear, but you received a spirit of adoption, through which we cry, *Abba, Father!*" (Rom 8:15) and again "And proof that you are children, God sent the spirit of his Son into our hearts, crying out, *Abba, Father!*" (Gal 4:6). Although Paul does not refer to the Lord's Prayer in his epistles, it is thought that these texts that invoke the Father with the words of Jesus himself in his prayer were perceived as an allusion to the Lord's Prayer and our special relationship to his Father, when we pray "Father."

The word Father is a metaphor for God. Those aware of the limitations of all metaphorical language and women in particular who are aware of the patriarchal connotations that a masculine word may arouse have questioned the viability of the Lord's Prayer as now spoken. Can it any longer be appropriate to speak of God in any gender-specific language? Should one at the least include female metaphors for God on an equal basis with male metaphors? "Our Mother who art in heaven" may sound strange in the recitation of the Lord's Prayer, but theologically there is no reality of a mother or father which God does not display in an eminent way. One might alternate male and female metaphors as occasion and appropriateness indicate. It has also been suggested that we abandon gender-specific metaphors of God in our prayer. "Our parent who art in heaven" avoids the partial nature of all gender-specific metaphor. Parent as a word, however, carries none of the emotional depth of mother or father. It has also been suggested that in prayer one avoid concrete metaphor as much as possible. Abstract words for God exclude no one. "Our Creator who art in heaven" captures much, but not all, of the meaning of "Our Father." Abstract words in praying to God, however, seem to distance God. The genius of the Bible has been its willingness to talk to God in humanly intimate terms, person to person.

Even if one were to suggest an acceptable alternative to "Our Father," the problem of usage and acceptable change is not easily resolved. William Tyndale gave us in the Lord's Prayer the word "trespasses," which while almost obsolete today continues to be said by both Catholics and Protestants worldwide. The tradition seems too long and strong to recommend a change of words. Perhaps one might instead reclaim the meaning of this word for the contemporary Christian. If Tyndale prevailed for almost five centuries, what hope is there to undo that word which of all the words attributed to Jesus in the gospels may be the one authentic word that Jesus himself actually spoke? Would feminists themselves, men or women, want to be deprived of such a unique treasure? Perhaps the issue remains one of reclaiming the univeral meaning of the word "Abba, Father." The discussion of Father that here follows tries to achieve a universally acceptable understanding of the word. It may well be beyond the scope of this book and the skill of this author to resolve to everyone's satisfaction the issue of gender language in the Lord's Prayer.

Prayer in the Old Testament referred to God as Father. Pagan religion also knew of a father-god, the source and sovereign of the gods. What is unique about the Lord's Prayer is that God is addressed directly and intimately as Father. Origen claimed he could find no instance in the Old Testament of God being addressed directly as Father.[2] Augustine in his commentary on the sermon on the mount claims that nowhere in the Bible is Israel directed to pray to God as "our Father." That God is compared to a father, or named Father, presents nothing new. After all, God was the source of all that existed, and God brought forth creation much like a father brings about the existence of his children. The biology of ancient times thought that the father was the generator, the direct source of tiny human beings that dwelt within the father's seed. The mother was as earth in which the seed once sown could be nourished and brought forth as the fruit of the womb. Moreover, the father was the provider, the line of defense and the origin of wealth and subsequent well-being. God the Father was the God of creation and the God of providence, the source of all life and the commonweal. Familiar are the images of God as Father seeking the obedience of sons. In lamenting the rebelliousness of Israel against its Father in heaven, Jeremiah typically writes: "I thought how I would set you among my sons, and give you a pleasant land, a heritage most beauteous of all nations. And I thought you would call me, 'My Father,' and would not turn from following me" (3:19). See also Is 63:16.

Mothers were, of course, equally hard-working contributors to the family, but in a patriarchal society they were dependent upon the male figure for the support of their lives. Moreover, pagan fertility rites so common in agricultural lands had debased the image of woman into an impersonal source of a pervasive fecundity. Childhood dependence upon a mother's care did not readily reflect the *transcendent* God that the Hebrews tried so hard to detach from the pagan gods, who personified the human powers of life and death, and whose role in human events was confused. Nevertheless, images of God as a mother can be readily found in the scriptures: "Can a woman forget her suckling child, that she should have no compassion on the son of her womb? Even these may forget, yet I will not forget you" (Is 49:15). Jesus laments over Jerusalem that refused him: "how many times I yearned to gather your children together, as a hen gathers her young under her wings" (Mt 23:37). The spirit of Wisdom and the whole Sophia tradition touching on Jesus amplifies the feminine aspects of God. We have not yet discovered the extent of the feminine side of God unsung in the biblical texts.[3]

The objection to God as Father comes from the one-sidedness of this metaphor. God does not have a body and thus cannot be either male or female, or only male or female. God imaged as dominantly masculine in behavior, however, will translate into a patriarchal God. God our Father thus appears to validate a patriarchy that does not grant equality to other human beings, women most of all. Reading the invocation by Jesus of Abba-Father, not as a descriptive label for God or just a metaphor to explain the ways of God, may help mitigate this problem of a patriarchal image of God. Jesus does not describe God as Father, but *calls* God "Abba, Father." Jesus uses Father as a proper name of the hidden God, heretofore known only with that ineffable name no one could utter (YHWH). Consider this text which undercuts patriarchy: "Call no one on earth your father; you have but one Father in heaven" (Mt 23:9). That Father in heaven, whom Jesus addresses by the name known only to the Son, is not a patriarchal father. The prodigal father of the Prodigal Son parable (Lk 15) comes out of his way to welcome home his wayward younger son, and goes out of his house to soothe his angry elder son. No patriarchal father would have put himself on the same level with either the sinful son or the dependent son. Jesus himself lived a life of not lording it over any man or any woman. Unlike a patriarch, he lorded it over nothing and over no one. He took as his own neither wife, nor children, nor goods, nor even a place to lay his head. He did not own; he did not dominate; he did not claim others were his servants. He proclaimed that he did not "come to be served but to serve and to give his life" (Mt 20:28). He died in loyalty and love of his own on the Calvary cross. He died in humiliation, crucified, and impotent to safeguard his own life.

The question might be asked, do we pray to the Father just as Jesus prayed to his own Father? Jesus says in John's gospel: "I revealed your name [the Father's] to those whom you gave me out of the world" (17:6). And further on: "I am going to my Father and your Father, to my God and your God" (20:17). Jesus promised the Samaritan woman at the well that "the hour is coming when you will worship the Father neither on this mountain nor in Jerusalem . . . the hour is coming, and is now here, when true worshipers will worship the Father in Spirit and truth; and indeed the Father seeks such people to worship him" (Jn 4:21–23). Does Jesus bring us into the same intimacy and relationship, insofar as possible, that he enjoyed with his Father in prayer? Surely the unique bond of Jesus with the Father is more than that of the disciple, but in an analogous way we pray "through him, with him, and in him." In support of our praying with the same prayer of Jesus, which is acceptable to the Father, consider this text from John: "Amen, amen, I say to you, whatever you ask the Father in my name he will give you. Until now you have not asked anything in my name; ask and you will receive, so that your joy may be complete" (16:23–24).

The prayer of Jesus in the Garden of Gethsemani would seem to give a glimpse of his soul naked before God. Jesus addresses the Father intimately, totally willing to be of one will with his Father. His Father's house, his work, his will, his glory were the purpose of Jesus' life on earth. Jesus cleaves to God's will. His Father sent him into the world, lived in him always, loved him even now, and would raise him up. In his human and earthly moment of seeming abandonment, he prays with a passion the secret proper name of his Father: *Abba*, Father! Behold my life. Look at my predicament. You alone are sovereign. All of human life is in your hands and follows your will. My Father, my Father, do not forsake me. Without you my life is nothing; my being has no relationship but to you. Jesus prays: "My God, my God, why have you forsaken me?" (Mk 16:34), and at the last "Father, into your hands I commend my spirit" (Lk 23:46). Jesus begins his manhood with the announcement in the temple that he "must be in his Father's house" (Lk 2:49), and he ends his life commending his spirit to his Father in the hope of his restoration to his Father's house.

This prayer of Jesus to his Father is radical and foundational prayer for us. It places us in the awareness that we are nothing without God, and can do nothing without God's sovereign will. Jesus draws us to pray alongside of him, to speak to the Father in the words he gave us, and to hope equally that our life is enfolded in God who would save us from all our enemies in this world. As Gregory of Nyssa says, the Fatherhood of God suggests accessibility and intimacy with God.[4] God our Father is not the hidden and unapproachable awesome God revealed to Moses on Mt. Sinai amid thunder and lightning. That God is almighty and able to do all things we have long known; that God is equally ready to save us we have not known as well. Jesus embodies that gracious love of the

Father and reveals it forthrightly in the Lord's Prayer. John Ruskin writes of the Our Father:

> And to declare that we have such a loving Father, whose mercy is over *all* His works, and whose will and law is so lovely and lovable that it is sweeter than honey, and more precious than gold, to those who can "taste" and "see" that the Lord is Good—this, surely, is a most pleasant and glorious good message and *spell* to bring to men—as distinguished from the evil message and accursed spell that Satan brought to the nations of the world instead of it, that they have no Father, but only "a consuming fire" ready to devour them . . . .[5]

If God is spoken of as our Father, Christian lives should show their parentage. If God our Father is holy, then we as God's children must display holy lives. Without this spiritual resemblance we sinners incredibly claim for Father the Lord who is without sin. Jesus complains to his sinful enemies: "You belong to your father the devil" (Jn 8:44). In our failure to live lives of virtue, we do not imitate our Father in heaven. "So be perfect, just as your heavenly Father is perfect" (Mt 5:48). Then only will our lives proclaim what our lips say when we call upon "our Father." "So be imitators of God, as beloved children, and live in love . . ." (Eph 5:1).

WHO ART IN HEAVEN

ACCORDING TO MATTHEW, the remainder of the initial invocation of the Father is "who art in heaven." God as a spiritual being was understood by ancient religion as God of light. Light could be seen, but not touched or weighed. It would seem to be the most spiritual of substances. Light came from the heavens, and thus the sky-God represented a God of sky-light who transcended the mundane and earthly. The heavens were distant like the stars whose light was eons away from us. The God in heaven was a spiritual and transcendent being. God dwelt in inaccessible light. When Jesus, the beloved only Son of the Father in heaven, is baptized, we read: "heaven was opened. . . . You are my beloved Son" (Lk 3:21–22). In his *Commedia* Dante writes: "Our Father in Heaven, not by Heaven bounded / but there indwelling for the greater love / Thou bear'st Thy first works in the realm first-founded."[6]

Heaven, of course, should not be read as a locality or physical space, since only bodies are in place. Heaven is a spiritual condition of transcendence proper to God. Heavens in the plural was a shorthand for far away and beyond this world. The rendition "our heavenly father" rather than "our father *in* heaven" perhaps avoid the illusion that God is *in place*. "Our *Father* who art *in heaven*" was thus a way of saying the Lord was both close (father) and beyond (in heaven), both immanent and yet transcendent. "The Lord has established his throne in the heavens, and his kingdom rules over all" (Ps 103:19).

John Henry Newman speaks of the implications of the transcendent God:

> I mean then by the Supreme Being, one who is simply self-dependent, and the only Being who is such; moreover, that He is without beginning or Eternal, and the only Eternal; that in consequence He has lived a whole eternity by Himself; and hence that He is all-sufficient, sufficient for His own blessedness, and all blessed, and ever-blessed. Further, I mean a Being, who, having these prerogatives, has the Supreme Good, or

> rather is the Supreme Good, or has all the attributes of Good in infinite intenseness; all wisdom, all truth, all justice, all love, all holiness, all beautifulness; who is omnipotent, omniscient; omnipresent; ineffably one, absolutely perfect; and such, that what we do not know and cannot even imagine of Him, is far more wonderful that what we do and can. I mean One who is sovereign over His own will and actions, though always according to the eternal Rule of right and wrong, which is Himself. I mean, moreover, that He created all things out of nothing, and preserves them every moment . . . It [theology] teaches of a Being infinite, yet personal; all-blessed, yet ever operative; absolutely separate from the creature, yet in every part of the creation at every moment; above all things, yet under every thing.[7]

The Hebrew scriptures labored mightily to establish this one and transcendent God, the God above all creation, the God so much other that God's name could not even be spoken, for this God was not merely one more being among many beings. Somehow the transcendent one God of the Old Testament was beyond all things and beyond all gods.

The Jewish Christians, however, for whom Matthew wrote, might have misunderstood the "Father" to be "our father Abraham," or even God who dwells in Zion and thus might seem to dwell on earth. Matthew warns his readers: "Call no one on earth your father; you have but one Father in heaven" (23:9). The Father in heaven would remind the Jewish-Christian reader of the transcendence of God who cannot be contained on earth, and whose saving and heavenly providence extends now beyond the chosen people to all humanity, to whom Israel was sent as prophet. Matthew's gospel chooses to address God as "heavenly Father" frequently. Rabbinic prayers of that time often addressed God as "Father in heaven." In contrast, the gentile Christians, for whom Luke wrote, would not need such a qualification in order not to identify the Father with an incomplete fulfillment of the Old Testament promises.

A study of the sixth chapter of Matthew reveals that the author refers to "your heavenly Father" (6:1) immediately prior to the Lord's Prayer, and to "your heavenly Father" who "also will forgive you" (6:14) immediately following the Lord's Prayer. Did Matthew add heavenly ("who art in heaven" in the RSV) to Luke's simple "Father"? Was the evangelist following the lead of the passages that surround the Lord's Prayer in his own gospel? Jewish prayers did not mention the revealed name of God, and heavenly was a circumlocution for the divine name. Thus, it can be argued that heavenly Father is a Hebrew way of saying "God our Father." Probably in Matthew we are dealing with adaptations to the Jewish prayer conventions. As it turns out, "our Father who are in heaven" is a convenient reminder that our God is both near and far, both Many and One, both immanent and intimate as a *Father*, and transcendent and utterly other *in heaven*.

HALLOWED BE THY NAME

"WHAT'S IN A NAME? That which we call a rose / By any other name would smell as sweet." Shakespeare's Juliette would go to the heart of the matter; she would love the man and not the family name that was forbidden to her. Are names, then, arbitrary labels or do they at times carry hidden meaning? In Genesis we read that Adam "gave names to all cattle, and to the birds of the air, and to every beast of the field" (2:20). Did these names reflect the very nature of the new creature named, or were they convenient labels for referring to this one and not that one? American Indians do not name a child until they perceive something about the child's way of being that seems to presage his destiny. The happy smiling child, for example, might be called "laughing waters." In the Bible a name given by God to someone had reference often to the person's destiny. The name referred to the mission or role they were to play in the history of the kingdom of God. Thus, Abram is called out of Mesopotamia to become the father of the new nation of God's people, and his name becomes Abraham. Jacob becomes Israel, because his life was a contending with God. Simon becomes Peter, because upon this rock (*petra*) Jesus Christ will build his Church. Saul, when converted to Christ, become Paul, the last but not least of the Apostles. Who can forget the story of Zechariah, struck dumb by an angel until the moment when he would be able obediently to say of his newborn son: "John is his name." And Jesus is called the Christ (the anointed one, the Messiah).

In the episode of the burning bush, Moses asks: "If I come to the people of Israel and say to them, 'The God of your fathers has sent me to you,' and they ask me, 'What is his name?' What shall I say to them?" God would not give a name to Moses but said to him: "'I am who I am' sends you" (Ex 3:13–14). The infinite God is beyond the limitation of any verbal name. Unbounded is God's Being and ineffable God's nature. That "name" of God given to Moses remained unspeakable in Hebrew worship. They wrote the sacred tetragrammaton, YHWH, but they spoke a more general name for God *Adonai* when they read the scriptures aloud. That word comes down to us in its translations as the English word Lord. But the proper name of God escapes us. The intimate name of God is God's being. God does not have a name; God is God's name, as God is God's knowing, loving, and so forth. God is not a subject to whom various qualities can be added. God is already everything. We do not ask what God exists? God is not one God among many gods. God is infinite. Similarly, we cannot ask what name God has. God cannot have one name among many; God is without limiting name. And in the Lord's Prayer, the hidden name of God, that which carries the weight of the boundless mystery of God, is *Father.* It is the name given God by the only Son, and "no one knows who the Son is except the Father and who the Father is except the Son and anyone to whom the Son wishes to reveal him" (Lk 10:22). And in John's gospel Jesus says: "I made known to them your name . . . that the love with which you loved me may be in them and I in them" (17:26).

In the Commandments that Moses gave to Israel, rooted in the revelation of the mysterious name of God, the second commandment reads: "You shall not take the name of the Lord your God in vain" (Ex 20:7). To have access to God's name, however poorly, was to be tempted to abuse it. God's name is holy in itself, but we abuse it in our rage or ignorance. To call upon God's name for revenge and evil purpose was to be careless of the privilege. God was holy, and the name of God was equally holy. It must be kept holy by anyone daring to use the name of God in any way. Israel was given access to God by being given something of the hidden name of God. We can address someone only if we know his or her name. To call upon the name of God is to enter into the mystery of God, and to know the power of God as well, whose word is always effective. God's word is always heard and always creative. His words do not describe; they prescribe. "Let there be light; and there was light" (Gn 1:3). Therefore, God's name must be kept holy.

Knowing the name of someone creates privileges and obligations. Only those who are intimate with us know our name in a way that exceeds its usefulness as a label to distinguish us from someone else. Only friends are given access to the inner thoughts of another that allow them to say the name with a profound communion behind it. Lovers often coin nicknames for each other because the previous name, known by so many other people, cannot carry the weight of the new discoveries prompted by mutual love. In many languages, such as French, there is a formal pronoun for direct address (vous) and a more intimate one (tu) for family and cherished friends. That God talks to us at all signifies how beloved we are, for God thus wishes to enter into an ongoing conversation with us. Revelation in the scriptures means precisely this. God chooses to reveal God's self in giving us God's name to invoke, for the inner secret of God and the name are one and the same. Thus, Jesus knew the Father's name in prayer and in deed: "I came in the name of my Father" (Jn 5:43) and the "works I do in my Father's name" (Jn 10:25). To this Father Jesus introduces his disciples. God's name remains wonderful, and to call upon it an enormous privilege. No wonder that the eucharistic liturgy introduces the Lord's Prayer with the phrase: "we *dare* to say, Our Father."

Does the hallowing of the Father's name constitute a prayer petition for God's holiness to be made manifest in the world and especially in humankind, or does it consist in a doxology? If the former, the text might be paraphrased: may your glorious works be recognized by everyone and be manifest to all creatures. If the latter, the line might be paraphrased: glorious is the name of the Father; glorious is God as God alone. Read as a petition, "hallowed be your name" is a request for something to happen that has not yet happened; as a doxology, the text is a declaration that yearns for God to be glorified as God before making each and every human request. Recall the doxology of the seraphim in Isaiah: "Holy, holy, holy is the Lord of hosts; the whole earth is full of his glory" (6:3). In Ezekiel we read: "I will prove the holiness of my great name" (36:23). Should we read "hallowed be your name" as this kind of recognition of the infinite One, the creator, who is acknowledged before praying any petition that the Many need to bring before God? Because we are creatures, however, we must ask for everything, including our need to come to recognize the holiness of God's name. Perhaps the knowledge of God is the one necessity that underlies all our specific requests for partial goods. Schurmann goes so far as to declare that the hallowing of the Father's name is the "essence of the Lord's prayer."[8]

The word hallow is an earlier form of the English word holy. Halloween is a shortened form of Hallows-evening, or the vigil of All Saints (All Holies) Day, when the souls of the dead were thought to roam this earth. The Greek word in the Lord's Prayer is *hagiasthēto*, which in its roots means a-earthly, or unearthly, that is, holy. Unearthly, purified, sacred, and unapproachable is the name of God. The burning bush is a holy setting for the theophany to Moses, for fire cleanses, consumes, rises to heaven as incense smoke. The verb is in the aorist tense, which suggests the holiness of the name of the Father once and for all, in a final and consummate way. In Greek, this tense was traditionally employed for reference to the sacred and divine.[9] The mood in English (and also in the Latin *sanctificetur nomen tuum*) implies *would that* thy name be hallowed. This form of the verb is a common Semitic device that avoids having to use the name of God. Thus instead of saying, "May you, O God, glorify your name," the sentence is turned to "May your name be hallowed," and by implication, hallowed by God. Consequently, whether or not the second line of the Lord's Prayer is the first of a series of petitions or a doxology, it is not primarily about human activity but about divine. If we ask God to tend to God's own cause and interest, that kind of petitionary prayer very closely resembles a doxology that praises God for the sovereign accomplishment of the divine purpose. If we are asking God to hallow God's name in us and to tend to our human cause and interest, that kind of prayer remains properly a petition. But in both instances it is the work of God we extoll. Mary prayed: "My soul proclaims the greatness of the Lord; my spirit rejoices in God my Savior" (Lk 1:47). In short, we do not wish to create God in our own image, using God's name as a way of hoping to manipulate the Almighty according to our ego-centered will. We want to let God be God.

Both Greek and Latin commentators on the Lord's Prayer widely agree that hallowed means glorified. God does not need to be sanctified, or made holy, but rather to be recognized as already awesome, either in human consciousness, or in the moral freedom of human beings, or both. To hallow the name of God is to recognize the great sovereign deeds of God in the creation of the world and its ongoing providence, and the redemptive deeds of Jesus Christ our Lord in his enfleshment through maiden Mary, his passion on the cross, and his resurrection and ascension to the right hand of the Father. We praise God's mighty deeds in our midst and thereby hold God's name as holy and awesome. In Matthew's gospel we read: "Your light must shine before others, that they may see your good deeds and glorify your heavenly Father" (5:16). And in John, "Holy Father, keep them in your name that you have given me, so that they may be one just as we are" (17:11). St. Ignatius would have his followers in the Society of Jesus do everything for the greater glory of God—*Ad Majorem Dei Gloriam*.

The Father is glorified by God's work in us, and not by our independent initiative before God. In the Torah we read: "Be holy, for I am holy" (Lv 11:44), and in Matthew we read: "So be perfect, just as your heavenly Father is perfect" (5:48). Ethics follows metaphysics; action follows being. Human beings who claim God as Father should be holy as God is holy, in witness to the relationship to their Father whom they thus resemble. In short, as Cyprian says, act like sons and daughters. To give all initiative to God means that God is glorified in us and not by us. Even our prayer is God's gift to us. In John's gospel Jesus prays: " 'Father, glorify your name.' Then a voice came from heaven, 'I have glorified it and will glorify it again.' " (12:28). We affirm in the Lord's Prayer that the name of God must be honored as already holy and awesome, always and everywhere. Thereafter we conclude that we should keep ourselves holy and glorify God's name in the deeds of our moral life as well as in our words of praise and worship. As Cyprian pointed out long ago, the name of the Father is hallowed "not because we wish for God that He be hallowed by our prayers, but because we seek from the Lord that His name be hallowed in us."[10] It is not religious rhetoric that counts but the praise embodied in works of justice and love. However, recognition of the glory of God and the holiness of the Father's name remains the dominant motif, rather than the ethical exhortation of human behavior, which can do nothing without God who sustains its every effort and indeed its very beginning. The Lord's Prayer is first of all a declaration of who the Father is, and only secondarily a recognition that human freedom must be enlisted in the unfolding of God's sovereign providence. Doxology and moral demand, sovereign providence and human freedom, are here thus reconciled. God who is the origin of all our good deeds brings them also to conclusion. To God be the glory, and in the end may God be all in all, and God's name hallowed.

One might conclude our consideration of this line of the Lord's Prayer by asking how invocation of the Father is related to the name that is hallowed. It can be argued that the name to be hallowed is precisely the name of the Father. In that sense, the prayer is peculiarly though not exclusively Christian and Trinitarian, bound up with the Father of Our Lord Jesus Christ. Another question might be asked. Is the *Father* a shorthand for the one God of Jew and Christian alike who is active and provident in our midst, and the *hallowed name* a reference to this same Father's infinite and awesome divine being? Does the *Father* represent the creator, infinite source of all being, and the *hallowed name* the mystery of the God who has no need to be creator other than the incomparable freedom of loving? Is holiness of being the source of fatherliness in activity? Does the name of the Father represent God turned toward this creation in a universal embrace, wishing to be known as Father by all humankind? Does the "hallowed" nature of this name contrastingly preserve the inaccessibility of the heavenly Father who cannot be known in an infinite way by any creature, howsoever elevated to friendship with God? There are suggestive questions, and I am inclined to answer them all in the affirmative, without wishing to suggest that the discussion is exhausted. The mystery of God is always and finally the mystery of the infinite One that created "in the beginning" by calling into existence the Many of creation. "Our Father who art in heaven, hallowed be thy name" invites the Father to finish what the Father has begun. Be our Father, hallowed in name. Be about the fulfillment of this love story. Accomplish the Kingdom of God to come.

THY KINGDOM COME

THE LORD'S PRAYER petitions that the Father's kingdom come. The implied request is that the kingdom might come as soon as possible and as fully as possible. The Greek verb tense suggests the advent of the kingdom once and for all in a final and consummate way. The mood in the English verb is subjunctive (and also in the Latin *adveniat regnum tuum*), implying *would that* your kingdom come. Here again is the common Semitic usage that avoids out of reverence using the name of God. Thus, instead of saying, "May you, O God, bring your kingdom to come into this world," it is "Thy kingdom come."[11]

The thou-petitions of this first half of the Lord's Prayer are not connected by conjunctions. This is unlike the we-petitions in the second part of the Lord's Prayer which are linked with "and": give us our daily bread *and* forgive us our sins *and* deliver us from evil. The three thou-petitions follow each other like a litany, like the famous sentence attributed to Julius Caesar: "I came, I saw, I conquered." Similarly in the Greek: your name be hallowed; your kingdom come; your will be done. The question might be raised whether this suggests three more or less parallel and synonymous versions of *one* petition. The hallowed name of the Father, the kingdom of God, and the will of heaven amount to the one mystery of God's salvific work in the created world. Do the thou-petitions amount to claiming may God be God in God's love for this world?

An eschatological reading of the thou-petitions tends to see each one of them as a variant form of the Christian's hope and perennial petition that God's reign be established on earth once and for all. Only when the kingdom comes in its consummate perfection will the name of the Father be fully hallowed. The emphasis is thus upon the final time and the ultimate victory and sovereignty of God. Then the Father's name will be fully hallowed, the kingdom completely come, and the will of God done to perfection on earth and in heaven. So considered, the three thou-petitions are variations on the one theme of the final coming. Christians would easily have prayed the Lord's Prayer in the light of the risen Lord Jesus, whose kingdom was soon to come to those "who will not taste death until they see the Son of man coming in his kingdom" (Mt 16:28). Their cry was *Maranatha*: "Come, Lord Jesus!" (Rv 22:20 and I Cor 16:22), and that simple prayer might sum up the thou-petitions succinctly. In Matthew's scene of the last judgment we read: "Come. . . . Inherit the kingdom prepared for you from the foundation of the world" (25:34).

The *regnum gloriae*, the kingdom of glory, is the kingdom of God in its final fulfillment, when "God himself will always be with them [as their God]. He will wipe every tear from their eyes, and there shall be no more death or mourning, wailing or pain, [for] the old order has passed away" (Rv 21:4). The kingdom of God will become the kingdom of heaven as this world will pass away. "Thy Kingdom come" thus becomes a way of praying for the final judgment and the second coming. The petition would be a way of praying for whatever is needed now so that that final and glorious day may come soon. That judgment is upon us; be ready for it. That fulfillment is coming; rejoice in it. Christ the King in the city of God, the kingdom prepared by the Father from all eternity, would be the answer to this second thou-petition. Let God be recognized in God's infinite being (your name be hallowed) *and in God's infinite doing* (your kingdom come), and also in the freedom of humans and angels who are ever encompassed by a sovereign providence and grace (your will be done, on earth and in heaven). Granted God's comprehensive salvation will one day be manifest in all its glory, yet God's irresistible grace is always and everywhere, even now, though hidden in this world. In sum, the Lord's Prayer in these opening petitions yearns for the revelation of who God is and what God does. The Paternoster prays in effect that the kingdom of God may come quickly: "Then comes the end, when he hands over the kingdom to his God the Father, when he has destroyed every sovereignty and every authority and power. For he must reign until he has put all his enemies under his feet. The last enemy to be destroyed is death . . . so that God may be all in all" (I Cor 15:24–28).

In this eschatological reading of the kingdom petition, God remains the infinite One, who is everything and does everything. Just as the Hebrews shouted the *alleluia* in praise of God (praise Yah!), Christians hallowed the name of the Father of Our Lord Jesus Christ, King of kings, whose kingdom will never end. Insisting that God is God, however, never denies that the creation does exist and is not God, and that human freedom does exist and is not the divine will. Creation enjoys its own being; human freedom its own doing. And yet, the creature cannot exist apart from God, and human freedom is always in the hands of God. Nonetheless, one must also enter the perspective of the creation that is not God. Particular in time and in space, human history is layered with individual freedom, partial strategies, chance events, and constant change. The kingdom of God on earth can be readily related to this Many of creation just as the hallowed name of the Father is related to the divine One.

Origen's advice about this petition was to persevere in prayer, because the kingdom of God was both now today and then to come. "Thy kingdom come" thus becomes not only a request for the triumph of God in that final day, but also a recognition that right now and *everyday to come* is within the holy providence of God, today as well as on *that day.* "For behold, the kingdom of God is among you" [within you in some translations] (Lk 17:21). God's name is hallowed on earth and in heaven to the extent that human beings worship God in recognition, praise, and service. Martin Marty suggests that to pray for the coming of the kingdom is to ask the Father for everything, in the hope that whatever we need God will provide in the kingdom come.[12] We read in Matthew how to avoid anxious prayers: "All these things the pagans seek. Your heavenly Father knows that you need them all. But seek first the kingdom [of God] and his righteousness, and all these things will be given you besides" (6:32–33).

"Thy kingdom come" recognizes that the Father's plan is worked out in the kingdom of justice and peace announced by and embodied in the Son, Jesus Christ. In that reign of God, the blind see (Lk 7:22). That kingdom is one of tending to the needs of one's neighbor, whom one can see, as well as loving the God whom one cannot see. *Ora et Labora*; work and pray. "You shall love the Lord, your God, with all your heart, with all your being, with all your strength, and with all your mind, and your neighbor as yourself" (Lk 10:27). In Plato's *Republic* Socrates yearns for a world where justice prevails, both in the internal and moral kingdom of the individual's freedom wherein both body and soul play their proper and integrated role, and in the external and political kingdom where what is rightly owed to each person is given in a responsible way. Plato speaks of the reign of justice. Paul writes of the reign of grace to the Romans: "Let not sin reign" (6:12). And Jesus proclaims: "Now the ruler of this world will be driven out" (Jn 12:31). The coming of the Lord's kingdom is involved with our being the continuation of the loving voice and healing hands of the savior, who upon the cross was crowned, but with only suffering in this world. "This is the King of the Jews" (Lk 23:28). The risen Jesus is the kingdom come now, the very beginning of a new heaven and earth. Therefore, as Cyril of Jerusalem points out, we pray that the Father's name be hallowed *in us*, that the kingdom come *in us*, and God's will be done *in us*.[13]

In some of the manuscripts of the Lord's Prayer, especially in eastern church texts, this petition for the coming of the kingdom is worded as a request for the coming of the Holy Spirit. "May the Holy Spirit come upon us and purify us." Tertullian in the West and Gregory of Nyssa and Maximus the Confessor in the East in their commentaries on the Lord's Prayer give witness to the substitution of the coming of the Holy Spirit for the coming of the kingdom. Nyssa writes "For what Luke calls the Holy Spirit Matthew calls the Kingdom." Most commentators believe this so-called Marcion interpolation is a liturgical gloss of the early church. In its use of the Our Father in baptism rites, the fusing of the coming gift of the Holy Spirit in the sacrament and the text of the Pater then solemnly recited by the catechumen would be readily understood. In Luke's gospel, there is a probable similar early-church interpolation at the end of his prayer sequence, where we read "how much more will the Father in heaven give the *holy Spirit* to those who ask him?" (11:13) for the more contextual line "will give *good things* to those who ask him" (Mt 7:11, which is the parallel passage).

A few commentators think that this interpolation in the Lord's Prayer may go back to something Jesus himself said. There seems no way to establish this reading, however, and the "kingdom come" manuscripts do predominate. It is true that the kingdom of God inaugurates the direct reign of God, who now gently rules through the Spirit dwelling in our hearts, rather than through a vicar outside us, such as the Old Testament Law or even the natural law in our sinful condition. It is also worth considering that all prayer petitions reduce themselves to a request for the Holy Spirit. Given the Spirit who is life itself, what more could be asked? "If God is for us, who can be against us?" (Rom 8:31). The epiclesis, the calling down of the Holy Spirit, in the eucharistic prayer shows a similar emphasis upon the descent of the Spirit of God as the essence of the power of the sacrament. The bread can become life-giving bread, and the body of Jesus Christ, only if the life-giving Spirit in response to the prayer of the church, which is the mystical body of Jesus, comes down upon this bread and the people assembled to receive it.

THY WILL BE DONE

DOES DOING THE WILL OF THE FATHER represent a plan of action in order to bring about the kingdom? This petition about the will of God on earth as in heaven is found only in Matthew. Does Luke miss a new meaning by not including this line? Or has Matthew added something, and how significant is this petition? Does the third thou-petition repeat in a redundant way what is already stated with "Thy kingdom come"? If the line is tautological, then Luke may have been omitting only what seemed inessential. If the line is more crucial, Matthew may have included a petition that should not be overlooked.

Those who favor the eschatological reading of the thou-petitions in the first half of the Lord's Prayer tend to see all three petitions as variations on one and the same motif: may God be God and show forth his wisdom and sovereignty over all creation. Accordingly, "thy will be done" is not a moral demand placed on human beings so much as another declaration of the sovereignty of God who moves this world. Think of the final lines in Dante's *Commedia* about the divine will as the love "that moves the sun and stars." The fulfillment of the divine providence does not depend upon the ethical decisions of human beings; their freedom is included in the divine plan that always precedes free will and sustains its exercise at every turn. Many of the first English translations of the Paternoster read "thy will be *fulfilled*." Krister Stendhal concludes succinctly that this third petition is "a prayer to God—not a disguised moral injunction or admonition."[14] Jesus himself identified his own free will with the salvific and sovereign will of his Father: "Because I came down from heaven not to do my own will but the will of the one who sent me, that I should not lose anything of what he gave me, but that I should raise it [on] the last day. For this is the will of my Father, that everyone who sees the Son and believes in him may have eternal life, and I shall raise him [on] the last day" (Jn 6:38–40). See also John 5:30.

Those who favor the here-and-now everyday approach to the thou-petitions of the Lord's Prayer rather than the eschatological argue that our doing the will of God is essential for the coming of the kingdom. God will not save the world without our cooperation. Tertullian points out that although God does always accomplish what the Almighty wills, nonetheless we must do the will of God, which is our salvation.[15] Human liberty is not just apparent; it is genuine moral freedom. "Not everyone who says to me, 'Lord, Lord,' will enter the kingdom of heaven, but only the one who does the will of my Father in heaven" (Mt 7:21). Our contribution towards the advent of the kingdom remains crucial. By doing the will of God we give flesh and blood to the coming to life of the kingdom. "So also faith of itself, if it does not have works, is dead" (Jas 2:17). Cyril of Jerusalem urged the newly baptized to purify themselves to be worthy of the kingdom.[16] "This is the will of God, your holiness" (I Thes 4:3). The kingdom come on earth depends upon the will of the Father being done on earth. The gift of God's grace creates a demand that we accept it and make it fruitful by our own choice, even though all virtue depends upon God in its beginning and its end. Richard Dillon argues that the entire sixth chapter of Matthew, where the Lord's Prayer is located, urges moral behavior and responsibility as the only proper response to the kingdom of God given to us and even now within us.[17] Do we not pray later in the Lord's Prayer: forgive us *even as we forgive*? In a parallel way, we might pray thy kingdom come even as we thy will make done.

To do the will of God is to collaborate with the creator in the cosmic work of love. The will of God, however, is never opposed to our own best interest. Any conflict is only an apparent one. No higher dignity accrues to human beings than to be an instrument of divine love in what they do with their life. Human beings are not the slaves of God but co-creators of the good and collaborators in solidarity with God. In the depth of the human heart an enormous self-giving love waits to be discovered and set free. God's will is also our own heart's secret desire. "This is the will of God, your holiness" (I Thes 4:3). Martin Marty argues that we must not say "thy will be done" as a prayer of resignation to the will of God judged as inimical to our own welfare. Rather we must shout "thy will be done" as a battle cry, a battle for God's sovereignty in our hearts and in our whole world. "The Christian seeks the peace of victory" not of reluctant acceptance of the inevitable.[18] The good must triumph in us and in the world, and only then God's will is done.

A reader of the gospels cannot but notice the similarity of "thy will be done" with the Gethsemani narratives. Often the will of God being done requires the strength to accept suffering. The absence of an explicit "thy will be done" in the Lucan Lord's Prayer might be explained by noting that the agony in the garden already contains the substance of this particular prayer petition. Did Matthew then add to the Lord's Prayer precisely by taking the other extended example of Jesus praying aloud that we have in the synoptic gospels, and inserting into the Lord's Prayer the crucial line, "not as I will, but as you will," from the Gethsemani account? The Greek text (*thelēma genēthēto*) is identical in the Gethsemani account of "thy will be done" (Mt 26:42) and in the Lord's Prayer (Mt 6:10). Or, conversely, was the Gethsemani episode built up by taking material from the Lord's Prayer? We find in the garden prayer the "Abba, Father" form of divine address and the "watch and pray that you may not undergo the test," a passage which so resembles the "lead us not into temptation" (or "put us not to the test") of the Paternoster. After all, there were no sound recordings of the words Jesus prayed in Gethsemani and of what he said to his Father. Even if he prayed aloud, the disciples, we are told, were all asleep. Did the evangelist therefore import a text into the paradigmatic prayer of Jesus in the garden story by borrowing from the quintessential prayer of Jesus? It was in that vein, before the passion narrative, that Jesus taught his disciples who asked him how to pray. In the psalms we also read: "But the steadfast love of the Lord is from everlasting to everlasting upon those who fear him, and his righteousness to children's children, / to those who keep his covenant and remember to do his commandments" (103:17–18).

Let us look at the Gethsemani narratives more closely. "Father, if you are willing, take this cup away from me; still, not my will but yours be done" (Lk 22:42). Or consider Mark's version: "Abba, Father, all things are possible to you. Take this cup away from me, but not what I will but what you will" (14:36). Is "not what I will but what you will" a prayer that the eschatological will of the Father for the salvation of the world go forward or is it a reference to Jesus' moral decision to obey his Father? Or both? Does the Father's providence embrace the crucifixion as the divine plan of redemption, or does the Father's will adapt to the crucifixion and so write straight with crooked lines? In some way does the prayer of Jesus include both the transcendent will of the Father and the human will of Jesus brought into harmony? Does Jesus mainly affirm the wisdom of the Father in the events of this world, or does the will of God have a directly personal challenge for Jesus at that moment? Does Jesus embrace the cross in acceptance of what cannot be avoided, or with recognition that the cross is his vocation mysteriously given him by his loving Father? In short, does the Gethsemani episode represent a worshipful recognition of the sovereignty of his Father over all of human history or an ethical triumph of the obedient will of Jesus? Or both? Consider the conjunction of the divine will or plan and the will or purpose of the human life of Jesus when he declares: "My food is to do the will of the one who sent me and to finish his work" (Jn 4:34).

In conclusion let us argue for both the will of God and the will of Jesus united in the recognition that the human heart's desire at its depth is precisely the will of God for the salvation of all flesh. The greatest miracle of God's sovereign will is the conversion of the human heart. Greater even than creation from nothing is the transformation of human free will from sin to grace. God works our salvation without denigrating the integrity of our freedom. God overcomes the handicap that is our sinful heart, already reluctant to do God's will. From a negative condition God's almighty freedom creates our freedom to say yes to God's will. That choice remains ours, while yet all God's, just as our very existence and being is truly ours and entirely from God and in God. Thy will be done says: O God, do not delay to include us in your kingdom, for outside your kingdom we remain nothing and no one. God willing we shall one and all respond to the Lord who called us out of nothing to dwell with the living God in inaccessible light. In the light of the resurrection, Paul would write: "In all wisdom and insight, he has made known to us the mystery of his will in accord with his favor that he set forth in him as a plan for the fullness of times, to sum up all things in Christ, in heaven and on earth" (Eph 1:9).

ON EARTH AS IT IS IN HEAVEN

THE USUAL INTERPRETATION of this second half of the third thou-petition assumes the will of God is being done in heaven and needs doing on earth. The will of God is already accomplished by the angels in heaven, and by the stars and planets of the heavens. In the Greek, heaven is singular in this petition, but plural in "Our Father who are in heaven" (the heavens). The reference in both cases is to the world beyond this terrestrial life. What appears lacking is that this sovereign will of God in heaven may equally prevail on earth over the will of humankind and a recalcitrant planet. Cyril of Jerusalem writes: "As in the angels thy will is done, so on earth be it done in me, O Lord."[19] Origen related the earth to heaven, as the flesh to the spirit, or body to the soul. When the Spirit triumphs over the flesh and God's will is done on earth "there will be no more earth but everything will have become heaven." When the will of God is not done and sin prevails, "the sinner is earth, and if he does not repent, will become earth." [20] Augustine follows him in this line of interpretation, and remarks that earth is related to heaven as sinners are to saints,[21] or as unbelievers to the faithful in Cyprian.[22] The will of God will be done on earth as it is in heaven when the sinful members of the church on earth are brought into the holy church in heaven. Those who do not do the will of the Father show in their lives the fruits of the flesh, which are "immorality, impurity, licentiousness, idolatry, sorcery, hatreds, rivalry, jealousy, outbursts of fury, acts of selfishness, dissensions, factions, occasions of envy, drinking bouts, orgies, and the like." But, those who do the will of the Father show in their lives the fruits of the spirit, which are "love, joy, peace, patience, kindness, generosity, faithfulness, gentleness, self-control" (Gal 5:19, 22). If one follows this line of thought, the *on earth as in heaven* will refer simply to the will of God which should be done on earth as it is already done in heaven. When earth is made sinless, earth will be heaven. In sum, may earth and heaven be as one under God.

Let us suppose that all three of the thou-petitions are variations on the one eschatological theme: may God be God. Were that so, then the will of the Father must be done both on earth and in heaven, then the kingdom must come both on earth and in heaven, and the name of the Father be hallowed both on earth and in heaven. Origen long ago thought that the earth-heaven clause referred not just to "your will be done" but to all three preceding petitions.[23] The Tridentine Roman Catechism (1566) also teaches that heaven-earth refers to all three petitions that precede it.[24] In Matthew we read: "Father, *Lord of heaven and earth*, to you I offer praise; for what you have hidden from the learned and the clever you have revealed to the merest children" (11:25).

Another reading of on earth as in heaven is possible. Consider that the heavens might also need to submit to the divine will. The powers and principalities above this earth are still to be fully overcome. Paul writes: "despoiling the principalities and the powers, he made a public spectacle of them, leading them away in triumph by it" (Col 2:15). Origen suggests that the heavens also need to be brought into the kingdom of God. He points to this text in the gospel of Matthew: "All power in heaven and on earth has been given to me. Go, therefore, and make disciples of all nations, baptizing them in the name of the Father, and of the Son, and of the holy Spirit, teaching them to observe all that I have commanded you. And behold, I am with you always, until the end of the age" (28:18). Thompson argues that the warfare in heaven with unseen powers and angels constitutes a predominant theme in Paul's writings: "For in him all the fulness was pleased to dwell, and through him to reconcile all things for him, making peace by the blood of the cross [through him], whether those on earth or those in heaven" (Col 1:19–20). Moreover, the creedal confession of the Father almighty, creator of heaven and earth, would support the reading of *both* heaven *and* earth. Similarly, the final judgment to come of the living and the dead might be read as a consummation of both the heavens and the earth, indeed, "new heavens and a new earth" (2 Pt 3:13). See also Revelations 21. The phrase heaven and earth in the Bible stands for the whole universe in which heaven is not free from opposition to the will of God. Thus the line might be read not as "let thy will be done on earth as it is already done in heaven," but rather "let it be done both on earth and in heaven," where God also would be recognized as sovereign.

Thompson also argues from an analysis of the Greek grammar that earth goes with heaven, and that earth does not refer directly to done.[25] *Hos-kai* in Greek, the argument claims, is equivalent to *tam-quam* in Latin, and both-and in English. He therefore recommends a translation such as both in heaven and on earth. Later in the Lord's Prayer we encounter the same Greek conjunction, *hos*, which is usually translated: Forgive us *as* we forgive others. One wonders if following the logic above, that line would be well translated: both forgive us and we forgive others. The point being made is that you cannot be forgiven without being forgiving, just as you must speak of the whole universe as both heaven and earth. The Latin "*sicut in coelo et in terra*" would also sustain the English translation "both in heaven and in earth."

SUMMARY: THE THOU-PETITIONS

HAVING SEEN THE SIMILARITY and the differences among the thou-petitions, can any general remarks be made? One might notice that we began with calling upon the Father in *heaven*, and that we finished with begging that the Father's will be done on earth as in *heaven*. The import of these words that surround the three thou-petitions might be this: Would that the Father be Father both on earth and in heaven, which will come about because the Father's name is hallowed on earth as in heaven, the kingdom comes on earth as in heaven, and God's will is done, on earth as in heaven. The holiness and hallowed name of the Father sets up a certain exclusivity or aloofness about God, who transcends this world. The name of God as Father sets up a certain inclusivity or intimacy about God, who cares as a parent does about his or her children. Given the holy name of God, we yet confess the approachable Father. The *heavenly* Father of the Lord's Prayer is the *hallowed* name and the *almighty* Father confessed in the creed. Heaven and earth, power and love, divine love and human love are yoked in these paired names of the God of revelation. Given the infinite and ineffable being of God, we yet confess the marvelous doings of the Father for the coming of the kingdom that is our salvation, on earth as in heaven.

An analysis of the thou-petitions reveals that there is a remarkable parallel construction. Hallowed be thy name, thy kingdom come, and thy will be done are all prayers in the third person, which allows God to remain in hidden mystery. We do not presume to interrupt God with a direct request about the affairs of God, about which we know almost nothing. Reverence for the mystery of God dominates the construction of these petitions. In contrast, the we-petitions speak to God of our needs and wants with the imperative voice, acknowledging the precariousness of the human condition and the urgency of our needs and overall predicament. Furthermore, in the Greek all the thou-petitions contain the same number of words, the same parts of speech, the same word order, and the same rhythms. None of them are prefaced by the conjunction "and," as are the we-petitions. It would appear that the parallel form of the thou-petitions reinforces the common meaning of each of them. They remain three different ways of asking God the same thing: may God be God on earth as in heaven.

Let us list a number of speculative questions that open ways of contrasting the thou-petitions. Can we compare the first thou-petition with the creator, the Father-almighty; the second thou-petition with the kingdom of his only Son, our Lord Jesus Christ, and the third thou-petition with the gift of the Holy Spirit that tunes our will to the will of the Father? Is there a trinitarian structure? Moreover, is the "hallowed name" more Johannine, the "kingdom" more the Synoptics, and the "will be done" more sanctification and transformation congenial with Paul's writing? Does the "hallowed name" prepare for the kingdom which will be spiritual, which in turn prepares the heart to embrace the will of the Father? Does each petition set up the following one? Or, should we speak of the "will being done" as the implementation of the kingdom, which is the created embodiment of the "hallowed name" of the Father who wills to bestow eternal life upon all flesh? These questions all suggest the amplitude of this inspired prayer.

Shall we argue that the "hallowed name" is in part a doxology rather than a petition, and remains a form of praise in the opening address of the Father? Shall we argue that the "will be done" tends to emphasize the play of human freedom in the bringing about of the kingdom in hearts converted to God? Accordingly, it would seem that *Your kingdom come* is the central line of the Lord's Prayer in its first half. To it the previous words tend, and from it the subsequent words flow. Thus, because the Father is holy and sovereign, the good kingdom can be given to us. Because we have genuine freedom and can cooperate with God, the coming of the kingdom demands that the Father's will be done in us and by us.

In sum, the thou-petitions embrace the mystery of the Trinity. To call upon the Father, whose name is hallowed, is indeed to call upon the almighty Father. The kingdom to come is that of the Father, but a kingdom embodied now in the Son of God made flesh. The will to be done is the reign of the Holy Spirit in the life of the world, the church, and the individual Christian. Maximus the Confessor saw the Trinity in even more economical terms, which also accommodate the Lucan Lord's Prayer. Accordingly, the Father is addressed, the name of the Father that is hallowed is the co-equal Word of the Father, and the kingdom to come is the reign of the Holy Spirit.[26]

PART TWO
The We-Petitions

GIVE US THIS DAY
OUR DAILY BREAD

I

GIVE US THIS DAY OUR DAILY *BREAD*, our bread for the coming day, our journey bread. Bread from grain, ground into flour and mixed with water, baked each day in sufficient amount for those who were to be nourished, that was the bread of the poor. Whatever was added beyond bread to the meal was a luxury. Bread was the staple, sufficient to keep one alive and to satisfy hunger. The just man could pray: "Give me neither poverty nor riches; feed me with the food that is needful for me lest I be full, and deny thee, and say, 'Who is the Lord?' or lest I be poor, and steal, and profane the name of my God" (Prv 30:8–9). Bread was baked daily, because journeymen lived on daily wages, because food spoiled if kept too long, and because fresh baked bread is specially satisfying. It was in that sense, a daily ration, a daily bread, the bread of the poor, the bread of all people.[1]

The Greek word for bread is *artos*, translated as *panis* in Latin, and as bread in English. Bread originally meant fragments or morsels, and when applied to food came by general use to indicate pieces of bread. Bread was broken from a large loaf, in order to divide it among those at table, and in order to feed oneself in small portions. When Jesus multiplies the loaves, we read they gathered up twelve baskets of fragments, i.e., of bread. Gradually the word for fragment of bread replaced the word for loaf as the common designation of what everyone now calls bread. The *Oxford English Dictionary* points out: "It thus appears that a word originally meaning 'piece, bit, frustum' [Latin for fragment] has passed through the sense of 'piece of bread,' 'broken bread,' into that of bread as a substance; while at the same time the original word for 'bread, loaf, panis' [Latin for bread] has been restricted to the undivided article as shaped and baked, the 'loaf.' " The Anglo-Saxon translation of the Lord's Prayer writes for daily bread the word *hlaf*, from which the word loaf descends (see the Anglo-Saxon text on page 217). From meaning fragment, bread has come to mean the whole loaf, and from meaning loaf of bread it has come to mean food in general, or a meal. To break bread together is to share an entire meal.

From food in general the meaning of bread has been extended to include all needs. To be hungry is to be needy, unsatisfied, and desirous of so many things. Bread for the stomach remains the first and most essential need, although Jesus would remind us that "One does not live by bread alone, but by every word that comes forth from the mouth of God" (Mt 4:4). Nonetheless we cannot live long without bread for the body. When bread refers to physical needs primarily, we have come to speak of bread as money. To earn a lot of bread is to make a lot of money that will buy many things to satisfy many physical needs. Human beings live in a web of material need and sustenance, and the whole cosmos contributes to the maintenance of those fragile and precarious conditions necessary for human life to thrive. Our body is material and belongs to a network of physical balances. We must receive everything; we are never self-sufficient. We must have our daily bread or die. Alfred Delp writes while awaiting death in a Nazi prison: "Only one who has known the effect hunger can have on every life impulse can appreciate the respect in which bread is held and what the perpetual struggle for daily bread really means."[2]

Jesus loved to break bread with others. He accepted many invitations from both friends and enemies to dine. He worked miracles to change water to wine, and to make bread out of a few loaves. He blessed bread, broke it, and shared it. He was invited as a guest, and he hosted his disciples to a dawn breakfast on the shores of the sea of Galilee (Jn 21). He spoke often of the kingdom as a feast of food and drink, "the banquet in the kingdom of heaven" (Mt 8:11). He told all kinds of stories about suppers, farms, food, hunger, and thirst. The parable of the "wedding feast" is poignant in its desire to fill all the places at table: "invite to the feast whomever you find" (Mt 22:9). Similarly, the parable of the "great feast" would include everyone: "make people come in that my home may be filled" (Lk 14:23). He gave prayers and blessings at meals. He said he was the bread of life (Jn 6). At his last supper he gave us his body as bread broken and food to be eaten.

When bread also satisfies spiritual needs, we speak of soul food. We break bread together in order to fill our desire for community, for conversation, for sharing of mind and heart with friends around a common table. Human beings are hungry to feed not only their bodies but also their hearts and souls. Think of Ruth, widowed and alone, gleaning amid the alien corn, or the sons of Jacob begging food in Egypt from their brother Joseph, whom they had left for dead. One wants reconciliation as well as nourishment. Jesus encouraged the disciples to seek spiritual food before physical bread: "So do not worry and say, 'What are we to eat?' or 'What are we to drink?' or 'What are we to wear?' All these things the pagans seek. Your heavenly Father knows that you need them all. But seek first the kingdom [of God] and his righteousness, and all these things will be given you besides" (Mt 6:31–33). Monika Hellwig writes of the words of Jesus fulfilling the overall needs of human beings:

> His message was to look not to self-defense but to the needs of the other; to be most concerned about those in greatest need; not to ask what people deserve but what they need; not to defend one's rights by violence but by a simple challenge to conscience; to be concerned at all times with seeing that the will of God is accomplished in the society, trusting that all other needs will be met; to judge people by what they do and not by the words and banners in which they declare their loyalties; to take no revenge but to de-escalate violence and evil by initiating a different style of life and pattern of relationships; to live simply and avoid grabbing and hoarding and enriching oneself because it does not increase happiness but only makes barriers against others and adds anxiety; not to be worried about saving one's life but always ready to give it.[3]

Spiritual bread has been understood to come in two principal ways: the word of God that feeds the heart, and the eucharistic bread of life that feeds the soul. Let us consider the word of God as bread: "One does not live by bread alone, but by every word that comes forth from the mouth of God" (Mt 4:4 and Dt 8:3). Just before Luke introduces his account of the Lord's Prayer, he tells the story of Martha who was preparing bread for the table, and Mary who was listening to the words of Jesus: "Martha, Martha, you are anxious and worried about many things. There is need of only one thing. Mary has chosen the better part and it will not be taken from her" (10:41–42). Immediately after the Lord's Prayer, Luke writes of the prayer of petition for food by children to their father: "If you then, who are wicked, know how to give good gifts to your children, how much more will the Father in heaven give the holy Spirit to those who ask him?" (11:13). On the road to Emmaus, after the breaking of the bread and the consequent recognition of the risen Lord, the disciples exclaim: "Were not our hearts burning [within us] while he spoke to us on the way and opened the scriptures to us?" (Lk 24:32).

Let us consider the bread of life as food for the soul. Jesus promised that he would be the bread of life for us, that his body would be broken and given us as bread. When we break bread in the eucharist we are fed with the life of the risen Lord Jesus. "So Jesus said to them, 'Amen, amen, I say to you, it was not Moses who gave the bread from heaven; my Father gives you the true bread from heaven. For the bread of God is that which comes down from heaven and gives life to the world.' They said to him, 'Sir, give us this bread always' " (Jn 6:32–34). Christians have thought that the spiritual meaning of bread culminates in the eucharist, which was itself prefigured by the manna in the desert. "I am the living bread that came down from heaven; whoever eats this bread will live forever; and the bread that I will give is my flesh for the life of the world" (Jn 6:51). In the Roman mass immediately before the communion bread is distributed, the assembly prays the Lord's Prayer. Daily bread and daily eucharist have long enjoyed an intimate association. Thus the spiritual meaning of bread brings the Lord's Prayer into the sacrament of the eucharist.

In the meeting with the woman at Jacob's well, "Jesus answered and said to her, 'Everyone who drinks this water will be thirsty again; but whoever drinks the water I shall give will never thirst; the water I shall give will become in him a spring of water welling up to eternal life.' The woman said to him, 'Sir, give me this water, so that I may not be thirsty or have to keep coming here to draw water' " (Jn 4:13–15). The woman at the well is the human soul before its Lord and its God. That soul is sensual; it has had five husbands; it has drawn endless buckets of water to quench a limitless thirst. The human body and soul thirst until they finally dry up and die. The well is tapped again and again, but one day it too will run dry. The human soul at the well yearns for deep draughts of both bodily satisfaction and soulful love. The woman comes to Jacob's well, the Jacob who desired Rachel so much that he counted the seven years of labor to win her like a day, so much did he love her. The woman at the well comes everyday with her jug hugged to her breast, and that jug runs dry again and again. Jesus speaks to her of filling her thirst once and for all, and fulfilling her soul's desire. Jesus invites her to know the Lord of love and to receive the gift of God, a fountain of the spirit's water that wells up within her unto eternal life. She leaves her own jug beside the well and goes with a mission to tell her own town what Jesus had told to her. She now carries the word of God within her heart, where it wells up as a fountain of spirit and truth. Her body now is the container that draws living water for others still thirsty as she once was.[4]

II

Give us this day our *daily* bread. The word translated as daily in English is *epiousios* in Greek. When we read "give us this day our daily bread" do we think of the two references to day as redundant? Does the phrase mean: give us this day our this day bread? Most commentators agree that "daily" bread is not a repetition of "this day" in Matthew, or "day by day" as Luke's Greek text is commonly understood.

Does *daily* bread add a further and spiritual meaning to this petition? Does it refer not only to physical bread but also to spiritual bread? What does the Greek *epiousios*, translated imprecisely in English as daily, truly mean? Origen, among the most learned of Greek scholars and the earliest commentator on the difficulties of *epiousios* in the Lord's Prayer, notes that the word seems to be a neologism, coined especially to render in Greek an Aramaic word (or possibly a Hebrew word) carrying some unique meaning. *Epiousios* does not appear again in the New Testament, nor could Origen or any subsequent investigator discover it elsewhere in Greek literature.[5] Attempts have been made to uncover an example of its use outside the Lord's Prayer in Matthew and in Luke, but in each instance scholars were divided on the validity of the alleged example. A recently reported discovery of a papyrus with *epiousios* (the Sayce transcription of the Hawara papyrus), which subsequently was lost, marks the frustrating effort to find an example of this word outside of the gospels.[6] Such a text would help to determine the meaning of this peculiar word, because dictionary meanings are derived from observing how a word is used.

Epiousios probably translates an Aramaic word that tries to capture what is unique about this Christian prayer for bread. *Epiousios* is the only adjective in the Lord's Prayer. To break bread with Jesus at the meals that he shared must have been a special experience. Lacking any examples of the use of *epiousios* outside of the Pater we can only surmise its proper meaning. In a reference to the mislaid papyrus Metzger says: "Until this papyrus is found again, therefore, the cautious lexicographer must perforce rely on the context of the Lord's Prayer, on etymological considerations, and on Patristic and versional evidence in seeking to ascertain the meaning of this elusive word."[7] C. W. F. Smith holds the "term is best read as having no simply limited meaning."[8] But there may be something misleading in this entire search. Were the word to be imprecisely translated from the Aramaic of Jesus into the Greek of the evangelists, we might have something of a false lead. However, various hypotheses remain about what *epiousios* may truly mean. Of its precise definition, after all is said and done, we may never know.

Although there is no complete agreement on the origin of *epiousios*, speculation has centered upon two possible roots for the word. One is that it derived from the word meaning to come or to be near, (*ep-ienai*), which suggests a translation of "the coming day" or "tomorrow."[9] Jerome claims that a Hebrew version of the now lost *Gospel to the Hebrews* uses the word *mahar (maar)*, which means tomorrow, as the equivalent word. It is argued that the word *mahar* is a Chaldean or Aramaic word written in Hebrew letters.[10] Since Jesus spoke Aramaic, this would seem to be an important clue to understanding the Greek word. However, by the fourth century, such a text of the Lord's Prayer, patterned as it was on Matthew's gospel, may already show influence of liturgical practice.[11] Because of liturgical usage *epiousios* may refer consistently to the bread of the coming day. When the Lord's Prayer was used for morning prayer, it referred to the then coming day. When the Lord's Prayer was used for evening prayer, it referred to the next day, which began at sunset. Perhaps counting against the various "morrow" readings is the warning that the gospel specifically sounds against worrying about the morrow. "So do not worry and say, 'What are we to eat?'. . . .Do not worry about tomorrow; tomorrow will take care of itself. Sufficient for a day is its own evil" (Mt 6:31, 34).

The other possible root word is *epi-einai*, related to the verb "to be" and meaning needed or required for subsistence. This root suggests a translation of "substantial" or "essential": bread that is necessary, or sufficient, or the bread which must be at hand, that is, *daily* bread. Werner Foerster claims that when all the derivation arguments are joined, it is safe to say *epiousios* somehow defines the amount of bread. The bread is for today, much as the manna in the desert was a daily gift of just what was needed, neither too much nor too little. Foerster concludes that the basic translation is "the bread which we need." Hemer suggests a similar rendition: "the bread for our coming day's need."[12] This latter wording captures both possible derivations, and "coming day" might be read both as today's ongoing day and tomorrow's day.

Whatever the exact definition of the word, there have emerged three families of interpretation for *epiousios*. (1) *Daily* bread can be read as literal, thus meaning physical bread that nourishes the body, sometimes with and sometimes without implications of a spiritual nature.[13] (2) *Daily* bread can be read symbolically as spiritual bread, soul food that nourishes the spirit, sometimes with and sometimes without implications of a physical nature. The wisdom of God and the Word of God would fall under such a category. Origen more than any other single commentator argued for the spiritual meaning of *epiousios*.[14] (3) *Daily* bread can be read as both spiritual and physical, simultaneously and inseparably, and perhaps even equally.[15] The agape meal of the early Christians that Paul alludes to in his letters was a blend of a large family meal and the eucharistic liturgy in its initial stage of development. Christian bread was a comprehensive daily bread, feeding body and soul. Human beings need bread for body and for soul. Augustine clearly opted for both meanings of *epiousios*. The spiritual bread may also include reference to the eucharistic bread, or it may refer to that spiritual communion available to every Christian by the indwelling of the blessed Trinity.[16] Krister Stendhal writes of this equilibrium: "And in the meals of the early church the eucharist and the nutrition were held together as we can see from I Cor. 11:17–33. The petition for the bread thus holds together material and spiritual needs without making one more important than the other. The daily bread was a token of the Messianic Banquet—and the Messianic Banquet a reminder of the sanctity of the daily bread. The eucharist and the grace at meals are distinct but also in continuity with each other."[17]

In Patristic literature, the Lord's Prayer was spoken of very early and often. Patristic writers in the West and the Greek Fathers in the Antioch school in the East generally interpreted *epiousios* as physical bread, or as both physical and spiritual bread. Gregory of Nyssa, John Chrysostom of Antioch, and Theodore of Mopsuestia all opt for a frugal and necessary daily bread for the sustenance of bodily life in this petition of the Lord's Prayer. We pray for what we need and what we must have to survive. Augustine, Cyprian of Carthage, and John Cassian insist on both material bread and spiritual bread.

When Jerome came to translate *epiousios* into Latin, he rendered it as *supersubstantialem* (supersubstantial) in Matthew and as *quotidianum* (everyday) in Luke. Jerome would seem to straddle the question, choosing the more spiritual word for Matthew's more eschatological Lord's Prayer, and the commonplace word for Luke's more everyday Lord's Prayer. John Cassian thought both of Jerome's Latin words were appropriate, since the bread is of both heaven and earth. Ambrose thought that the Latin which referred to today and the Greek which referred to tomorrow both belonged in the comprehensive Lord's Prayer. Although the liturgy uses Matthew's text, it actually follows an earlier pre-Jerome Latin translation, which used the word *cotidianum*, also translated as daily.[18]

The Greek Patristic writers in the East for the most part prefer the spiritual meaning of *epiousios*.[19] Give us this day our daily bread prays for the life of our soul. Starting with Origen the influence of the translation *morrow bread* was widespread. Cyril of Jerusalem concurred in such a reading. Morrow bread was understood as spiritual bread for tomorrow given even today. The bread of the kingdom of heaven was even now and yet to come.[20]

There is something attractive in including both the physical and the spiritual meaning of bread in the reading of *epiousios*. This *daily bread* that we ask is surely a wonder bread, a food that is saving, a food that we need. As more than one commentator has noticed, to read *epiousios* as both body food and soul food, is to have one's cake and eat it too. Yet, surely in God it ought to be possible to join body and soul with such abundance. Human sexuality generously addresses both body and soul. Surely the breaking of the bread of the kingdom ought to include the needs of both body and soul, both this world and the world to come, brought into one communion by the God who created the Many in order to bring all into the One who is God. As the woman at the well wanted the life-giving water so that she would not be thirsty again (Jn 4) so the crowd wanted the bread of the multiplication of loaves so that they would not be hungry for food again. But Jesus said to them: "I am the bread of life; whoever comes to me will never hunger, and whoever believes in me will never thirst" (Jn 6:35).

Having seen so many translations of *epiousios* in the Lord's Prayer, let us suggest one of our own. Give us this day our *journey bread*. In a first reading journey bread is bread for the journey of life. It resembles the manna in the desert, the journey bread of the exodus from Egypt to the promised land. Dante renders the Paternoster: "Give us this day Thy manna" (*Purgatorio* 11:3). As the manna-bread ceased to be given when Joshua and the Israelites cross the Jordan river and enter the promised land at Jericho, so the journey bread of Christians will not be needed when we reach the heavenly Jerusalem. The Israelites called their mystery food, manna, which means in Hebrew, "what is it?" Similarly, *epiousios* remains a mystery word, and the journey bread more than food for just the body. It is a marvelous waybread, a holy *viaticum (via* as way), the "daybread that matters" to strengthen us until we have crossed the Jordan, crossed the bar from this life to the eternal ocean of God's infinitude. One is reminded of the journey in Tolkien's *Lord of the Rings* when Frodo and his party, tired and hungry, are given a provision of elfin bread. This bread of the elves of the forest had a marvelous quality; it gave strength to the body and courage to the soul, but it did not satisfy human hunger pains. Journey bread is also mystery bread. Journey bread picks up connotations of "our daily bread," for the journey is a day's journey. *Jour* in French is the word for day, and journal is a daily diary or a daily newspaper. Give us our daybread. Give us our journey bread. As the worker seeks the journeyman's wage, we seek our bread for today, our journey bread to nourish us through the desert of this life until we reach the land flowing with milk and honey. The Lord's Prayer is our daily prayer for that journey bread that we all need and must have lest we perish of hunger in the wasteland. The bread that we need, give us today and day after day. Give us today our journey bread.

III

Throughout the we-petitions of the Lord's Prayer Matthew favors the aorist tense. That leaning toward the eschatological can be found again in the phrasing of "give us *today* our daily bread." The decisiveness of the kingdom yet to come breaks in even now. Now is the hour; this is the day the Lord has made. The kingdom come in faith even now permeates Matthew's prayer. "Today when you hear his voice, do not harden your hearts as in the rebellion" (Psalm 95 as quoted in Hebrews 3:15). Many Patristic commentaries read the today in parallel with Matthew's comments that follow the Lord's Prayer: "Do not worry about tomorrow; tomorrow will take care of itself. Sufficient for a day is its own evil" (6:34). Hence today was all that the Christian should be concerned about, entrusting tomorrow to God's providence that feeds the birds of the air and clothes the lilies of the field. Evangelical poverty is a virtue that trusts in God to provide. Not to worry anxiously for tomorrow, but to let God minister to our need this day so that we never forget the continual providence of God, would capture the sense of "give us *today* our daily bread." Today is eternal for God, who created time in the beginning and will judge and fulfill time in the ending, and for whom there is no yesterday or tomorrow, but only today.

In place of the today (*sēmeron* in Greek) in Matthew, Luke introduces a different phase (*kath hēmeran* in Greek) which might be translated everyday or each day or day by day. That everyday is spirit-filled in the life of the Christian colors much of Luke's gospel. The day of the Lord is not just *then* in the kingdom, even in anticipation, but rather here and now in the everyday of historical existence. The kingdom is even now within us. Luke was fond of adding throughout his writings allusions to the ongoing historical struggle to be a Christian. History counted with Luke, who saw the need of the church to come to terms with an extended future. The end was not yet. Luke adds daily to the section in Mark and in Matthew: "If anyone wishes to come after me, he must deny himself and take up his cross *daily* and follow me" (9:23). And in Acts, Luke in a typical way writes: " *Every day* they devoted themselves to meeting together in the temple area and to breaking bread in their homes. They ate their meals with exultation and sincerity of heart" (2:46).

In summary, let us compare Matthew and Luke on the matter of the day as a time-frame. Matthew stands more in the eternal now (*kairos*) and Luke more in the passing time (*chronos*). Today in Matthew is the day the Lord has made; everyday in Luke is a miracle of grace, whose historical reach is wonderful. In Matthew, today is the first day of the coming age; the final times have begun. In Luke, each day adds a precious gift of grace from God for those with eyes to see the indwelling of the Spirit amid the mundane and everyday. Matthew would hold all is new by the sovereignty of God in the today; Luke would urge thanksgiving day by day that is making all new from within. In the Matthean gospel the bread is the food of the messianic banquet, tomorrow's bread given even today. In the Lucan gospel the bread is the manna for the journey across the desert of this life, and even up to Jerusalem. Today in Matthew feels the pull of tomorrow and the fulfillment of the kingdom drawing all things even now to Christ, who sits at the right hand of the Father. Day by day in Luke feels the push of the here and now bringing about the consummation of all things from within, because Christ is hidden and incarnate in our flesh. In an attempt to reconcile both perspectives Origen writes: "He who 'to-day' prays to God, who is from infinity to infinity, not only for 'this day' but also for 'each day,' will be prepared to receive him, who is able to give more abundantly than we desire or understand, things greater even—if I may use hyperbole—than the things that eye hath not seen . . . ."[21]

IV

Give *us* today *our* daily bread. The Lord's Prayer is a community prayer from the very beginning. Without bread, physical and spiritual, *all of us* hunger. To be human is to hunger for bread, for food and for fellowship, to receive and to give. Give bread to the hungry, and hunger to those with bread. We could be either physically starving or spiritually. Those who have bread and meet the need of others who hunger also satisfy their own spiritual hunger. And those who are physically hungry need also to satisfy their own spiritual hunger by receiving in order to give. Both Matthew and Luke use the plural, give *us* instead of give *me*. A story is told about conditions in hell: the people in hell were seated before a banquet table with silverware so long that no one could put anything into their own mouths. In contrast, the people in heaven were seated at the same banquet table with the same silverware, but they were feeding each other.

To share bread with everyone is the only way to have a happy meal. If other people are seen to be left out and hungry, we cannot eat our bread with a joyful heart. When Jesus fed the multitude, they each had enough to eat and there were yet twelve baskets of fragments left over. Were we to share the goods that we now hoard from each other out of fear and distrust, there would be bread in plenty for everyone to attend the feast of life. "I got mine" is a selfish phrase that ignores the needs of others. "Give *us our* bread" is a phrase that reminds us how cooperative an effort life on earth always remains. We need each other in the growing, harvesting, grinding, baking, and distributing of bread, and all other goods as well. How foolish it would be to eat all alone, or to feast when others are left on the steps of the house starving for bread, as Lazarus before Dives, who dined sumptuously everyday and never saw the hungry beggar on his own doorstep (Lk 16:19–30).

To receive a blessing is to be a blessing for others. To be forgiven is to become so goodhearted as to forgive others. All gifts are reciprocal. They are not received unless the person is enabled to give. We love others, not to make them indebted, but to enable them to love in return. Gifts are given so that new givers will be raised up. We might read this first we-petition in sympathy with the next petition in the Lord's Prayer, "forgive us as we forgive." Thus, we might say: Give us our daily bread as we give daily bread to others. May we receive the love of God so that we may love our neighbor as ourself. If you would know Jesus as the person for others, you will know him as such only by living as a person for others. Some of the most valid insights in liberation theology center on this perspective. Watch the way a person lives and you will know what they believe and whom they love. When we see people feeding each other and giving in the many ways of humble and loving service, we know God must have fed them well so to enable them to feed others in return. What can you give that you have not received? We are humbled and awed by the love we see in some human beings, and we ask God to love us as we see they love one another. We know that such self-giving loving must already be the reflection of God's way of loving.

Let us look at the miracle of the multiplication of the loaves in connection with "give *us our* daily bread." One interpretation would have the action of God upon the bread as central. Jesus works a physical miracle and multiplies the bread to feed the hungry crowd. There is no doubt that God who made bread from nothing can make bread from seven loaves. That Jesus who is Lord worked a wonder does not injure the gospel text. Another interpretation, however, would have the miraculous grace of God directed to the closed hearts of the assembled multitude of people. Accustomed to protecting their food supply when they travel, lest they run short and lest they find no hospitality along the way, they all carried a hidden reserve somewhere in their possessions. Jesus teaches them about the sisterhood of man and the fatherhood of God. Their hearts are changed from isolated self-defense to collaboration for the common good. They now are enabled to share all they have for the needs of others, trusting that each man and woman there will do likewise, and thus God will provide enough bread. When everyone opens their heart and their knapsack, they discover there is enough food to feed all the thousands, and with abundance left over. Jesus works a yet greater miracle, a spiritual miracle. More miraculous even than making much bread from little bread is the making of a generous heart from a hard heart, or a magnanimous soul from a frightened and self-enclosed one. To make a giving and holy heart from a selfish and unholy one, God must not only create from nothing, but must straighten a human freedom that is distorted and work with broken hearts that must be mended first, and then re-created anew. Only God writes straight with crooked lines.

In John's account of the last supper Jesus like a slave washes the feet of his disciples. They protest, but he insists that if they cannot understand that he wishes to serve and not be served, they cannot be disciples. In the wisdom of Jesus, to serve another's needs is to wash their feet. Similarly, to serve food stands for meeting the multiple needs of others who hunger for so many things both physical and spiritual. Jesus as the paschal lamb is all consumed in self-giving. His body is broken and given, as bread at the table is broken in many pieces and given out for many. We live for and from each other. To receive the eucharist body and blood of Jesus Christ is to be enabled to feed others. We are given to so that we may give, forgiven so we may forgive, and only truly consume bread when we ourselves become bread consumed for others. Forgive us just as we in moments of tenderness know human forgiveness from one another. Give us our journey bread just as we in moments of gratitude know human kindness and generous sharing with each other.

V

Give us today our daily bread. Matthew in his gospel puts the Greek verb for give in the aorist tense. Give us in principle everything. In Jesus who is Lord, who is the bread of life, the Father has indeed given us everything. Consubstantial with the Father, Jesus is the one and only Son. In him everything has been fulfilled. Luke, however, puts give in the present tense. An ongoing awareness is suggested by the present tense. Give us this day and every day to come in the history of the world the wherewithal to live. Day by day give us our daily bread.

Give us this day our daily bread. God's providence provides food, both physical and spiritual, for the creation which God loves. Moreover, in giving us Jesus Christ, the only beloved Son, God intended to give us a self-gift in which giver and gift were identical. This gift of God's self is God's universal gift, and therefore all men and women have access to their creator in their own time and place. Grace works its ways everywhere, although we know more of its ways inside the church than outside it.

To address God with the words "give us" seems to assume many things about God. It seems to assume that God wishes to be asked for what we need, and that God will answer our prayers. Why would God wish to be asked? Parents do not require their children to ask for their bread; they provide it willingly and spontaneously, knowing full well their offspring need food and cannot provide it from their own resources alone. Immediately before the Lord's Prayer we read: "Your Father knows what you need before you ask him" (Mt 6:8). How does God answer prayers? Does God intervene within the laws of nature to provide a better harvest? Does God inspire cooperation among human beings so that our needs are met by each other because of the generosity implanted in us by God? Does prayer do any good, since harvests at times fail and human beings often enough use their freedom to harm the well-being of their neighbors rather than foster it? These are fair questions about all prayers of petition, and especially of that paradigmatic prayer: "*Give* us this day our daily bread."

Faith in the infinite and sovereign providence of God must cope with two seemingly insurmountable obstacles: chance events in the physical world and human freedom in the spiritual world. Both of these seem to rob God of the kind of sovereignty necessary to guarantee us our daily bread. God may be benevolent, but in the face of these factors God seems to be helpless. Or contrarily, if God does direct physical chance and human freedom with an infinite sovereignty, the hunger of this world would seem to indicate that God, who is able to do all things and thus feed all creatures, is not always benevolent in our regard.

Although prayer remains always a mystery, there are some aspects of petition to God that can be stated. Prayer should not be a last resort. Prayer to God is a first resort. We should give thanks to God always and everywhere. We should ask for our daily bread always and everywhere. We must not take our next breath for granted. It is a personal gift from God, just as is the sun rising every morning. Nothing happens without the mind and heart of God inspiring its very being and its every movement. Nothing escapes the constant loving attention of God. Creation is sustained at every turn by the deliberate wisdom and goodness of the creator. Thus, we should pray always and for everything. We pray for our daily bread; we pray for the daily care of our life. If we are hungry or if we are ill, we pray that God will take care of us nonetheless. We even suggest how God might take care of us by providing food for our table and by making us well if we are sick. But, we remain open to God's ways and the mystery of God's response to our prayer. We trust in God's care, and we know that whatever happens we remain within that loving providence. "Your father knows what you need before you ask him" (Mt 6:8). In the garden of Gethsemani Jesus prayed that the cup might pass and that he might live. He trusted in God's care. And his prayer was answered. The resurrection was not the mortal life he had asked for, but it exceeded whatever he might have dreamed of as the Father's love and care for him.

God's providence provides food, both physical and spiritual, for the creatures whom God loves. How does the bread of the eucharist differ from the bread of this world? How does supernatural bread exceed natural bread? First of all, the sacrament of the eucharist asks of the assembly that they purify their hearts and turn from the sins that may be obstacles to belief in God's love. The readings and prayers clarify the image of God and God's goodness, so that there are no unnecessary blocks between us and the love of God. The eucharist surrounds the assembly with the story of God's bread in the scriptures, lest we forget how much God loves us. It disposes the heart of the participant with the many resources of song and music, the beauty of architecture and overall decor, and the group support of a common faith and love. The eucharist amplifies the promises of God by sounding them out loud and clear. Thus the sacrament maximizes the reception of that nourishment which God offers always and everywhere. We concentrate all our attention and prayer on begging God's presence here and now. We say well of God, we bless God, we acknowledge his agape in our regard. We give thanks always and everywhere for the work of the Holy Spirit in all times and places. We focus our awareness of who God is and what God is doing. We call upon Jesus' promise not to leave us orphans and to give us this sacramental bread as the promised gift of his body and blood, his real presence in our life. We do all this in memory of him. If then God does not feed us abundantly in the eucharist with its claim upon the promise of the Lord, with all that preparation and concentration for its reception, who could believe that God nourishes us anywhere else? If not here and now, where and when?

Eating with friends feeds our soul, and the food that is prepared for us to eat will become our body. We wish to receive that nourishment from someone we love and who loves us, so that the food that will become our body is given as a gift of life and love to us personally. Our *companions* are literally the ones with whom we break bread together (companion from *cum-panis* in Latin, which means with bread). The mother who feeds her newborn child the milk of her breast knows that she gives more than nourishment. She gives life and love; she gives her own body; she gives herself.[22] In the eucharist we eat the bread of life given by the Lord Jesus who said "this is my body given for you" and "I am the bread of life . . . whoever eats this bread will live forever." This bread, his body that is our food, will become our body and we shall live with his own life, the eternal life of the living God.

Giving food to another human being involves always an access to their body. It is this access to the body of the one being fed that makes food always a sacramental event. Eating together is another way of making love together but in community that is wider than the sexual union. It is similar to the love of man and woman that brings new life into the world. Bread is given from a body and received into a body that delights in its reception. We should not presume an access to another's body; that can only be given as a gift when we ask to love them or to feed them. We do not break bread with our enemies; we do not let our enemies prepare our food. We wish to make the birth of our body and the growth and nourishment of that body a matter of exchanging the love of human persons, who are freely given access to ourselves because of the love we share together.[23] John Ruskin writes: "For all true Christianity is known—as its Master was—in breaking of bread, and all false Christianity in stealing it."[24]

FORGIVE US OUR TRESPASSES

THE SECOND WE-PETITION joins a theme of forgiveness which is essential though not unique to the Gospels. Forgiveness of injuries represents an ethical ideal not always found outside the New Testament writings. "Love your enemies . . . . Be merciful, just as [also] your Father is merciful . . . . Forgive and you will be forgiven" (Lk 6:35–37). Forgiveness should be universal and continual. Everyone should be forgiven, regardless of the offense. Offenders might need to be forgiven repeatedly, even "seventy times seven." We need daily forgiveness as much as daily bread. Our body each day hungers for food; our soul each day hungers for forgiveness. Mercy is the soul food of our daily communion with one another. We grow weary in body each day and need to ask our bread; we grow sorrowful in soul each day and need to ask forgiveness. We hunger for that love that will accept us as we are, and call us to be more in the belief that we are children of one Father. Each eucharistic meal begins with the confession of sins and the proclaiming of forgiveness. To sit at the same table with an offender declares he or she is already forgiven. After the resurrection, Jesus who had been abandoned to his passion and death by his friends did not seek first their repentance and sorrow. In the resurrection appearances, he sought them out and broke bread with them. Their hearts were on fire with a new-found hope when he explained to them the scriptures, and in the breaking of the bread they recognized him and his love so often known this way before.

Reform of behavior is not a prerequisite for true forgiveness, though it may be a consequence. One need not first become loving in order to be loved, nor give in order to receive. One need not be good first in order to have goodness bestowed. God who created us out of nothing in God's own goodness can recreate us out of even the negative valence of our sins. The goodness resident in the forgiving person reaches out to the sinner precisely in their need and despair. We are not loved because we made ourselves good and loveable, but because God who is good loves us and makes us thereby good. Forgiveness is because of God, not because of us. Sinful misery calls forth forgiveness from God, who came in Jesus Christ to call sinners. They need and hunger for forgiveness. They are forgiven, not because they are deserving, but because they are desperate and at heart sorrowful. All human beings, sinful though they be, deeply want forgiving love. So seldom have they experienced divine acceptance. Christians are invited to forgive the sinner, just as Jesus who is Lord forgives them.

What are we to forgive? Matthew writes of forgiving *debts*, and Luke of forgiving *sins*. Matthew's Greek word, *opheilēmata*, is translated in the Latin Vulgate as *debita* and in the King James and the contemporary Revised Standard Version as debts. Luke uses the Greek word, *hamartias*, that is translated as *peccata* in Latin, and sins in English. Matthew's debts shows a more Semitic usage. The Aramaic word for sins was debts, with the primary analogue financial debts. To the Greek gentile Christians of Luke's community, however, *sins* would be more understandable. The Greeks knew sin, or *hamartia*, as literally a missing of the mark, an arrow gone astray, an error or mistake, a falsity of some kind.

The Lord's Prayer in the English liturgy speaks of forgiving trespasses, a word we have kept through the centuries since its adoption in the first English translation of the New Testament from the Greek. That particular word was introduced into the Lord's Prayer in William Tyndale's translation of the Bible in the early sixteenth century. The "father of the English Bible" probably took the word trespass from previous English translations of the Latin Bible, which employ that word in Matthew's commentary immediately following the Lord's Prayer. In the Wycliffe translation (1380) of that commentary we read: "For if ye forgeuen to men ther synnes: youre heuenli fadir, schal forgeue to you youre trepassis" (Mt 6:14). A contemporary of Chaucer, Wycliffe was the first to translate the New Testament in its entirety into English, and into an English yet understandable today. He translated from the Latin Vulgate text, for so many centuries the only authorized church version. Jerome translated the Greek word *paraptoma* (transgressions), which is repeated several times in the Matthean commentary following the Lord's Prayer by an alternate use of two Latin words, *peccata* (sins) and *delicta* (offenses). Wycliffe rendered those two Latin words with the English words "sins" and "trespasses." Wycliffe was the first to use that particular word, and Tyndale took it over as his word of preference in the Lord's Prayer itself and in the following Matthean commentary. Tyndale even used the same word in his translation of Luke's Pater, where the Greek is yet different: "And [if] ye wyll not forgeve men there trespases, no more shall youre father forgive youre trepases." Subsequent translations of the Lord's Prayer in Matthew for liturgical use have kept that peculiar word trespasses to this day. No other widely used English Bible translation employs it in the Lord's Prayer itself, though in the King James version it is found in the Matthean commentary. Nonetheless, in the *Book of Common Prayer* and in actual practice with the faithful both Catholic and Protestant the word trespasses has perdured in the Lord's Prayer to this day.[25]

A trespass is a violation of what is owed to someone or something. One can trespass on another's property by unlawful entry. One can trespass the spiritual boundaries of another's privacy. Trespasses are transgressions, offenses, violations of the integrity of what does not belong to the transgressor. "No Trespassing" signs indicate private property and private lives. Justice would give what is due where it is due. Trespasses are thus injustices. Etymologically the word comes from Old French, *trespasser*, to pass beyond or to pass across. In early English there were variant spellings of trespass, and it is possible that the word trapesing, or traipsing, is related. Accordingly, to trespass implies an invasion of the space of another in a careless and irreverent way. To forgive trespasses is therefore to forgive offenses of a wide and inclusive range. W. H. Auden writes of forgiving love as an unpresumed overcoming with the beloved of all fear of trespasser's reproach: "And love's best glasses reach / No fields but are his own."[26]

In the time of Jesus the tax collectors were considered great sinners. They defrauded people of their money. The gouged excessive taxes with the connivance of the occupying Roman establishment. Whatever they could collect above their quota, they could keep as their own profit. Tax collectors were thieves in positions of office and power just as insider traders of our own day take advantage of their position to steal. Tax collectors were unjust and unmerciful. They would not forgive debts. They would add burdens. The apostle Matthew was called to follow Jesus when he was Levi the tax collector. His story is one of conversion. Luke's story of Zaccheus, the fraudulent tax collector, shows forgiveness and repentance expressed in the repayment of the monies taken from others unjustly.

The primary analogue in the biblical literature for forgiveness was the remission of financial debts. To write off a debt was to forgive. Jesus tells two great stories of the forgiveness of debts. In one story Jesus was dining at the house of a Pharisee, who did not extend the usual guest hospitality of foot washing to Jesus. A woman, thought to be sinful, washes the feet of Jesus with her tears and wipes them with her hair. Jesus explains to his host that gratitude for forgiveness is in proportion to the magnitude of the debt that is forgiven. "So I tell you, her many sins have been forgiven; hence, she has shown great love" (Lk 7:41–50). In the other story, the master of a household forgives a debtor a huge sum. He in turn refuses to forgive his fellow servants debts of a much smaller amount. The master is irate saying: "You wicked servant! I forgave you your entire debt because you begged me to. Should you not have had pity on your fellow servant, as I had pity on you?" (Mt 18:23–35).

Most translations of the Lord's Prayer in Matthew use the word *debts*: "Forgive us our debts as we forgive our debtors." *Debts* carries a wider connotation than sins. To be indebted to someone is often to owe a debt that cannot be paid back. I am much obliged for endless favors from innumerable known and unknown benefactors. One is indebted to parents who give life, and the debt cannot be remitted. Who can repay the creator for their existence? Who can give back to life as much as they have received? Our very material being, occupying this place and asserting this personality, is a burden to others who must make room for us. For being a burden to others we remain indebted even if not always guilty. We impinge on each other for better and for worse, and we remain responsible to and for each other. We are in their debt and they remain in ours. Our neighbors carry our burdens even if our behavior is ideal, and we carry theirs as well. "Bear one another's burdens." We carry not only the burdens of each other, but also each other as burden. Simone Weil writes: "Our debtors comprise all beings and all things; they are the entire universe. We think we have claims everywhere. In every claim we think we possess there is always the idea of an imaginary claim of the past on the future. That is the claim we have to renounce."[27]

Origen writes that a human being is always a debtor. The human condition is one of indebtedness. If we cannot pay our innumerable debts then we live in default. We thus stand in need of continual mercy. Debts capture the idea of sins not only of commission, but also all our sins of omission. Think of all the good we might have done, and the debt to others who must put up with a world that might have been a better place had we been more generous. We are indebted to one another for our shortcomings as well as for our crimes, for what we are as well as for what we do. We are estranged and thus indebted. We owe others and we owe God for the burial of our talents. Either we have contributed to the welfare of others or we have been part of their general impoverishment. We sin every day and need to be forgiven seventy times seven. If our behavior is self-serving and unlawful, we are all the more indebted. Even if I am forgiven, I am still indebted. Human life entails being in debt, and regardless of innocence or guilt, we are one and all much obliged. Peter captures that feeling of being overwhelmingly in debt when he says to the Lord by the lake: "Depart from me, Lord, for I am a sinful man" (Lk 5:8).

No disciple can love God with all their strength, all their soul, and all their heart. "When you have done all you have been commanded, say, 'We are unprofitable servants; we have done what we were obliged to do'" (Lk 17:10). No disciple can give to the community and to the commonweal all that the request for charity demands. "Owe nothing to anyone, except to love one another; for the one who loves another has fulfilled the law" (Rom 13:8). And who can love without failures, who can love with boundless generosity, and who then does not need to be forgiven and in turn to forgive? When the woman with the hemorrhage touched the cloak of Jesus as he passed by in the crowd, she sought a healing from him that would restore her from the isolation that her constant flow of blood imposed on her. Anyone she touched in her condition was contaminated, and she had dared to touch Jesus. But the Lord healed her, restored her to the community, took away her alienation, and dismissed her in peace: "Daughter, your faith has saved you; go in peace" (Mk 6:34). Sin is like that; it contaminates us, and we infect others. Only when others embrace us with forgiveness, no matter their risk, are we restored to health of soul.

Sins, which in Luke's version of the Pater correspond to debts in Matthew, carry clearly the additional connotation of deliberately guilty behavior. Origen calls sins our unpaid debts. When Christians settled down into the long haul of history, they were conscious that daily sins would always be a burden. Daily forgiveness was the remedy. The Greek word for sin, *hamartia*, suggests moral activity that is off target. In Walker Percy's *Love in the Ruins* a sinful liaison is set in the sand bunker beside the eighteenth hole of a golf course. That location in a trap off the green perfectly mirrors the moral trajectory of errant behavior, which misses its intended aim. Sinfulness accounts for all our stray arrows. Luke's everyday Christianity knew sins as misses, frequent and deplorable occurrences. The word was easily understood by the Greek-speaking gentile Christians of the Lucan community, whose traditional ethics were the product of such a moral philosophy.

The etymology of forgive suggests a giving with intensity. To *for*give was to give in a sustained way. To forbear insult is to endure insult. Thus to forgive is to give up thoroughly one's resentment. To forgive is to perdure in giving. The gift of forgiveness is pure gift. To forgive a debt was to give up absolutely the claim to repayment. In Luther's catechism the word for forgive is *verlasse*, which is to let go thoroughly. To dismiss a debt might also suggest undoing an overwhelming indebtedness that cannot be calculated. Thus pardon or forgiveness presents a gift, a give-back, a full give, a *for*give of the claims in justice for retribution. One commentator on the Lord's Prayer writes: "Forgiveness is a state of mind and heart, a condition of gratitude, one might say, to *all* the manifestations of life, inner and outer, no matter how negatively they may affect ourselves. It is absolutely unconditional or it is nothing."[28]

We ask God to "give us our daily bread." God gives initially to us. The whole first part of the Lord's Prayer promises the Father's kingdom to come in our midst. Our very creation from nothing is the Father's pure gift. To love God in return for such divine giving is to be a forgiving person. Our life is gift; our *for*giveness is to return a pure gift for a pure gift. As we have been loved so we love in return. As we have been given, so we give. As we have been forgiven, so we forgive. Human forgiveness is as close as human beings will come to the divine creation from nothing, brought forth in pure love, for to forgive is to find within us a Godlike goodness that asks no return but only wishes to bestow itself for the good of the beloved.

To ask what the forgiveness of God might be like brings to mind the stories that Jesus told of human acceptance. Consider the parable of the prodigal son (Lk 15) and the equally prodigal father, whose mercy is lavish and extravagant. Here is no patriarchal father who will claim all that is owed to him. Here is a tender and heart-given father who wants nothing but his sons around him and a loving bond among them. Think of Jesus himself in the story of the woman taken in adultery (Jn 8). Here is a compassionate and sensitive man, unwilling to embarrass or condemn, who asserts nothing but the common indebtedness of all flesh in the weakness of its sexuality. Her sin is understandable even if not excusable. No harsh judgment, only patience and gentle acceptance without humiliation. She is not innocent, but she is not condemned to die; she is forgiven. Or, take the words of Jesus in agony on the cross as a paradigm of divine mercy: "Father, forgive them, they know not what they do" (Lk 23:34). And to the repentant thief in agony he promises a total remittance of debts: "Amen, I say to you, today you will be with me in Paradise" (Lk 23:43). To forgive means to have a vulnerable soul, a sympathetic eye, a truthful heart, a love for the other that overrides any claim for one's own goods, or rights, or interests. They are forgiven, not because they have earned it, but because they are a brother or sister whom we have accepted as one of our own, unconditionally and gratuitously. Our commitment to the sinful person is based on who they are and not on what they do. We forgive them, not because they are so sorry, but because they are so miserable and so in need of our love.

Political realists remind us that there is no such thing as a "free lunch." Someone must pay for it. The law of Karma is a law of compensation. Every human activity has its consequence and sooner or later its price must be paid for better or for worse. Our whole world is one cosmic web, an enormous network of cause and effect. The teacup broken today is heard in the stars tomorrow, however far and howsoever faintly heard. Our lives are intertwined. In the gospels Jesus calls for forgiveness and mercy repeatedly. "Be merciful, just as [also] your Father is merciful" (Lk 6:36), and Paul says "as the Lord has forgiven you, so must you also do" (Col 3:13). Jesus is thought to be "a friend of tax collectors and sinners" (Mt 11:19) and he says that "I did not come to call the righteous but sinners" (Mk 2:17). "Forgive and you will be forgiven" (Lk 6:37) and "Blessed are the merciful, for they will be shown mercy" (Mt 5:7). Forgiving love is a pervasive atmosphere in the life of Jesus Christ. The multitude on the hillside was hungry and far from home. They sought their daily bread but they received a change of heart. Jesus' words changed their selfish hearts and they shared with one another their meager provisions. And behold there were baskets of leftovers. From some loaves and a few fish a large crowd was fed. They knew they had received a free lunch, not only food for their body, but a free heart that enabled them to have mercy upon their neighbor as themselves. God's forgiveness that melts our hard hearts is our daily bread, given us freely and freeing us everyday to love in mercy and to forgive "those who trespass against us."

AS WE FORGIVE THOSE
WHO TRESPASS AGAINST US

THE PETITION FOR FORGIVENESS in the Lord's Prayer concludes: Forgive us our debts, *as we forgive our debtors*. On a literal level the text would seem to say: forgive us *insofar as* we forgive others. May we receive a vertical forgiveness from our Father in heaven to the extent that we extend horizontal forgiveness to one another. The problem raised by this interpretation, however, is formidable. Forgiveness is never dependent on our initiative; it begins with God's grace first given to us while we are yet sinners. Nor does God's love wait for the sinner to repent, but rather God's love touches our hearts while sinful in order that we may repent. Thus God forgives us when we are hard-hearted and unforgiving, precisely so that our souls may become forgiving towards others. Only when we are forgiving can we be free of the fearful selfishness and isolation that is our sinfulness. Human forgiveness, therefore, is never an adequate cause for divine forgiveness, which is antecedent to our response, unconditional in its offer, and always given gratuitously. God does not love us because we are good and forgiving, but because God is good and forgiving. Divine love and forgiveness holds all the initiative. Our very sinfulness attracts God to us, because our hard-heartedness cries out for salvation. Being loved is not a reward with God for being on good behavior, although moral integrity is not a matter of indifference to God. Our forgiveness of others is not a cause, nor a precondition, nor a promise of God's loving us but a consequence.

A first reading of Matthew's brief commentary after the Lord's Prayer would seem to reinforce "forgive us *insofar as* we forgive." The evangelist writes: "If you forgive others their transgressions, your heavenly Father will forgive you" (6:14). We read in Mark: "Therefore I tell you, all that you ask for in prayer, believe that you will receive it and it shall be yours. When you stand to pray, forgive anyone against whom you have a grievance, so that your heavenly Father may in turn forgive you your transgressions" (11:24–25).

In Mark's text the example for forgiveness is put "anyone against whom you have a grievance," whereas in Matthew the example is put "your brother has anything against you" (5:23). Nonetheless, it remains unacceptable to read the Lord's Prayer as divine forgiveness *because of* our human forgiveness. Even human forgiveness cannot strictly speaking be earned. It is gift; it is given. That is why it is called for*give*ness. Repentance may be the necessary condition for receiving the gift in reality, for forgiveness is a relationship. Repentance, however, is never the adequate cause of forgiveness. What then is the intimate connection between our forgiving hearts and God's forgiveness of us?

"Forgive us as we forgive" need not imply human initiative with God's mercy. It may rather point to a parallel in the kind of forgiveness being asked. Forgive us *just as* or *even as* we forgive others. Forgive us in a similar way as we forgive others. All we know of forgiveness comes from our own human experience of being forgiven by others. We ask that God forgive us as we have known forgiveness so graciously and tenderly from others. In that same breath we acknowledge that forgiveness received from others but reflects the forgiveness given them by God. Human forgiveness is a pale reflection, though a real one, of the much more profound divine forgiveness. Nevertheless, we learn of God's ways by analogy with the human ways we have known. It is hard to imagine how anyone could comprehend God's forgiveness if they had never been forgiven during their lifetime by good people around them.

At a communal penance service of my own community, the Congregation of Holy Cross, a large number of priest-confessors were placed in a wide circle around the sanctuary of the church. The penitents were invited to approach them and make a simple confession of sins, in view of everyone. The congregation watched as people began lining up for each confessor. The congregation witnessed those confessors reach out and embrace each penitent. "Forgive us as we forgive each other" took on a new meaning for me. It became possible to grasp how tender and how universal must be the loving embrace and forgiveness of God when one could see a religious family acknowledge before each other their need for forgiveness and watch them publicly receive a warm and reconciling embrace from a representative of that whole community, and of the church beyond the confines of that place or that moment in time.

One might even propose another reading: may we forgive as God the Father forgives. Such a reading, however, may make the petition seem an exhortation to us rather than a prayer to the Father.

Let us change our reading: give us to forgive in a similar way as the Father forgives. Better yet: give us to forgive as Jesus who is Lord forgives. When Jesus hung in torment upon the cross, he prays for forgiveness in Luke's gospel: "Father, forgive them, they know not what they do" (24:34).[29] If human beings are created good and know goodness because God has given it to them, then sinfulness is somehow a distortion. Human beings were meant to love one another, and not to harm each other. We are tangled lovers, who have somehow become entangled in sinful motives and actions. Consequently our goodness is paralyzed and tied up. In such a knot of confusion, we do not know what we do. We are immobilized like Gulliver tied to the earth by many strands of floss. We are giants of spiritual awareness tangled in a thousand slight webs of our fickle attachments and loyalties. We are stranded in the snarls of our overall human history, both sinning and mightily sinned against. Our actions are not innocent, but they are forgivable. Even when we do our very best, we burden the future with our sins in the present that we judge now to be virtues. We are all mixed up in our place and time and can see only a small portion of what we do and what we fail to do. Thus we are victims of our circumstance at least in part; yet we are responsible for our freedom. In the Lord's Prayer we ask God to forgive us as we (Jesus) forgives, for tangled lovers know not what they do.

Finally, being forgiven and forgiving in turn would seem to be a reciprocal relationship. You know you have received forgiveness when you find yourself giving it. No one gives what they have not received. No one who has truly received does not give. Therefore we pray: let our forgiveness rise at the very instant we are forgiven. Let there be no discontinuity between being forgiven and offering forgiveness to all others. To be forgiven is to be changed at heart, to become ruthful and compassionate, to see offense from the point of view of God who loves the sinner. If we have received forgiveness in a way that touches the depth of our soul, we will be forgiving in turn. The one sets up the other, as a gift truly received brings about a return gift in gratitude. Manson writes: "If you cannot give forgiveness you cannot begin to receive it."[30] If we remain angry and unforgiving with others in their sin, we cannot forgive ourselves either. Nor do we appreciate that God can forgive us when we sin. Sebastian Moore writes of the Lord's Prayer: "forgive us our sins, *in the way of* us forgiving each other" or again "forgive us our sins *as* us forgiving each other, that is to say, truly."[31] When we are hard-hearted, our image of God, of ourself, and of the other is negative, closed, and unreceptive. When we forgive our brother and sister we acknowledge the forgiveness of the Father in a fuller way. When we have been profoundly forgiven by the Father, we offer forgiveness to our neighbor as a simple consequence. Love of God and love of neighbor go hand in hand. To love God is to love neighbor, and to love neighbor is to love God. To be forgiven by the Father is to forgive all others, and to forgive all others is to know forgiveness from the Father. The initiative and the grace is always God's, but the sign of the reception of grace is this new life. If you do not forgive, you have not received forgiveness in the way that gives new life. God's forgiveness enjoys a sovereign power to change our hearts of stone into hearts of flesh, our old unforgiving way into a new pattern of abundant mercy.

In the story that Jesus tells to Simon the pharisee, Jesus asks him which of the two people whose debt was cancelled will love their benefactor the most. Simon replies logically: "The one, I suppose, whose larger debt was forgiven" (Lk 7:43). Jesus then points out the sinful woman who in sorrow for her sins was bathing his feet with her tears and drying them with her hair. And he concludes: "So I tell you, her many sins have been forgiven; hence, she has shown great love. But the one to whom little is forgiven, loves little" (7:47). In the footnote to this verse in the NAB, we read: "literally, 'her many sins have been forgiven, seeing that she has loved much.' That the woman's sins have been forgiven is attested by the great love she shows toward Jesus. Her love is the consequence of her forgiveness."

The translation that most of us are familiar with is misleading: "I tell you, her sins, which are many, are forgiven; for she loved much." She is not forgiven, however, *because she loved much*. Rather *because she was forgiven*, she loved much. Moule argues that the crucial word because (*oti*) depends on the verb to tell rather than the verb to forgive. Thus: "The reason [Jesus is saying] why I [am able to] tell you that her many sins are forgiven is the fact that she is showing so much love."[32] This interpretation indeed fits the logic of the whole parable and its central point: forgiveness is the source of one's love. The one who is forgiven much loves much, and in a parallel way the one who is forgiven little (like Simon in the parable) loves little. Zerwick translates *oti* as *considering that*, which also supports this argument.[33] Van Linden renders the words of Jesus: "I tell you, her many sins are forgiven. Her great love shows this. The one who is forgiven little loves little."[34] In short, because human beings first receive love when forgiven, they are enabled to give love and be forgiving. No one loves before they themselves are loved. If anyone forgives, it is because they are forgiven. The initiative is always from God, who is the source of all goodness, even though there remains a paradoxical truth in the claim that the one who loves much will be forgiven much.

Sin is an offense both against God, and against the human victim of our sin, as well as against our own better self that never is provided a way to love because of our selfishness. Thus, forgiveness is the restoration of a bond of intimacy with God, with our neighbor, and also with our own inner soul where love and generosity are ever born and all too often starved. The text of the Lord's Prayer wishes to say that moments of forgiveness are all of a piece; you cannot have forgiveness from God unless you are en route to forgiveness that touches others and most of all oneself. To be loved is to love in return, and that is how we know we have been open to receive love. Readiness to receive calls forth readiness to give. Being loved softens our disposition so that we love in return. Always we are challenged to find the meaning of forgiveness in giving it. Paul writes: "bearing with one another and forgiving one another, if one has a grievance against another; as the Lord has forgiven you, so must you also do" (Col 3:13). The gospels counsel us to love our enemies, for God makes the sun to shine on the good and the bad alike. As Augustine says, it is not for those who ask our pardon that we are told to pray.

The Old Testament also knew there was a close relationship between giving forgiveness and receiving mercy from God. "Forgive your neighbor the wrong he has done, and then your sins will be pardoned when you pray" (Sirach 28:2). The Torah law of Jubilee that required every seven years a release from indebtedness in money, in land, and in servants, may throw light on this petition of the Lord's Prayer. Thirtle cites the Jubilee law as a likely source for "as we forgive." Accordingly, Christian Jewish disciples would pray in the spirit of the Mosaic law: "Release us from our debts, even as we also were in the habit of making release to those who were indebted to us."[35] The forgiveness given by the Father of Jesus was thereby compared to a perennial Jubilee year, the new age to come, the day the Lord has made, the time of grace. Lachs makes the same argument, while also noting the commonplace failure to keep the Law. To encourage a lender to loan money during the time right before a Jubilee year, the rabbinic tradition of *prosbul* allowed a creditor to file a document with the court in order to circumvent the intent of the remission of debts in the Jubilee year.[36] Thus, the

Lord's Prayer would ask for the disciple truly to keep the Jubilee year law of total forgiveness and to expect God to do no less.

In the New Testament spirituality, baptism is understood as a bath of regeneration. One is reborn. The "old man" dies. The newly baptized is a new creation. The baptized receive a complete remission of their sins. They know in the immersion in the pool of graceful waters a total washing that cleanses them of all guilt. They are forgiven from head to toe; they are clean in body and soul. As they emerge from the birthing waters of life, they pray for the first time in the community the Lord's Prayer. Would it not be the golden moment to forgive all others as God has just forgiven them? Having received unconditional forgiveness, they offer unlimited forgiveness. Having been forgiven, they are prompt to forgive. Having been so gifted, one responds with offering to share the wealth. Forgive others as God has just forgiven you. Forgive us, O Lord, even as we are forgiving one another. "Receive the holy Spirit. Whose sins you forgive are forgiven them . . ." (Jn 20:23). Baptism is the Spirit's gift of a new and merciful heart, a soul conformed to the image of the compassionate God. Forgive us our sins so we can live in a new community of love. Release our hearts with divine pity, for only then and thus do we have kindness for others. "When the pardon of God is received, it enables us to forgive."[37]

In the Western eucharistic liturgy, after we pray the Lord's Prayer we exchange the sign of peace as brothers and sisters. To address God as Father demands being at one in peace and forgiveness with each other. Jesus said: "Therefore, if you bring your gift to the altar, and there recall that your brother has anything against you, leave your gift there at the altar, go first and be reconciled with your brother, and then come and offer your gift" (Mt 5:23–24). Anyone who has tried to share a meal with an enemy or someone disregarded will know what a bitter experience it can be. The whole symbolism of a meal shared, bread given and taken, is that the good given me comes as a gift from loved ones around me who wish that given food to become my very body. Thus after asking in the Lord's Prayer for the Father to give us bread, we ask for forgiveness of our indebtedness. No one should break bread without prior reconciliation. The bread will be bitter food otherwise. Each eucharist is preceded by the "Confiteor," wherein we beg forgiveness of God and one another. After the crucifixion of Jesus, whose spear-raped body had been wounded by those whom he came to befriend, he takes the initiative to break bread again with his faithless and cowardly disciples as they lovingly used to do. Nothing else the risen

Christ could have done for them would have given the experience of being forgiven for the abandonment of their friend and lord.

Matthew and Luke exhibit several verbal differences in the second we-petition. Matthew uses the Greek conjunction *hos*, which in English means as, and Luke uses a somewhat less precise word, *gar*, which might be translated for or even as. Matthew employs the aorist tense in the verb, and Luke, as we have seen before, favors the present tense. Moreover, Luke adds "as we *ourselves (autoi* in Greek) forgive *everyone (panti* in Greek) indebted to us." *We ourselves-everyone* seems to intensify the human component in the divine forgiveness, just as the present tense emphasizes the everyday component in human mercy. Origen thought that the text in Matthew might be read mistakenly "as we forgive those *who repent* their sins against us," whereas Luke made it clear "as we forgive *everyone* who sins against us."[38] Matthew uses a noun for "as we forgive [have forgiven] our *debtors*," whereas Luke employs a participle, "even as we ourselves forgive everyone *indebted* to us."

The verb forms in Luke all contribute to the ongoing quality of forgiveness, which is a daily matter for the Christian living in history. Matthew's text favors an eschatological reading, in which the saving and sovereign deeds of God are called upon in their triumphant and decisive once and for all intervention in human history. The end times break into the moment, just as the infinite God, who encompasses all Being, created time and space in the beginning and even now sustains everything at every turn. Matthew, as we have seen before, emphasizes God as the One. Luke favors the Many. Matthew would have Christians forgiven by the Father and forgiving brother and sister in turn so that they are prepared for the judgment soon to come. Luke would have Christians forgiven by the Father and forgiving brother and sister in turn as the answer to one's prayer for forgiveness now and the validation of one's hope for tomorrow.

LEAD US NOT INTO TEMPTATION

THIS LAST OF THE WE-PETITIONS proves no less open to multiple interpretations than its predecessors. The most striking puzzle about the final petition is this. God leads no one into temptation. God does not even consider it, and thus needs no coaxing to resist. "No one experiencing temptation should say, 'I am being tempted by God'; for God is not subject to temptation to evil, and he himself tempts no one. Rather, each person is tempted when he is lured and enticed by his own desire" (Jas 1:13–14). The text of the petition as we have received it seems misleading. Moreover, everyday life leads everyone into temptations of one kind or another. All earthly life is a temptation to an exaggerated self-love and self-importance without God. Even the right thing can be done for the wrong reasons. Everything and anything can be a temptation to move away from God, or an opportunity to move closer. The Bible has been called the Book of Temptations. The many trials or tests or temptations of the chosen people in the desert come readily to mind. "Blessed is the man who perseveres in temptation, for when he has been proved he will receive the crown of life that he promised to those who love him" (Jas 1:12). Temptations overcome increase one's virtue, and in any event, they cannot be avoided. Thus, a distinction might be made between being inevitably exposed to temptations and entering into a consensual identification with an habitual vice or some grand seduction. "I sent to learn about your faith, for fear that somehow the tempter had put you to the test and our toil might come to nothing" (I Thes 3:5).

Origen in his commentary on the Lord's Prayer notes that the issue is not to avoid all temptation outright, but rather not to be entangled and overpowered by temptation. Tertullian and Cyprian both explain that God permits temptations, while not actually leading anyone into them. The Old Latin text before Jerome's (Vulgate) translation reads: *ne nos patiaris induci in tentationem*, or do not suffer us to be lead into temptation.[39] The petition thus becomes a plea to the Father not to allow temptation to ruin us. God permits temptation only to punish wrongdoing by allowing its inevitable consequences or to test virtue as gold is tried in the refiner's fire. All unworthy dross is burnt away and only pure virtue remains. Temptation from God's perspective is a revelation of virtue or its lack. As Tertullian insisted, even the just man Abraham was sorely tempted, or "tried." And in the Book of Judith we read:

> Besides all this, we should be grateful to the Lord our God, for putting us to the test, as he did our forefathers. Recall how he dealt with Abraham, and how he tried Isaac, and all that happened to Jacob in Syrian Mesopotamia while he was tending the flocks of Laban, his mother's brother. Not for vengeance did the Lord put them in the crucible to try their hearts, nor has he done so with us. It is by way of admonition that he chastises those who are close to him (8:25–27).

Job was lead into temptation by Satan and God permitted the trial to manifest despite suffering the deep perseverance in the virtue of Job. "My son, if you come forward to serve the Lord, prepare yourself for temptation" (Sirach 2:1). Satan was more successful with Eve, whose heart in Paradise was open to temptation. And Adam just as well. Israel fared no better in the desert:

> Remember how for forty years now the Lord, your God has directed all your journeying in the desert, so as to test you by affliction and find out whether or not it was your intention to keep his commandments. He therefore let you be afflicted with hunger, and then fed you with manna, a food unknown to you and your fathers, in order to show you that not by bread alone does man live, but by every word that comes from the mouth of the Lord. (Dt 8:2–3)

Augustine and Jerome interpreted the Lord's Prayer to mean that the Father would not allow one to be tempted beyond one's ability. The grace necessary to overcome temptation would be given. Paul writes: "No trial has come to you but what is human. God is faithful and will not let you be *tried* [a derivative form of *peirasmos*, which is the Greek word for temptation in the Lord's Prayer] beyond your strength; but with the trial he will also provide a way out, so that you may be able to bear it" (I Cor 10:13). God writes straight with crooked lines. "We know that all things work for good for those who love God, who are called according to his purpose" (Rom 8:28). Tyndale comments: "let us not slip out of thy lease, but hold us fast; give us not up, nor cease to govern us, nor take thy Spirit from us."[40] Even Jesus was tempted. In the beginning of his public ministry he is led into the desert to be tempted by the devil. In the end of his life when he is being tested by the agony of the cross Jesus prays: "Father, if you are willing, take this cup away from me; still, not my will but yours be done" (Lk 22:42). Jesus was always led by God, who sorely tested him.

Not only is the verb, "lead us not," apparently misleading, but temptation may also be an unfortunate translation of the Greek word, *peirasmos*. The English follows the Latin, *tentationem*. The Greek *peirasmos* very likely translates an Aramaic word, which cannot now be ascertained with certainty. The Syriac version of the Lord's Prayer uses a word that could be singular or plural. If plural, the petition may be talking of the many temptations in the life of humankind on earth. Job refers to the moral life as a "constant warfare" (7:1). If singular, the reference may be to one overwhelming temptation, which is the time of crucial trial. Such an endtime catastrophe was expected in the ultimate struggle between good and evil, between God and the Devil. This apocalyptic time of catastrophic suffering was referred to as the "Messianic woes,"[41] into which the individual might be drawn. And, always for a believer, the great temptation is to deny one's whole faith. The martyr's victory was seen as the triumph of God who did not allow the trial to overcome the beloved.

Let us assume that the Gethsemani account is the model for this petition in the Lord's Prayer for deliverance from temptation. Jesus tells the disciples in the Garden: "Watch and pray that you may not undergo the test [enter into temptation in the RSV]. The spirit is willing, but the flesh is weak" (Mt 26:41). Is he telling them to rise up and pray lest they come to deny him out of fear during his great trial, or lest they fall into any of a thousand moral temptations? Or, is Jesus telling them to pray that they may never be brought to the crucifixion in their life, to having to lay down their life for their friends with whom they shared the bread of life at the one table? In sum, is temptation in the Lord's Prayer the moment of ultimate temptation, the threat to one's very life and one's very faith in God? The "hour of death" is a moment of truth, a moment of testing our acceptance of God, a temptation to despair. The final temptation is a spiritual one. Should the Pater read: that you may not enter into the ultimate temptation, the time of *trial*? Should this petition read: *Save us from the time of trial*, as several Bible translations render it?[42] Is the temptation of the Christian in the Gethsemani gospel account a fall from moral virtue, or a shipwreck of an entire life caught in some intolerable predicament? Is the temptation to sin or to apostasy? Is the temptation to unlawfulness or to perdition, to wrongdoing or to the mystery of iniquity? Krister Stendhal writes of "lead us not into temptation": "Here is the non-heroic prayer. Not: When temptation comes, give me strength! Rather: We know that if Satan tightens the screws we have no chance. The spirit is willing, but the flesh is weak."[43]

Suffering is sometimes a good thing for human beings. It can deepen a person's soul, make them appreciative of life's blessings, evoke the hidden strengths in their heart. Athletes like to speak of the benefits of being pushed beyond one's physical limits; no pain, no gain is a proverb. To endure hardship, to accept challenge, to overcome pain remain triumphs of the human spirit and often deeply enriching experiences of human community, assistance, and the raw courage and perseverance of the human spirit. But the petition in the Lord's Prayer to be spared the trial is not about this kind of therapeutic suffering. In the Pater we pray not to be broken. We pray not to be so tortured that we become like an animal. We pray that we will not be deprived of food and sleep so severely that we cannot remember who we are. We pray that we will not be excruciatingly and systematically burned, and shocked, and stretched to pieces on a rack. We pray that our very freedom and our mind will not be massacred. That is the trial that one could fear from the bottom of one's soul. Thus, "do not put us to the test." One of the early English versions of the Lord's Prayer asks not to be lead into the "fandinge." The word is related to our word for foundering, as when a ship founders and it sinks on a reef. That shipwreck of soul is what we ask not to be lead into in the Lord's Prayer. "Out of the depths I cry to you, O Lord" (Ps 130:1). And, "From the days of John the Baptist until now, the kingdom of heaven suffers violence, and the violent are taking it by force" (Mt 11:12). Jesus promises those who suffer with him: "It is you who have stood by me in my trials, and I confer kingdom on you, just as my Father has conferred one on me, that you may eat and drink at my table in my kingdom; and you will sit on thrones judging the twelve tribes of Israel" (Lk 22:28).

All sin is finally a lack of faith. Adam and Even did not believe that God was looking after their happiness, and in mistrust they reached out to help themselves. Satan tells Jesus in the desert: "*If* you are the Son of God, command this stone to become bread" (Lk 4:3). Already tempted to despair on the cross as revealed in his cry of "My God, my God, why have you forsaken me?" (Mk 15:34), a last temptation was put to Jesus as a test of his faith in his God despite the awful suffering: "Let the Messiah, the King of Israel, come down now from the cross, that we may see and believe" (Mk 15:32). Everyday moral temptations may be a fair fight for a Christian, although the grace of God is yet needed. Crucifixion, however, in whatever form such a catastrophe comes to the Christian, is an unfair fight. Such a trial remains an overwhelming danger to lose faith in the Father altogether. Think of the holocaust of World War II as a time of *trial* rather than temptation for a contemporary Jew. Martyrdom for the individual in time of persecution is an ultimate *trial*. Torture is unspeakable; it can rip a healthy body and a strong spirit to shreds. How to cling to the spirit despite the weakness of the flesh. Nuclear holocaust, should it ever come to pass, will be a time of great *trial* for all humanity. Think of the end-of-the-world battle between good and evil described in the Apocalypse. "I will keep you safe in the time of trial that is going to come to the whole world to test the inhabitants of the earth" (Rv 3:10). Accordingly, the last we-petition of the Lord's Prayer might well read: "Save us from the time of trial" rather than "lead us not into temptation." If we are not saved from that *trial*, who can stand? "For at that time there will be great tribulation, such as has not been since the beginning of the world until now, no, nor ever will be. And if those days had not been shortened, no one would be saved; but for the sake of the elect they will be shortened" (Mt 24:21–22).

It has been noted that the noun *peirasmos* (temptation/trial/test in English) in the Greek of the gospel text might not refer to anything specific. *Peirasmos*, however, almost always means *trial* rather than temptation in the New Testament, although the Devil's temptations of Jesus in the desert remain a notable exception. *Peirasmos* is used there for what appears to be straightforward temptation. Unlike the Israelites unfaithful in the desert to their God, Jesus perseveres throughout forty days of hunger followed by Satan's temptations to distrust God and grasp power regardless of obedient faith. Perhaps we are here given a clue to the reconciliation of the terms temptation and trial. Temptations are over time; they belong to the realm of creation and the world of the Many. The trial is a moment of eternity that breaks into time; its outcome belongs to the realm of God as sovereign, and the world of the One. The temptations throughout the life of Jesus culminated inevitably in the showdown trial of the crucifixion. The temptations of Israel in the desert after the exodus from Egypt lead to the moment of crisis.

They demand food and water. They then fashion a golden bull to adore. The covenanted Jews fail God's test of their fidelity to the Covenant. Temptations encountered in the desert of this world lead the people of God to moments of trial. Our collective guilt draws even the innocent to the moment of trial, the testing of spirits, from which we beg deliverance in the Lord's Prayer. The test is of faith; the temptation is to apostasy.

One might conclude that there is only a fine line between temptation and trial, or between tempting to sin and testing the spirit. Some ambiguity about this petition of the Lord's Prayer is attested by the variant English translations themselves that range from "do not lead us into temptation" to "subject us not to the trial." The common liturgical practice of adding a coda (the so-called embolism) to the Lord's Prayer in the various elaborations that precede the doxology reveals how the community itself tried to clarify what it thought the prayer implied in its closing words. As I understand the matter, temptation is allurement to what is sinful. It has a negative connotation. Temptation is enticement into evil and seduction into sin. A test or a trial, on the other hand, has a positive connotation. God invites human beings to declare by their behavior in trying moments who they really are in the depths of their hearts. It is a test if one leaves a hundred dollar bill on the desk while the secretary closes the office. It is a temptation if one whispers to the secretary a solicitation to rob the bank.

Our whole life is a trial or test, an opportunity that we are given to work out in our expression of self the identity that we forge in the passing of the days of our lifetime. We need time to try out our life and to test whom we want to become. To parody the emergency broadcasting system: "this life is a test; it is only a test; if it were not you would have been told what to do and where to go." In our decisions lies our unique name. We are what we choose. In moments of jeopardy, in times of life and death, we declare in an especial way where we stand with the love of God. Hence moments of great suffering or danger are desired because they do distill the essence of our life in one response, and feared because they take on a conclusive quality. In this moment of trial I reveal myself. I declare who I am. I choose in a way that may not readily allow another choice. I commit myself. Hence in the Lord's Prayer we pray that we be not tried or tested (tempted) in a manner that threatens our ruin. If we must be tested, we pray for the moment of grace and the propitious way, a providential care that will help us with the crucial yes or no of our days in the eyes of our God.

BUT DELIVER US FROM EVIL

DOES THIS REQUEST FOR DELIVERANCE FROM EVIL, found only in Matthew's gospel, add further meaning to the preceding petition that requests not being lead into temptation or put to the test? Is this last line of the Lord's Prayer the positive statement of what the previous line expresses negatively: deliver us from evil, i.e., lead us not into evil temptation? Is the petition for deliverance from evil already contained in the words that ask to be saved from temptation or trial? Does Luke omit this line because he perceived that it was redundant, and he was in the habit of retelling the gospel story in more succinct ways? Origen thought "deliver us from evil" implied the "lead us not into temptation." Tertullian and Augustine maintained that the two lines were roughly equivalent. Maximus the Confessor in his commentary on the Lord's Prayer argued for a distinction. Temptation should be read as the law of sin, but evil as the devil, the evil one.

To complicate this matter further, does *evil* in this text refer to evil in general, a kind of abstract power of evil, or does it refer to the *evil one,* to the devil? The Greek word, *tou ponerou,* could be either the evil one or the evil thing (evil in general).[44] The conjunction in "*But,* deliver us" follows regularly after a negative verb, and thus need not set up a grammatical contrast: lead us not into, but on the contrary deliver us from. From a logical point of view, the translation of deliver us from the *evil one* does seem to distinguish this line from its predecessor more clearly. Temptation suggests an impersonal evil; the evil *one* points to our personal adversary the devil. And yet, the great *tempter* of humankind is the evil one. However, if the preceding line is read, "Save us from the time of *trial,*" it would seem that deliver us from the evil *one* might be the preferred translation. The "time of trial" is frequently conceived as a diabolical intervention and Satanic temptation. Paul writes to the church of his "fear that somehow the tempter had put you to the test and our toil might come to nothing" (1 Thes 3:5). The evil one would correspond aptly to the instigator of the great *trial* we wish to be saved from. Moreover, the sense of being "saved *from*," and not merely "not lead *into*" would fit the "deliver us *from* the evil one." Karl Barth comments that the Greek, *rhusai*, which means deliver, in its customary usage has the force of "snatch us from these jaws" of the evil one.[45]

Thus, the translation "Save us from the time of trial" instead of "lead us not into temptation" would seem readily to support the "deliver us from the evil *one*." The trial and the evil one are with reason associated. The eschatological dimension associated with Matthew would tend to yoke together "trial" and "evil one." The Lucan gospel, which lacks the "deliver us from evil / evil one," might more easily render the last petition of the Pater either "lead us [to enter] not into temptation" or "save us from the time of trial." While not ruling out the trial or test reading, *temptation* might appear more congruent with the everyday demands in the Lucan text and spirituality.

In many of the manuscripts of the Lord's Prayer there are glosses written to explain what this last petition might mean. In the Roman eucharistic liturgy there is an addition made after the recitation of the Lord's Prayer, which elaborates what the deliverance from evil might specifically mean: "Deliver us, Lord, from every evil . . . and all anxiety as we wait in joyful hope for the coming of our savior, Jesus Christ." Both the glosses on the scriptural text of the prayer and the add-on liturgical commentary that follows the Lord's Prayer in the eucharist today would indicate that questions of how to read the final petition are not new and have been addressed in many ways before.

Frederick Chase argues that the preposition *apo* more accurately refers to being protected *from*, rather than a deliverance *out of* a morass already encountered. The preposition *ek* would more properly fit the reading of delivering us out of the evil already encountered, that is, the evil of everyday temptations. The Lord's Prayer is thus read to ask that we be *saved from* the time of trial, and protected *from* the *evil one* who is instigator of such a test. "For our struggle is not with flesh and blood but with the principalities, with the powers, with the world rulers of this present darkness, with the evil spirits in the heavens" (Eph 6:12). In summary, the last petition asks for a prevention of a great evil, rather than a rescue from an already experienced evil. In such a reading the preposition *apo* supports the third we-petition as a plea for deliverance from an evil not yet encountered which would be disastrous, rather than for deliverance from the entanglements of a wicked world all around us and in which we are already immersed.

The early Latin commentators on the Lord's Prayer, and virtually all the Greek Patristic writers translate *ponērou* as the evil one.[46] The evil one was, of course, identified with the Devil, or Satan, the "adversary of man," the "prince of this world." Cyril of Jerusalem argued that if it were read as evil in the abstract, the clause became redundant: "If 'lead us not into temptation' referred to not being tempted at all, He [Jesus] would not have said: 'but *deliver* us from the Evil One.'" Gregory of Nyssa thought "temptation and the evil one meant one and the same thing." He argued: "if a man prays truly to be delivered from evil, he asks that he may be far from temptation. For no one would swallow the hook unless he had first gulped down the bait in his greed." Peter Chrysologus blends both understandings when he points out that "sin [is] from the devil, from whom all evil comes."[47] Augustine in his "Sermon on the Mount" thought that "lead us not into temptation" indicated a petition to preserve us from evil, whereas "deliver us from evil" was a petition to rescue us when already in trouble. Tyndale writes of deliverance as being plucked out of the world, the flesh, and the devil when we are fallen.

The Protestant tradition has tended to read the *evil one*, and to conceive of the struggle between good and evil as an apocalyptic one, a personal combat between God and the Devil as imaged in so much biblical writing. Nevertheless, the interpretation of evil in the abstract is clearly grammatically possible and was not absolutely unknown in early times.[48] Biblical evidence to this point can be given: "The Lord will rescue me from *every evil* threat and will bring me safe to his heavenly kingdom. To him be glory forever and ever. Amen" (2 Tim 4:18). In the Latin West from the time of Augustine, we find more readings supporting a generalized reading of evil. Later Scholastic theology would be more in sympathy with the mystery of evil metaphyscially investigated, than with the metaphorical and biblical imagery. In summary, however, evil in the abstract and evil personified would seem in their effect equivalent. The devil is readily seen as the essence of evil and font of all evils.

The Bible has a penchant for personifying evil. Philosophy is more likely to talk of evil in essential ways. Thus the Garden of Eden story that begins the Bible portrays the tempter in the form of a snake, and the Apocalypse that ends the Bible shows the Satanic figure as a dragon pursuing the woman to eat up her child.

The biblical world loved the color and forcefulness of metaphor. The New Testament is full of descriptions of the evil one, who is referred to as Satan, the Devil, the father of lies, murderer from the beginning, Mammon, Beelzebub, the prince of this world, the tempter, the accuser, your adversary the devil, the enemy.[49] In the commentary on the parable of the sower, Jesus says "the evil one comes and steals away what was sown in his heart" (Mt 13:19), and later on "the weeds are the children of the evil one, and the enemy who sows them is the devil" (Mt 13:38–39). Jesus saw his life as a combat with the devil, succinctly summarized in the three temptations in the desert that precede his public life. Jesus speaks of the devil and his angels frequently. In John we read this prayer of Jesus: "I do not ask that you take them out of the world but that you keep them from the evil one" (17:15). See also 1 John 2:14. The word in Greek here is *ponērou*, and the New American Bible in a footnote suggests this text, like the Lord's Prayer, refers to the "devil rather than to abstract evil." And Paul writes: "In all circumstances, hold faith as a shield, to quench all [the] flaming arrows of the evil one. And take the helmet of salvation and the sword of the Spirit, which is the word of God" (Eph 6:16–17). See also 2 Thessalonians 3:3. Alfred Delp comments on this text of the Pater: "In the natural course of existence we are again and again brought up against both the agony in the Garden and the temptation of the wilderness. There, too, genuine temptation had to be met, because our Lord was weak with hunger and because the devil found him vulnerable. The devil. Yes there is not only evil in this world, there is also the evil one; not only a principle of negation but also a tough and formidable anti-Christ."[50]

In conclusion, the final petition would seem to be a prayer for the Father's providence to save us from a trial beyond us, as well as for a remedy to our moral temptations. In the Book of Wisdom it is written: "Let us see if his words are true, and let us test what will happen at the end of his life; for if the righteous man is God's son, he will help him, and will deliver him from the hand of his adversaries. Let us test him with insult and torture, that we may find out how gentle he is, and make trial of his forbearance" (2:17–19). The plea is more to protect us from entering the trial or the clutches of the evil one, rather than a plea to rescue us who are already implicated with evil. Cyprian echoes Paul when he writes that if God is for you against the devil and the world, what is left to pray for? If one has God, one has everything. One is reminded of Paul's poignant hope:

> If God is for us, who can be against us? He who did not spare his own Son but handed him over for us all, how will he not also give us everything else along with him? . . . What will separate us from the love of Christ? Will anguish, or distress, or persecution, or famine, or nakedness, or peril, or the sword? . . . For I am convinced that neither death, nor life, nor angels, nor principalities, nor present things, nor future things, nor powers, nor height, nor depth, nor any other creature will be able to separate us from the love of God in Christ Jesus our Lord. (Rom 8:31–39)

I do not wish to enter the metaphysical question of whether or not the devil, commonly referred to under the proper names of Satan [the name means adversary in Hebrew] or Lucifer [the name means light-bearer in Latin] enjoys substantial existence as a spiritual person. Angels function as messengers of God, and they may be only metaphors for the actions in the world of the transcendent God. Biblical scholars argue among themselves, and most conclude that the metaphysical status of the devil cannot be decided by scripture alone. Philosophers and theologians have long theorized about angels, both good ones and bad. Their affirmative conclusion can stand on its own argument, but no one would claim such theorizing is beyond dispute. Helen Luke, a Jungian theologian, writes that the devil is "the identification of God in the ego's will to power."[51] Systemic social evil that traps good people in a web of bad deeds has seemed to many persons a diabolical evil. Regardless of how one answers the question, surely evil in its awful mystery of dark iniquity and the evil one in his or her malice converge toward a common ground. This is the kingdom of darkness, the kingdom opposed to God, the mystery of evil, of primordial sin that comes not from muddled human reasoning and tired bodies, but from wickedness that chooses the bad with knowledge and not with bodily concupiscence.

The angelic sin is the best example of the mystery of evil as inexplicable, unintelligible, a surd in a rational world. Adam and Eve in their original sin remain comprehensible. Although the first parents lacked nothing, they were outsmarted, and their bodies were complications. But the original sin of the angels defies all explanation. They were supremely intelligent, without physical passion or fatigue, and their freedom followed without the intervention of a bodily train of emotion-laden thought. Why ever would they fall away from God, the source of all being and goodness? Here is the mystery of evil, from which "delivery us, O Lord." Barth thought evil was in the last analysis the "infinite menace of the nothingness that is opposed to God himself" in the mystery of the One and the Many.[52] The mystery of the infinite God involves created beings taken out of nothing. The residue of that nothingness accounts for evil. Adam and Eve were delivered to evil because they wanted to be like gods, although they were human beings and they were creatures.

Deliver *us* from evil is in the final analysis not so much a plea for individual salvation from disaster as a prayer for the community, the church, and the whole world to whom it is sent in mission. Jesus promised that the "gates of the netherworld shall not prevail against" this church community (Mt 16:18). Evil will not triumph in the end over good, nor the Adversary over the sovereign Lord. The "one begotten by God he protects, and the evil one cannot touch him" (1 Jn 5:18). There are not two kingdoms; there is only the kingdom of heaven within which evil is permitted by God a certain space for a certain time. The church community is not guaranteed that it will be free of evil and its consequences. It may indeed wound itself with sin, mutilate itself with schism, suffer persecution and all manner of abuse, from without or from within. None of this evil will be fatal. That is the promise. The church community, the body of Jesus Christ, will perdure despite these evils and the evil one. Otherwise God is undone by evil and God's promises fail, and our hope is in vain. But the Lord's Prayer which ends with a plea for deliverance from evil began with the recognition of that hallowed name which is sovereign both on earth and in heaven. From that almighty Father and through our Lord Jesus Christ whose Kingdom has come does this prayer of prayers have its warrant to hold out for us its invincible hope. Deliver us from evil once and for all.

SUMMARY: THE WE-PETITIONS

WE BEGIN WITH ASKING FOR BREAD, the staff of life, and we close by asking to be delivered from evil, whose wages is death. The gift of bread includes all that we could ever need to sustain our life in all its multiple dimensions: physical, social, intellectual, spiritual. Deliverance from evil includes all that we could ever fear would end our life physically or spiritually. The we-petitions are thus comprehensive. They cover all our concupiscible desires to consume and to live, and all our irascible desires to preserve ourselves from any diminishment of our being. These requests in the Lord's Prayer remain most simple and forthright. They reveal the essence of all petitionary prayer, which is need, that is known and recognized, to reach beyond one's own resources. For our daily bread we need faith; for a forgiving heart we need charity; for deliverance from all evil we need hope. The we-petitions do not primarily instruct us; they do not insistently urge us to live better lives. These succinct prayers ask only for what we must have to live, and they ask as children who turn for the only support of their lives to their father and mother.

The we-petitions contain the essence of all petitionary prayer. Reliance on God for bread, heart, and deliverance from evil that is beyond us makes up the basic attitude of faith. Similarly, the essence of temptation and sin is to trust in oneself rather than in God. In the temptations of Jesus in the desert we can somewhat see a parallel with the we-petitions of the Lord's Prayer. (1) Jesus is tempted to turn the stones into bread. He counters the devil with the belief that not by bread alone does one live. Thus, "Give us this day our daily bread." (2) Jesus is tempted to test God's special love and protection of himself by casting his body down from the pinnacle of the temple. He counters the devil with the belief that one ought not test God. Thus, "Lead us not into temptation." (3) Jesus is led up to a high mountain and tempted with the promise of all the kingdoms of the world if only he will fall down and adore Satan, the prince of this world. Jesus counters the devil with the belief that only the Lord God is to be adored. "Deliver us from the evil one."

Jesus chose bread as the symbol of his body, broken and given for the life of many. The choice was well suited to a hungry world, where half the global population goes to bed with empty stomach. Our life comes from the Father, creator of heaven and earth, and we appropriately call to that same Father to give us our daily bread. The air we breathe, the food we eat, the clothes we wear, the family who sustains us, the friends who draw us forth, the language and learning that instruct us, and the faith and sacraments that nourish us are all gifts of the provident Father. Nothing comes to us without the core gift of God that surrounds it. We are endlessly needful, and never truly self-sufficient without God. The infinite One, the almighty-Father shares his being as food for us and with us. Luther writes in the *Short Catechism*: "God gives daily bread indeed without our prayer, also to all the wicked; but we pray in this petition that He would lead us to know it, and to receive our daily bread with thanksgiving."[53]

The plea for forgiveness touches the human family deeply, for the lack of bread shared keeps us apart. The gift of bread offers us the chance to break bread in a meal together that is a token of our reconciling. Forgiveness is the bread of the soul. We need to be at one with God and with our brothers and sisters. Our spiritual hunger for unity and friendship begs its bread just as our physical hunger asks for plain food. Division, enmity, and hatred starve our soul-life, and we die within. Hatred is a gradual poison that kills not only its victim but its source. The oppressor saps the life of the oppressed, but consequently the oppressed cannot nourish the life of the oppressor, who is starving alone and from within. Think of all the hungry and victimized children on this planet. Think of the world wars, the genocidal massacres, the two hundred million violent deaths of the twentieth century. Inspect the bundle of iron keys in your pocket that lock out others who might steal, and lock in those who live in fear. If women have been oppressed by a patriarchal order, men have distorted themselves with violence and competition to make themselves oppressors. No one wins, unless everyone wins. We are entangled lovers, wanting to reach out, to be tender and giving, trustful and cooperative, but never achieving such forgiveness for long. We are sinned against as well as sinning. Our guilt is so understandable, even if not excusable. To know all is to forgive everything. The terrible things we do to each other make up our sins; our failure to do enough to reach out to others makes up our boundless indebtedness. We pray, therefore, for our daily forgiveness after we have asked for our daily bread. Our body must live, but so must our soul. Give us daily bread just as we feed others; give us daily forgiveness even as we forgive others.

We are so vulnerable to evil. Even before we are born, the air our mother breathes and the food she eats, the emotional love she is given or denied, will touch the marrow of our bones and the depths of our soul. Any man or woman can so easily be undone by life. Any man or woman can so easily be wounded by evil that traps them. Our body is but warm water cupped in soft tissue stretched over breakable bones. Put someone on the rack, burn her breasts, crush his testicles, inject poisonous drugs into their veins and you can change anyone into a shambles. Starve them, confine them, deprive them of sleep. Or, let nature have its way with cancer, with a blood clot to the brain, with automobile smashes that mash fragile flesh. Chemicals in tobacco smoke, addictive drugs ingested, alcohol imbibed in excess, we hardly need our neighbor to ruin our body and soul. Our life is wide open to evil all around us. We live in fear of the nuclear cloud poised above us, and the earthquake beneath us. Augustine writes: "In adversity I long for prosperity, in prosperity I fear adversity. What middle place is there betwixt these two, where the life of man is not all trial? Woe to the prosperities of the world, once and again, through fear of adversity, and corruption of joy! Woe to the adversities of the world, once and again, and the third time, from the longing for prosperity, and because adversity itself is a hard thing, and lest it shatter endurance. Is not the life of man upon earth all trial, without any interval?"[54] Life is a "vale of tears." "Deliver us from evil" is a prayer we continually murmur in our sleep when we unconsciously grind our teeth, and clench our jaw tightly against the terrors of our dreams. Our bodies are so vulnerable, our virtues so perishable. Life so easily becomes terrible, and death is dreadful. We are unable to defend ourselves from catastrophe from within as well as from without, from enemies as well as from our own flawed and foolish freedom. Every prayer ends like the Lord's Prayer: God help us! "Deliver us from evil."

If an infant child could formulate a prayer to its mother, it would ask three things. Feed me; change me; do not drop me. When we pray, our petition is more sophisticated but the basic human predicament still prevails. (1) "Give us our daily bread" is an acknowledgment that God our Father feeds us. Fledgling birds in the nest clamor for their food. Their entire being becomes seemingly a mouth that can never be filled with enough nourishment for the demand from within to grow. We nurture ourselves persistently and insatiably at the breast of life, whether mother earth or holy mother church. There is no more profound icon of the needful human condition before God the Father than the child Jesus at the breast in his mother's arms. The madonna and child is a tender and human picture of hungry life needful in the arms of God who gives us our daily bread.

(2) "Change us" is a child's plea to a parent to refresh their body. Make us clean again. Too often our sinful society is a wasteland, and our inner life is soiled like our linen. Bathe us clean and dress us in white garments. Forgive us our sins against our God and one another. It is the fear of death that makes us mangle life with our strangleholds that reveal our anxiety. We cannot let go of our self-serving and self-defensive ways. We spoil the beauty around us in our attempt to cling to it. We make love to others willing or not, for we need to love God and cannot find our way. The woman at the well was thirsty for the living water Jesus would give her; her five husbands left her thirsty. There is no more profound icon of the sinful human condition before God the Father than Jesus on the cross with John and Mary at his feet, and the thieves, one repentant and the other unrepentant, crucified on either side of him. Sin crucifies our living self, and we bleed to death. Jesus who dies for us with forgiveness on his lips and concern for the others around him is a tender and human picture of our sinful life in the arms of the Lord Jesus, who will not let go of the drowning man or woman among us, even if in our sinfulness we drag him down with us.

(3) Children in the arms of another know when they are secure. They fear falling even before they can recognize danger. "Do not drop us" is a plea to God to keep us from falling into a perdition we cannot even imagine, but can only be terrified of. Don't let us fall. "I have observed Satan fall like lightning from the sky" (Lk 10:18) is a frightening text. If the angel of light has fallen into darkness, what of lesser lights? Protect us, do not let us be lost, or drop out of sight. In the Psalms we read: "hide me in the shadow of thy wings" (17:8). The image is one of being enfolded and overseen. The mother bird hides her defenseless young under her wings at night to keep them from the enemy. No one wants to lose their life. We fear the death of our body; we should fear even more the death of our soul. The Lord's Prayer directs us to say: "deliver us from evil." Carry us in your arms and we shall be safe. There is no more profound icon of the fearful human condition before God the Father than the dead body of Jesus on his mother's lap. The pieta presents mother and

son seemingly defeated by death, yet soon they will be triumphant in the resurrection. God will not let us drop from his arms. The pieta is a tender and human symbol of our mortal life in the arms of God, whom we pray to hold us up from falling and to deliver us from every evil.

Just as the thou-petitions yield the image of the Trinity with a little accommodation of the text, so the we-petitions might also be aligned with the work of the Trinity. All the operations of God in the world are the work of all the divine persons together. Even the incarnation of the Son is the work of the Trinity, the one God, even though only the Son became flesh. Nonetheless, we conveniently assign the work of creation to the father, redemption to the Son, and sanctification to the Holy Spirit. Similarly, the work of the Father belongs "in the beginning," the work of the Son in the church time, and the work of the Spirit especially in the end times of the world when creation is finally transfigured and lifted up into God. The petition for daily bread fits the need of all creation from the beginning for its existence and its sustenance. The petition for the forgiveness of sins fits the new creation that rises out of the death of sin itself now undone by the death and resurrection of Jesus Christ. The petition for deliverance from evil fits the renewal of the face of the earth by the Holy Spirit and the final consummation "in the ending" when God will be all in all. In sum, bread is the creation of human life; forgiveness is the re-creation of human life; and deliverance from evil is the transfiguration of human life in union with the Father, the Son, and the Holy Spirit. In the Lord's Prayer we are throughout mindful that we address the Father, Son, and Spirit. We ask for ourselves the bread of new life, the heart of new flesh that comes from receiving and giving forgiveness, and the new heaven and new earth that rises from the fulfillment of the whole creation in the beatitude that eye has not seen and which God has prepared for all those who love goodness.

THE THOU- AND WE-PETITIONS COMPARED

HAVING LOOKED AT EACH OF THE PETITIONS of the Lord's Prayer separately, what more might be said of them as a group in conclusion? Peter Chrysologus writes that the Paternoster gives the Christian "the theme of praying, the subject matter to ask for, and the norm of making petition."[55] John Chrysostum claimed of the Lord's Prayer that "each of the petitions encloses all Christian perfection."[56] The *Roman Catechism* concludes that the petition "deliver us from evil" contains the substance of all the rest. Clearly one might have expectations that the petitions of the Our Father capsulize the essence of petitionary prayer. The words are few and the purity and simplicity of what is asked reminds the believer of who God is and what constitutes the human condition.

Augustine noted that the first three petitions concern God's desires and interests, and the second three concern us human beings.[57] Thy name (1), Thy kingdom (2), and Thy will (3), establish a vertical and divine dimension to the prayer. Our daily bread (4), forgiveness of our sins (5), and our deliverance from evil (6) establish a horizontal and human dimension. In the former we attend to eternity, and in the latter to time in this life. The former address the One and the latter the Many. In the first set of petitions of the Pater we acknowledge the One infinite God, and in the second set of petitions we pray for the needs of the Many in creation. Let God be God; let creatures be creatures. It was the original sin to want to be as God. Love God and love neighbor, a creature as oneself, sums up the Lord's Prayer.

In the incarnation of Jesus Christ the One and the Many come together in a marvelous communion. In the prayer of the Lord Jesus the vertical and the horizontal, the divine and the human, the eternal and the temporal are reconciled because they are reconciled first of all in his flesh. We in turn pray the petitions of the Lord's Prayer in the Lord Jesus and with him and not alone. We do not understand how the concerns of God and the concerns of this world dovetail perfectly, but in the death and resurrection of Jesus we have a demonstration of that integration and at*one*ment. The Lord's Prayer manifests then not two causes, the divine concern and the human, but rather one cause and one concern—the kingdom of God which enfolds the creation of the world and which has been irrevocably bonded to its creator in the enfleshment of the beloved and the only Son.

In the Lord's Prayer one can also discover the lineaments of the Old Testament promises made to Israel. For Christians Jesus is the messiah long awaited, and in him are fulfilled the hopes of the covenanted people of God descended from Abraham. Early in this history of salvation Moses was told the sacred name of *YHWH* on the holy ground of the burning bush. In the invocation of the Father in heaven whose name is hallowed one can recognize the completion of that revelation. Here is the priestly access of Moses to the throne of God brought yet closer in the Son who is drawn to the bosom of the Father. In "thy kingdom come" one can recognize the kingdom promised to David and to his successors forever. Here is the royal role that Jesus as Son of God made flesh was given. As King of kings he would inaugurate the final kingdom of God. In God's "will be done" one can recognize the restoration of Israel, and the spiritual role given it after the Babylonian exile to bring inner salvation through holiness of life to all the nations. Here is the prophetic role that Jesus as "the way, the truth, and the life" embodied in his days among us. And when Jesus left this world, he sent the Holy Spirit into our hearts to teach us all these things that he spoke of so that the truth, holiness, justice, and peace of the prophets might be enfleshed in the hearts of the new people of God. In sum, in the name (1), the kingdom (2), and the will (3), one can draw a parallel with the priest, the king, and the prophet. These were the traditional roles of the messiah of God, whom Christians believe to be Jesus who is Lord.[58]

The petitions also lend themselves to other parallels with the Old Testament. To Moses was revealed the unknown name of God, "I am who am." That hallowed name answered the cry for bread of the people in the desert with the gift of manna from heaven, their "daily bread." To David was given the kingdom that has no end. His sin was ever before him. He would yearn to forgive his sinful son Absalom's rebellion, just as David had himself been forgiven by God for his sin that failed to acknowledge the kingship of God. To Isaiah was given the hope of deliverance. He suffered the Babylonian exile and the terrible cost of evil in his own people. The prophets prayed for God's deliverance of their people from the evils that confronted them. Daily bread, forgiveness of sins, and deliverance from evil parallel the holy name, the kingdom of the Father, and the doing of God's holy will on earth as in heaven. Moreover, in the bread, the forgiveness, and the deliverance, one can draw a parallel with the messianic priest, the king, and the prophet. In the daily bread received with thanksgiving and adoration the name of God is hallowed; it is a priestly role. In the forgiveness of sins in a world when what is done to the least of my brethren is done to me, the kingdom of God has come upon us; it is a kingly justice. In the day that evil is undone and we are liberated from sin, the will of God will be done, and earth and heaven will be as one; it is a prophetic judgment. The good prevails over the evil. In the holy name and the holy bread we know the Father and the creator. In the kingdom come on earth and the forgiveness of sins we know the Son and the redeemer. In the will of God done on earth and our deliverance from all evil we know the Holy Spirit and the sanctifier of the human heart, whose descent upon us renews the face of the earth.

One need not find all such comparisons of the petitions of the Pater a matter of precision. These are suggestive ways of relating the petitions of the Lord's Prayer. The richness of the prayer lies in its adaptability to a wide range of interpretation.[59] Although there remains a constant content to the Our Father, there are also endless ramifications that give a momentary glimpse into a religious world that ultimately is as simple as just one word, the Word of God made flesh in Jesus Christ who is Lord. Simone Weil writes: "The Our Father contains all possible petitions; we cannot conceive of any prayer not already contained in it. It is to prayer what Christ is to humanity. It is impossible to say it once through, giving the fullest possible attention to each word, without a change, infinitesimal perhaps but real, taking place in the soul."[60]

PART THREE

Other Commentary

INTRODUCTION

Not only is the bibliography through the centuries about the Lord's Prayer enormous, the interest in this prayer is attested also by the large number of Patristic authors who have written commentary upon this gospel prayer. Both Greek and Latin, East and West have contributed mightily to the study of the Lord's Prayer. Commentaries on the gospel of Matthew and of Luke add further study of the gospel text itself. I have chosen for this anthology, however, more comprehensive works about the Lord's Prayer.

For the invocation, "Our Father who are in heaven," I have chosen a selection from the commentary of Cyprian of Carthage. His writings are influenced by Tertullian, and together they represent the earliest ample Latin Patristic commentary on the Lord's Prayer. To this day Cyprian's commentary remains among the best of all the Latin commentaries through the centuries.

Cyprian was born probably at Carthage between 200 and 210. He was a wealthy and well-educated pagan who was converted while a brilliant rhetor, or lawyer, in Carthage. He was baptized probably in 246 and shortly thereafter designated bishop of Carthage. He was beheaded in 258 during the persecution of Decius. His "De Dominica Oratione" ("About the Lord's Prayer") was composed early in 252. Similar to the commentary of Tertullian, Cyprian's work was also intended for catechumens. He also wrote for the entire Christian community, whose unity under the bishop remained fragile.

"Hallowed be Thy name" is discussed in a selection from the commentary on the Lord's Prayer by Gregory of Nyssa. He is an early and outstanding Greek Patristic author. His work is known for its spiritual and allegorical emphasis. His mystical words seem fitting appreciation of the "hallowed name."

Gregory of Nyssa was born circa 335 in Cappadocia in present-day Turkey. Together with his older brother, Basil the Great, and his friend, Gregory Nazianzus, he completes the trio of Cappadocian fathers of the church. His sister, Macrina, remains an important figure in the history of monasticism. Gregory was an educated rhetor.

He was influenced by Plato's philosophy, Origen's theology, and the allegorical bent of the biblical school of Alexandria. In 371 he was made bishop of the small see of Nyssa in Caesaria in Cappadocia. He was a leading theologian at the second ecumenical council, held in Constantinople in 381. His *Life of Moses* and commentary on the *Canticle of Canticles* give expression to his mystical theological insights. He died circa 394. Gregory of Nyssa's commentary on the Lord's Prayer consists of a series of five homilies; I quote from the first part of the third homily.

"Thy Kingdom come" is discussed in a selection from Maximus the Confessor. He is a late and less-known Greek Patristic author. His commentary on the Lord's Prayer is fulsome and magisterial. It seems to me in style and content praise well suited to the "kingdom." The importance of this commentary by Maximus has been generally overlooked, and indeed it has only recently been available in English.

Maximus was born circa 580 in Constantinople and died at Lazica on the Black Sea in 662. His tongue and right hand were cut off by Emperor Constans II because of the refusal of Maximus to change his teaching about the Monothelite controversy in Christology. The subtitle of his commentary on the Lord's Prayer reads: "A Brief Explanation of the Prayer Our Father to a Certain Friend of Christ by Saint Maximus, Monk and Confessor." His commentary was probably written between 625 and 630.

"Thy will be done" is discussed in a selection from the theological commentary on the Lord's Prayer by Thomas Aquinas. He represents the height of medieval theological wisdom. His scripture commentaries, though abundant, are less well known. The combination of his theological reflection on the implications of doing God's will and his commentary on the biblical text itself makes the selection from Aquinas well yoked to this petition of the Lord's Prayer in Matthew.

Thomas Aquinas was born circa 1224 in Naples and died in Fossanuova in 1274 while en route to the Council of Lyons. His *Summa Theologica* is a monumental work of medieval theological synthesis. His theological writings are voluminous and masterful. His integration of ancient Aristotelian philosophy with classical Christian theology represents an enduring contribution to Catholic theology to this day. The "Collationes super Pater Noster" are collected in the *Opuscula Theologica* of Thomas Aquinas. These sermon-conferences were delivered in the vernacular in the parish church of the Dominican priory in Naples during the Lent of 1273, some months before his death. They survive in Latin translation with editing by his secretary, Reginald of Piperno.

For the much discussed and still mysteriously worded petition, "give us our *daily* bread," I have used a long selection from Origen's commentary on the Lord's Prayer in his masterful commentary on Christian prayer. Origen is a very early and brilliant Greek Patristic author, roughly contemporary with Cyprian in the West. Origen's commentary is the most outstanding one of all the Patristic commentaries, and the earliest in the East. To this day it remains quite possibly the single most helpful commentary on the Lord's Prayer.

Origen was born in Alexandria in Egypt circa 185. His father died as a martyr in 202. Origen conducted a school of catechetics and produced a prodigious amount of theological commentary and scriptural exegesis. Almost all of the Bible is commented upon, and with more than one approach. Origen may be the greatest theologian of the Greek Church, although not all of his writings proved to be orthodox. He died in Tyre in Asia Minor in 253. Origen's commentary "On Prayer" was written after 230 and probably in Caesaria in Palestine. It was dedicated to Ambrose the deacon and to Tatiana. The commentary on the Lord's Prayer is contained therein as a principal part.

"Forgive us our trespasses" is covered with a selection from both Teresa of Avila and Simone Weil. Saint Teresa is known both as a mystic and as a reformer of the Carmelite Sisters during the Counter-Reformation. She sees the Lord's Prayer as a map of contemplative prayer in its essentials. Teresa of Jesus was born in Avila in 1515 and died in 1582. She began the wide reform of the Carmelite Order with the nunnery in Avila in 1562. Her writings on the mystical life have been exemplary and Teresa was declared a doctor of the church. The *Way of Perfection* was finished in 1566 and then revised in 1569. It was published at the end of her life about 1579. In this outstanding work on prayer written to her Carmelite sisters, the entire Lord's Prayer is commented upon in passing.

Simone Weil is a twentieth-century French mystic and a woman of extraordinary intellectual and spiritual insight. Her commentary on the Lord's Prayer probes the depth of the mystery of human and divine forgiveness. Simone Weil was born in Paris in 1909. In her life and writings she was both a mystic in pursuit of God and an activist compassionate for the poor and oppressed. She died in England in 1943 of malnutrition, in part because she maintained her food ration should not exceed that of her compatriots who had been unable to escape Nazi-occupied France. *Waiting for God* consists mainly of letters and essays written to Jean-Marie Perrin, O.P., a priest and spiritual mentor in the last years of Weil's life, 1940–42. At this time she was living in Ardèche in France as the guest of Gustave Thibon. After a conversion to prayer during a visit to Assisi in 1937, Simone Weil recited the Lord's Prayer daily and with deliberate concentration. Her commentary on the Lord's Prayer is a short essay within this anthology of her spiritual writings.

"Lead us not into temptation" is discussed in a selection from a commentary by St. Augustine on Matthew's Sermon on the Mount, within which is found the Lord's Prayer. Augustine is a giant of theological writing whose influence stretches from late antiquity through the Middle Ages. Along with Aquinas he is probably the most influential of Church writers with regard to overall theological understanding in the Church in the West.

Augustine was baptized by Ambrose, Bishop of Milan, in 387. The account of his twenty-year conversion is given in Augustine's own *Confessions*. He was ordained a priest in 391 and consecrated bishop of Hippo near Carthage in North Africa in 395. Augustine died in 430, having written voluminously of Christian theology, pastoral sermons, and scriptural commentary. Augustine's commentary on the Sermon on the Mount (Mt 5–7) is a written treatise, composed in the several years between his ordination to the priesthood and his elevation to the episcopacy.

"Deliver us from evil" ["Put us not to the test"] is discussed with selections from Alfred Delp's commentary on the Lord's Prayer and from Leonardo Boff's book on the same subject. Alfred Delp was a Jesuit in Nazi Germany who died in prison because of his criticism of the war. He was born in Mannheim, Germany in 1907. He was a convert to Catholicism in 1923 and became a member of the Jesuit Order in 1926. He was ordained a priest in 1937. During the crucial years of World War II, 1939–42, Delp was editor of the influential magazine *Stimmen der Zeit*. Because of his participation in the Kreisau Circle, an anti-Nazi group devoted to a Christian social order to be established after the war, he was arrested in July 1944. He was later condemned to be hung to death in prison on February 5, 1945. Delp's commentary on the Lord's Prayer was written from his prison cell. The first pages are dated from Advent 1944.

Leonardo Boff is one of the leading liberation theologians of Latin America. He was born in 1938 in Concordia (Santa Catarina State) Brazil. In 1964, after theological studies, Boff was ordained a

Franciscan priest in Petropolis, where he currently teaches theology at the major seminary there. He received a doctorate in theology in 1971 from the University of Munich. Leonardo Boff is considered a controversial major figure in Latin American theology. His commentary on the Lord's Prayer has been reviewed as an "inaugural eschatology" that does not exempt the Christian believer from social responsibility to the poor here and now. The work has been described as "simultaneously a helpless cry from a broken world and a clarion call to believe unto justice." His interpretation of the Lord's Prayer in light of the evil encompassing the oppression of the poor is a fitting companion piece to the Delp selection. Both authors warn us of complacency in the face of massive evil, as does the final petition. Both authors, at the close of the prayer, draw us into the contemporary world and into active care and concern. Indeed Christian prayer should always lead to conversion of life and tireless love for the children of the one Father who through us and with us would give us each and all our daily bread.

CYPRIAN OF CARTHAGE

The Lord's Prayer*

Chapter 1

THE PRECEPTS OF THE GOSPEL, most beloved brethren, are other than divine teachings, foundations for building hope, supports for strengthening faith, nourishments for encouraging the heart, rudders for directing our course, helps for gaining salvation, which, as they instruct the docile minds of believers on earth, conduct them to the heavenly kingdom. God wished many things also to be said and heard through the prophets, His servants; but how much greater are the things which the Son speaks, which the Word of God, who was in the prophets, testifies with His own voice, no longer commanding that the way be prepared for His coming, He Himself coming and opening and showing the way to us, that we who thus far have been wandering in the shadows of death, improvident and blind, illumined by the light of grace, may hold to the way of life with the Lord as our leader and guide.

Chapter 2

He who, among His other salutary admonitions and divine precepts by which He counsels His people unto salvation, Himself also gave the form of praying, Himself advised and instructed us what to pray for. He who made us to live taught us also to pray, with the same benignity, namely by which He has deigned to give

---

*"About the Lord's Prayer," in *Saint Cyprian Treatises*, translated and edited by Roy J. Deferrari (New York: Fathers of the Church, Inc.: 1958), 127–36. This book is volume 36 of the Fathers of the Church series. Copyright © the Catholic University of America Press. Reprinted with permission of the Catholic University of America Press. The English translation was based on the critical Latin edition of W. Von Hartel, *Corpus Scriptorum Ecclesiasticorum Latinorum* 3:1–3 (Vienna, 1868–71).

and bestow the other things, so that, while we speak to the Father with that prayer and supplication which the Son taught, we may more easily be heard. Already He had foretold that the hour was coming when "the true adorers would adore the Father in spirit and in truth";[1] and He fulfilled what He promised before, so that we, who by His sanctification have received the Spirit and truth, may also by His teaching adore truly and spiritually. For what prayer can be more spiritual than that which was given us by Christ, by whom the Holy Spirit was sent to us, what prayer to the Father can be more true than that which was sent forth from the Son, who is truth, out of His mouth? So to pray otherwise than He taught is not ignorance alone but even a sin, since He Himself has established and said: "You reject the command of God, that you may establish your own tradition."[2]

Chapter 3

So let us pray, most beloved brethren, as God the Teacher has taught. It is a friendly and intimate prayer to beseech God with his own words, for the prayer of Christ to ascend to His ears. Let the Father acknowledge the words of His Son, when we make prayer. Let Him who dwells within our breast Himself be also in our voice, and since we have Him as the advocate for our sins before the Father, let us put forward the words of our Advocate. For since He says: "Whatsoever we shall ask the Father in His name, He will give us,"[3] how much more effectively do we obtain what we seek in the name of Christ, if we ask with His own prayer?[4]

Chapter 4

But let those who pray have words and petitions governed by restraint and possessing a quiet modesty. Let us bear in mind that we stand in the sight of God. We must be pleasing in the sight of God both with the habit of body and the measure of voice. For as it is characteristic of the impudent to be noisy with clamors, so on the other hand does it benefit the modest to pray with moderate petitions. Finally, in His teaching the Lord bade us to pray in secret, in hidden and remote places, in our very bed-chambers, because it is more befitting our faith to realize that God is everywhere present, that He hears and sees all, and by the plenitude of

His majesty penetrates also hidden and secret places, as it is written: "I am a God at hand and not a God afar off. If a man hide himself in hidden places, shall I not see him? Do not I fill heaven and earth?"[5] And again, "In every place the eyes of the Lord behold the good and the evil."[6] And when we are gathered together with the brethren in one place and celebrate divine sacrifices with a priest of God, we ought to be mindful of modesty and discipline, and not toss our prayers about at random with uncouth voices and not cast forth with turbulent loquaciousness our petition, which should be commended to God in modesty, because the hearer is not of the voice but of the heart, and is not to be admonished by shouts, who sees our thoughts, as the Lord proves when He says: "Why do you think vainly in your hearts?"[7] And in another place: "And all the churches shall know that I am a searcher of the desires and the heart."[8]

Chapter 5

This does Anna in the first Book of Kings, portraying a type of Church, maintain and observe, who prays to God not with a noisy petition but silently and modestly within the very recesses of her heart. She spoke with a hidden prayer but with manifest faith; she spoke not with the voice but with the heart, because she knew that so the Lord hears, and she effectually obtained what she sought, because she asked with faith. Divine Scripture declares this saying: "She spoke in her heart and her lips moved, but her voice was not heard, and the Lord heard her."[9] Likewise we read in the psalms: "Speak in your hearts and in your beds be ye sorrowful."[10] Through Jeremias also the Holy Spirit suggests and teaches these same things, saying: "In the heart, moreover, O Lord, you ought to be adored."[11]

Chapter 6

Moreover, most beloved brethren, let him who adores not ignore this, how the publican prayed with the Pharisee in the temple. Not by impudently lifting his eyes to heaven nor by insolently raising his hands, but striking his breast and testifying to the sins inclosed within did he implore the help of divine mercy, and, although the Pharisee was pleased with himself, this man rather deserved to be sanctified who thus asked, who placed the hope of salvation not in confidence in his innocence, for no one is innocent, but confessed his sins and prayed humbly, and He who forgives the humble heard him as he prayed. This the Lord lays down in his Gospel saying: "Two men went up to the temple to pray, the one a Pharisee, the other a publican, the Pharisee stood and began to pray thus within himself: 'O God, I thank thee that I am not like the rest of men, dishonest, robbers, adulterers, or even like this publican. I fast twice a week; I pay tithes of all that I possess.' But the publican standing afar off would not so much as lift up his eyes to heaven, but kept striking his breast, saying 'O God be merciful to me a sinner!' I tell you, this man went down to his home justified rather than the Pharisee; for everyone who exalts himself shall be humbled and he who humbles himself shall be exalted."[12]

Chapter 7

Learning these things most beloved brethren, from the sacred reading, after we have learned how we should approach prayer, let us learn also, with the Lord as our teacher, what to pray. "In this manner," He says, "Pray ye: Our Father who are in heaven, hallowed be thy name. Thy kingdom come, thy will be done on earth, as it is in heaven. Give us this day our daily bread, and forgive us our debts, as we also forgive our debtors. And suffer us not to be led into temptation, but deliver us from evil."[13]

Chapter 8

Before all things, the Teacher of peace and Master of unity did not wish prayer to be offered individually and privately as one would pray only for himself when he prays. We do not say: "My Father, who art in heaven," nor "Give me this day my bread," nor does each one ask that only his debt be forgiven him and that he be led not into temptation and that he be delivered from evil for himself alone. Our prayer is public and common, and when we pray, we pray not for one but for the whole people, because we, the whole people, are one. God, the Teacher of prayer and concord, who taught unity, thus wished one to pray for all, just as He himself bore all in one. This law of prayer the three children inclosed in the fiery furnace observed, united in prayer and harmonious in the agreement of the spirit. The faith of the divine Scripture so declares, and, when it tells how such did pray, gives an example which we should imitate in our prayers, that we may be able to be such as they. It says: "Then those three as from one mouth were singing a hymn and blessing God."[14] They were speaking as from one mouth, but not yet had Christ taught them to pray. And so their words were availing and efficacious as they prayed, because a peaceful and simple and spiritual prayer deserved well of the Lord. Thus also do we find that the Apostles with the disciples prayed after the ascension of the Lord. Scripture says: "They were all with one mind continuing steadfastly in prayer with the women and Mary, who was the mother of Jesus, and with His brethren."[15] They were with one mind continuing steadfastly in prayer, declaring alike by their constancy and unity in prayer that God, who makes men of one mind to dwell in a home,[16] does not admit into the divine and eternal home any except those who are of one mind in prayer.

Chapter 9

Moreover, of what nature, most beloved brethren, are the sacraments of the Lord's prayer, how many, how great, collected briefly in words but abounding spiritually in virtue, so that nothing at all is omitted which is not included in our petitions and in our prayers in a compendium of heavenly doctrine! Scripture says: "Thus pray ye: Our Father who art in heaven." A new man, reborn and restored to his God by his grace says in the first place "Father," because he has now begun to be a son. "He came," He says, "unto his own and his own received him not. But as many as received Him, He gave to them the power to become the sons of God, to those who believe in His name."[17] He, therefore, who has believed in His name and has become the son of God, thereafter should begin to give thanks and to profess himself the son of God, when he declares that his father is God in heaven, also to testify in the very first words of his new birth that he reverences his earthly and carnal father and that he has begun to know and to have as father Him only who is in heaven, as it is written: "Those who say to their father and mother: I do not know you, and who do not recognize their children, these have kept thy words, and observed thy covenant."[18] Likewise the Lord in His Gospel has bidden us to call not our father upon earth, because one is our Father, who is in heaven.[19] And to the disciple who had made mention of his dead father, He replied: "Let the dead bury their own dead."[20] For he had said that his father was dead, when the father of believers is living.

Chapter 10

And, most beloved brethren, we ought not to observe and understand this alone, that we call Him Father who is in heaven, but we join in saying "Our Father," that is, of those who believe, of those who sanctified through Him and restored by the birth of spiritual grace have begun to be sons of God. And this voice also reproaches and condemns the Jews, because they not only faithlessly spurned Christ who had been announced to them through the Prophets and had been first sent to them, but also cruelly slew Him; who now cannot call the Lord father, since the Lord confounds and refutes them, saying: "You are born of the devil as father, and you wish to do the desires of your Father. He was a murderer from the beginning and has not stood in the truth, because the truth is not in him."[21] And through Isaias the prophet God exclaims with indignation: "I have begotten and brought up sons, but they have despised me. The ox knows his owner, and the ass the crib of his master, but Israel has not known me, and my people has not understood. Woe to the sinful nation, to a people laden with iniquity, a wicked seed, ungracious children. They have forsaken the Lord and have blasphemed the Holy One of Israel."[22] And in condemnation of these we Christians say, when we pray, "Our Father," because He now has begun to be ours and has ceased to be of the Jews, who have forsaken Him.[23] Nor can a sinning people be a son, but to those to whom the remission of sins is granted is the name of sons ascribed, to these also is eternity promised when the Lord himself says: "Everyone who commits sin is the servant of sin. But the slave does not abide in the house forever, the son abides there forever."[24]

Chapter 11

Moreover, how great is the indulgence of the Lord, how great the abundance of His regard for us and His goodness, that He has thus wished us to celebrate prayer in the sight of God, so as to call the Lord "Father" and, as Christ is the son of God, ourselves also so to be pronounced the sons of God, which name no one of us would dare to take in prayer, had not He Himself permitted us so to pray. So, most beloved brethren, we ought to remember and to know that, when we speak of God, we ought to act as sons of God, so that, just as we are pleased with God as Father, so too He may be pleased with us. Let us live as if temples of God, that it may be clear that the Lord dwells in us. Let not our acts depart from the Spirit, that we who have begun to be spiritual and heavenly may ponder and do nothing except the spiritual and the heavenly, since the Lord God Himself has said: "Those who glorify me, I shall glorify; but they that despise me, shall be despised."[25] The blessed Apostle also in his Epistle has laid down: "You are not your own, for you have been bought at a great price. Glorify God and bear him in your body."[26]

NOTES

[The notes have been emended for this reprinting]

1. Cf. Jn 4:23.
2. Cf. Mt 15:6; Mk 7:8.
3. Cf. Jn 16:23.
4. Cf. Jn 14:6.
5. Cf. Jer 23:23.
6. Prv 15:3.
7. Cf. Mt 9:4.
8. Cf. Rv 2:23.
9. 1 Kgs 1:13.
10. Cf. Ps 4:5.
11. Bar 6:5.
12. Lk 18:10–14.
13. Mt 6:9–13. Instead of *et ne nos induces*, Cyprian has *et ne patiaris nos induci*.
14. Cf. Dn 3:51.
15. Cf. Acts 1:14.
16. Cf. Ps 68:6.
17. 1 Jn 1:11,12.
18. Cf. Dt 33:9.
19. Cf. Mt 23:9.
20. Cf. Mt 8:22.
21. Cf. Jn 8:44.
22. Is 1:2–4.
23. The author of the book in which these pages are reprinted would like to disown any condemnation of the Jews, who remain the chosen

people, and their exclusion from the overall intent of the Lord's prayer. Allowances for sex-exclusive language must also be made with Patristic authors.

24. Jn 8:34, 35.

25. Cf. 1 Kgs 2:30.

26. 1 Cor 6:19–20.

GREGORY OF NYSSA

Sermon 3*

Hallowed be Thy Name, Thy Kingdom come.

THE LAW HAVING A SHADOW OF THE GOOD THINGS TO COME[1] prefigures the truth in types and allegories. When it introduces the priest into the Holy of Holies in order to pray to God, it purges him before entering by purifying aspersions. It then puts on him the priestly robe beautifully decked with gold, purple, and other brilliant colourings, places the girdle round his breast and suspends the pomegranates from the borders hung with bells. It then fastens the tunic on his shoulders, adorns his head with a diadem, lavishes ointment on his hair,[2] and thus brings him into the Holy of Holies to perform the sacred rites.

But the spiritual Lawgiver, Our Lord Jesus Christ, strips the Law of its material veils and lays bare the types and allegories. First of all, He does not give communion with God only to one whom He separates from everyone else, but He bestows this honour equally on all, offering the grace of the priesthood as common to those who desire it. Secondly, He does not manufacture the priestly beauty from alien adornments produced from dyes and curious devices of weaving, but He puts on him his own native adornments, decking him with the graces of virtue rather than with an embroidered purple robe. Not with earthly gold does He adorn his breast, but his very heart He makes beautiful through a perfectly pure conscience. He also fits the diadem with the rays coming from precious stones; they are the lustre of the holy commandments, according to the Apostle. He also covers with breeches that part of the body which is adorned

---

St. Gregory of Nyssa: The Lord's Prayer: The Beatitudes, translated and annotated by Hilda C. Graef (Westminster, Maryland: Newman Press, 1954), 45–50. This book is volume 18 of the Ancient Christian Writers series. Copyright © Paulist Press. Reprinted with permission of Paulist Press. The English translation was based on the Greek edition of 1840 by J. G. Krabinger.

by this garment;[3] for you surely know that this part is clothed with the covering of chastity. As to the spiritual pomegranates and bells which He suspends from the borders of life, these one might rightly conceive to be the evidence of virtuous living by which such way of life may become widely known. In the place of the bells, therefore, He suspends from the borders the melodious word of the faith; instead of the pomegranates the hidden preparation of the future hope still covered over by the more material bodily life instead of the flowers, the glorious gift of paradise; and thus He leads him to the *adyton*,[4] that is, to the innermost part of the Temple.

This *adyton* is not inanimate nor made by hands; but it is the hidden inner chamber of our heart if it be truly *adyton* (impenetrable) to evil and inaccessible to vile thoughts. The head, too, He adorns, not with the shape of letters embossed with gold leaf, but with a heavenly mind on the highest faculty of which, that is to say, reason, God himself is impressed.[5] Ointment He pours on his hair distilled from the interior virtues of the soul. A sacrificial victim, too, He prepares for him to offer to God in the mystic[6] rite, which is none other than Himself. Being thus led by the Lord to this sacrifice, he mortifies his fleshly mind with *the sword of the spirit, which is the word of God,*[7] and thus appeases God. Being in the *adyton*, he immolates himself in such a sacrifice, *presenting his body a living sacrifice, holy—pleasing unto God.*[8]

But someone might perhaps say that this is not the obvious meaning of the prayer we are interpreting; that we are wangling the words and fail to adapt our interpretation to the text before us. Therefore it should be remembered what we have said about prayer before. We said that he who has prepared himself so that he may boldly call God his Father is precisely he who is clad in such a robe as described in this sermon. He rings with bells and is adorned with pomegranates; his breast shines with the rays of the commandments and he bears on his shoulders the patriarchs and prophets themselves instead of only their names; for he has made their virtues his own adornment. He has placed on his head the crown of justice and soaked his hair with heavenly ointment; he dwells in the supercelestial *adyta* which are *adyta* to all profane thought and truly inaccessible.

But by briefly examining this, the sermon has sufficiently shown how a man ordained to the priesthood should be prepared; now there remains to consider the petition itself which the person within the sanctuary has been ordered to offer to God. For in my opinion the words of the prayer that are so concisely proposed to us do not yield a meaning that can easily be understood at first sight.

Hallowed be Thy Name, He says, *Thy Kingdom come*. What has this to do with my needs?—somebody might say who is doing penance because he repents of his sins or invokes the help of God in order to escape from his besetting weakness, because he is always aware of the temptations of the enemy. For on the one hand, fits of anger upset reasonable moderation; on the other, unnatural lusts enervate the soul's strength; from yet another direction covetousness blinds the clear sight of the soul; conceit, pride, hatred, and the rest of the catalogue of the forces fighting against us encircle us like a hostile army and endanger the final destiny of the soul. Now if a man is anxious to enlist the help of a Stronger One in order to escape from these dangers, what words would he be likely to use? Not those of the great David—*Deliver me from them that hate me*[9] and, *Let my enemies be turned back*,[10] and, *Give us help from trouble*,[11] and similar petitions by which one may procure God's help against one's enemies? What, however, says the pattern of prayer? *Hallowed be Thy Name*. Now even if I did not say that, would it be at all possible that God's name should not be holy? *Thy Kingdom come*. What is there that is not subject to the power of God, who, as Isaias says, holds the whole heaven in His palm, who compasses the earth, whose hand rules the moist nature,[12] who embraces the whole mundane and supramundane creation? But if the name of God is always holy, and nothing escapes His powerful dominion; if He rules all things, and nothing can be added to His holiness, since He is in all things absolutely perfect—what does it mean to pray: *Hallowed be Thy Name, Thy Kingdom come?* Perhaps by using such form of prayer the Word intends to set forth something like this: namely that human nature is too weak to achieve anything good, and that therefore we can obtain nothing of the things for which we are anxious unless the good be accomplished in us by Divine aid. And of all good things the most important for me is that God's name should be glorified through my life. But perhaps our meaning will become clearer if we start from the opposite end.

I have heard Holy Scripture somewhere condemn those who are guilty of blaspheming God. *Woe to those*, it says, *through whom my Name is blasphemed among the Gentiles*.[13] Now the meaning of these words is something like this: Those who have not yet believed the word of truth closely examine the lives of those who have received the mystery of the faith. If, therefore, people are "faithful" only in name, but contradict this name by their life, whether by committing idolatry for the sake of gain or by disgracing themselves by drunkenness and revelry, being immersed in profligacy like swine in the mud—then the pagans immediately attribute this not to the free choice of these evil-living men, but to the mystery[14] which is supposed to teach these things. For, they say, such and such a man who has been initiated into the Divine mysteries would not be such a slanderer, or so avaricious and grasping, or anything equally evil, unless sinning was lawful for them. Therefore the Word holds out a grave threat to such men, saying to them: *Woe to those through whom my Name is blasphemed among the Gentiles.*

Now if this has been properly understood, it will be time to consider the opposite. For I think it is necessary to make this before all else the principal part of prayer that the Name of God might not be blasphemed, but hallowed and glorified through my life. The prayer says, in effect, let the Name of His dominion which I invoke be hallowed in me, *that men may see your good works and glorify your Father who is in Heaven.*[15] Who would be so absurdly unreasonable as not to glorify God if he sees in those who believe in Him a pure life firmly established in virtue? I mean a life purged from all stain of sin, above any suspicion of evil and shining with temperance and holy prudence. A man who leads such a life will oppose fortitude to the assaults of the passions; since he partakes of the requirements of life only as far as necessary, he is in no way softened by the luxuries of the body and is an utter stranger to revelry and laziness as well as to boastful conceit. He touches the earth but lightly with the tip of his toes, for he is not engulfed by the pleasurable enjoyments of its life, but is above all deceit that comes by the senses. And so, even though in the flesh, he strives after the immaterial life. He counts the possession of virtues the only riches, familiarity with God the only nobility. His only privilege and power is the mastery of self so as not to be a slave of human passions. He is saddened if his life in this material world be prolonged; like those who are seasick he hastens to reach the port of rest.

How could anyone who sees such a man fail to glorify the Name invoked by such a life? Therefore I pray *Hallowed be Thy Name,* I ask that these words may effect in me things such as these: May I become through Thy help blameless, just and pious, may I abstain from every evil, speak the truth, and do justice. May I walk in the straight path, shining with temperance, adorned with incorruption, beautiful through wisdom and prudence. May I meditate on the things that are above and despise what is earthly, showing forth the angelic way of life. These and similar things are comprised in this brief petition by which we pray to God: *Hallowed be Thy Name*. For a man can glorify God in no other way save by his virtue which bears witness that the Divine Power is the cause of his goodness.

NOTES

[These notes have been emended for this reprinting]

1. Cf. Heb 10:1.

2. Cf. Ex 28:4,39 (Lv 8:7–12), the account of the vestments and anointing prescribed for Aaron as high priest.

3. *Periskelis* given as leg-band, garter, or anklet by Liddell and Scott, but more probably "breeches," as in Ex 28:42.

4. *Adyton*, the Holy of Holies of the Temple, inaccessible to any save the high priest, which impenetrability made it a suitable symbol for the inner region of the soul, in which the mystical life is lived. . . .

5. *Hēgemonikos*, adj., more frequently as subst., *hēgemonikon*, a term taken over from Stoic philosophy denoting the highest part of the soul. As in the present passage, it is often equated with mind or reason. . . . Hence from Origen . . . onwards it is regarded as the seat of the spiritual life *par excellence*, on which prophetic and other visions are impressed. . . .

6. *Mustikos*, a word of many connotations. Its root meaning (from *muo, close the eyes*) is *secret, not easily accessible*, hence it is used for anything of a sacred character. . . .

7. Cf. Eph 6:17.

8. Cf. Rom 12:1.

9. Ps 68:15.

10. Cf. Ps 55:10.

11. Ps 59:13 and 107:13.

12. Cf. Is 40:12.

13. Cf. Rom 2:24 (Is 52:5 and Ez 36:20).

14. *Mustērion*; the word was taken over from the pagan mystery religions, in which sense it is often used by the Fathers. . . . It was early adopted by the Christians for their own doctrines and rites. . . . The Latins first used *sacramentum*, with the same range of meaning as *mustērion*, which was also transliterated into *mysterium*. . . .

15. Mt 5:16.

MAXIMUS THE CONFESSOR

Commentary on the Our Father*

THY KINGDOM COME. It is right, then, that after the elimination of anger and lust there comes, according to the prayer, the victory of the kingdom of God the Father for those who, having rejected them, are worthy to say, "thy kingdom come," that is to say, the Holy Spirit, for by the principle and path of meekness they have already become temples of God by the Spirit.[1] For it is said, "On whom shall I rest if not on the one who is meek, on the one who is humble and who fears my words?"[2] From this it is obvious that the kingdom of God the Father belongs to the humble and the meek. For it is said, "Blessed are the meek, for they shall inherit the earth."[3] It is not this earth which by nature occupies the middle place of the universe which God promised as an inheritance to those who love him since he speaks the truth in saying, "When they rise from the dead they neither marry nor are given in marriage but are like the angels in heaven,"[4] and, "Come, blessed of my Father, inherit the kingdom prepared for you since the foundation of the world."[5] And again elsewhere to another who served with devotion, "Enter into the joy of your Lord."[6] And after him the divine Apostle says, "For the trumpet will sound, and those who have died in Christ will rise first, incorruptible; then we the living who remain here will be taken up together with them into the clouds to meet the Lord in the air, and thus we shall always be with the Lord."[7]

Since such promises have been made to those who love the Lord, who would then say, if he has his mind fixed squarely on the word of Scripture, if he is moved by the Word and wishes to be his servant, that heaven, the kingdom prepared from the world's

---

*Reprinted from "Commentary on the Our Father" in *Selected Writings of Maximus Confessor*, translation and notes by George Charles Berthold (New York: Paulist, 1985), 107–112. The book is part of the Paulist series Classics of Western Spirituality. Copyright © 1985 by George Berthold. Used by permission of Paulist Press. The English translation was based on the Greek edition of the seventeenth-century Dominican, François Combefis. See Migne, *PG* 90:871–910.

foundation, the joy of the Lord mysteriously hidden, the continuous and completely uninterrupted dwelling place and home with the Lord for those who are worthy, is in any way identical to the earth? On the contrary, I think I can now say that the earth is the solid and thoroughly unalterable habit and force of inflexibility in the good which the meek possess.[8] Because they are always with the Lord and possess an endless joy, they have acquired a kingdom prepared from the beginning and have been judged worthy of a place and position in heaven as a kind of land occupying the mid-point of the universe, that is, the principle of virtue. According to this principle the meek man, situated midway between the good and evil said of him, dwells in tranquillity, without being puffed up because he is well spoken of nor saddened because he is ill spoken of. For since reason is free by nature it has rejected appetite and is not sensitive to its regard and has settled the complete force of its soul on the immovable divine freedom. Wishing to give this to his disciples the Lord says, "Take my yoke upon you and learn of me for I am meek and humble of heart, and you will find rest for your souls."[9] He calls rest the victory of the divine kingdom, insofar as it produces in those who are worthy a sovereignty released from any bondage.

If the indestructible might of the unfading kingdom is given to the humble and the meek, who would at this point be so deprived of love and desire for the divine gifts as not to tend as much as possible toward humility and meekness to become, to the extent that this is possible for man, the image of God's kingdom by bearing in himself by grace the exact configuration in the Spirit to Christ, who is truly by nature and essence the great King? In this configuration, says the divine Apostle, "there is neither male nor female,"[10] that is to say, neither anger nor lust. Indeed, anger tyrannically destroys the exercise of reason and makes thought take leave of the law of nature. And lust takes beings which are inferior to the one and only desirable and impassible cause and nature and makes them more desirable than it. Thereby it sets up flesh as more valuable than spirit, and renders the enjoyment of what is visible more delightful than the glory and brightness of spiritual realities. By the sensual softness of pleasure it leads the mind from the divine perception of spiritual things which is connatural to it. Rather, there is reason alone which has by an abundance of virtue stripped itself of that tenderness and affection which are not only supremely without passion but are natural for the body as well. The spirit is then perfect master of nature and persuades the mind to take leave of moral philosophy whenever it should unite itself to the super-essential Word by simple and undivided contemplation, even if practical reason contributes to it for an easy separation and transition from the course of temporal events. Once this transition is accomplished it is not reasonable to impose as a heavy coat[11] the burden of a moral condition on the one who has shown himself unrestrained by sensible things.

And this is the mystery which the great Elijah clearly shows in the actions which he accomplished by way of figure.[12] For during his rapture he gives Elisha his coat (that is, mortification of the flesh in which the magnificence of the good moral order is firmly grounded) as an ally of the spirit in the struggle against any enemy force and as a blow against the unstable and flowing nature figured by the Jordan so that the disciple be not held back from crossing over to the Holy Land by being swamped in the mud and slipperiness of the craving for matter. As for himself, he advances toward God free and uncontrolled by any attachment to beings at all, simple in his desire and uncomplicated in his intention, and makes his dwelling with the one who is simple by nature through general virtues spiritually harnessed to each other as fiery horses. For he knows that it is necessary for Christ's disciple to keep away from unequal dispositions whose differences prove an estrangement since the passion of lust produces an outpouring of blood around the heart and a movement of anger evidently produces a boiling of blood.[13] When he reaches the point of having life, movement, and being[14] in Christ, he has put far from him the monstrous origin of inequalities and he no longer carries within himself the contrary dispositions of these passions, as I was saying, after the manner of the male-female opposition. In this way reason is not enslaved by them, having remained aloof from their unstable fluctuations. In it the holiness of the divine image has been naturally included to persuade the soul to transform itself by its free will to the likeness of God and to belong to the great kingdom which subsists substantially with God, the Father of all. It becomes a radiant abode of the Holy Spirit and receives, if one can say it, the full power of knowing the divine nature insofar as this is possible. By this power there is discarded the origin of what is inferior, to be replaced by that of what is superior, while the soul like God keeps inviolable in itself by the grace of its calling the realization of the gifts which it has received. By this power, Christ is always born mysteriously and willingly, becoming incarnate through those who are saved. He causes the soul which begets him to be a virgin-mother[15] who, to speak briefly, does not bear the marks of nature subject to corruption and generation in the relationship of male and female.[16]

No one should be astonished to hear corruption placed before generation. For the one who examines without passion and with a correct reason the nature of things which come to be and which pass away will clearly discover that generation takes its beginning from corruption and ends up in corruption. The passions associated with this generation and corruption, as I was saying, do not belong to Christ, that it, to the life and logic of Christ and according to Christ, if we can believe the one who says, "For in Christ there is neither male nor female," thus clearly indicating the characteristics and the passions of a nature subject to corruption and generation. Instead, there is only a deiform principle created by divine knowledge and one single movement of free will which chooses only virtue.

"Neither Greek nor Jew." This refers to a difference, or more properly a contradiction, in opinions about God. The Greek notion foolishly introduces a multiplicity of principles and divides the single principle into contrary energies and forces. It fashions a polytheist cult which becomes factious by reason of the multitude of its objects and ludicrous because of the various ways of veneration. The Jewish notion introduces a single principle but one which is petty and imperfect, almost impersonal as deprived of reason and life. Through opposite ways it results in the same evil as the first notion, a disbelief in the true God. It limits to a single person the one principle which would subsist without the Word and the Spirit, or which would be qualified by the Word and the Spirit. It does not see what God would be if he had no part with the Word and Spirit, nor how he would be God in having part with them as if they were accidents, by a participation close to that of rational beings subject to generation. In Christ, as I have said, there is none of these things, but only the reality of genuine piety, a steadfast law of mystical theology which rejects any expansion of the divinity as the first notion does, while not allowing any contraction as does the second.[17] Thus there is no dissension by a plurality of natures, the Greek error, nor an affirmation of the oneness of hypostasis, the Jewish error, because being deprived of the Word and the Spirit or qualified by the Word and the Spirit, God is not honored as Mind, Word, and Spirit. This teaches us, who have been introduced to the perfect knowledge of truth by a calling of grace in faith, to recognize that the nature and the power of the divinity is one, and therefore that there is one God contemplated in the Father, Son, and Holy Spirit. This means a single Mind essentially subsisting without being caused, who begot the one Word subsisting by essence without a principle, and who is the source of the one eternal life essentially subsisting as Holy Spirit. Trinity in Unity and Unity in Trinity: not one in the other, for the Trinity is not related to the Unity as an accident in an essence, nor conversely the Unity in the Trinity, for it is unqualified. Nor as one and the other, for the Unity does not differ from the Trinity by a difference of nature since it is a simple and single nature. Nor as one after the other, for the Trinity is not distinguished from the Unity by a lessening of power, nor the Unity from the Trinity. And the Unity is not distinguished from the Trinity as something common and general considered only by the mind as distinct from the parts which make it up, since it is an essence which exists properly by itself, and a force which is absolutely mighty. Nor as one through the other, for there is no mediation of relation as from effect to cause between what is completely identical and absolute. Nor as one from the other, for the Trinity is not a derivation of the Unity, since it is without origin and self-manifesting.

On the contrary, we say and know that the same God is truly Unity and Trinity: Unity according to the principle of essence and Trinity according to the mode of existence.[18] The same reality is wholly Unity without being divided by the Persons, and wholly Trinity without being confused in unity. In this way polytheism is not introduced by division, nor atheism by confusion. By avoiding both, the understanding of God in the light of Christ shines forth. I call Christ's understanding the new proclamation of truth, "In him there is neither male nor female," that is, no signs or passions of a nature subject to corruption and generation; "neither Jew nor Greek," that is, no conceptions opposed to God; "neither circumcision nor uncircumcision," that is, no different religions issued from these opposed conceptions. The religion of circumcision, through the symbols of the Law, considers the visible creation evil and accuses the Creator of being the author of these evils. The religion of uncircumcision deifies the visible creation through the passions and sets the creature against the Creator. Both of these together end up at the same evil, insolence against God. "Neither barbarian nor Scythian," that is, no tension of will pushing the single nature to revolt against itself, by which there has been introduced among men the unnatural law of mutual slaughter. "Neither slave nor freedman," that is, no division of the same nature by opposition of will, which makes dishonored what is by nature of equal honor and has as an auxiliary the attitude of those who exercise a tyrannical sway over the dignity of the image. "But Christ is in all," creating by what surpasses nature and the Law, the spiritual configuration of the kingdom which has no beginning, a configuration characterized, as has been shown, by humility and meekness of heart. Their concurrence shows forth the perfect man created according to Christ.[19] For every humble man is also thoroughly meek, and every meek man is also thoroughly humble: humble because he knows that his being has come to him as a loan, meek because he knows how to use the natural powers which have been given to him, since he gives them over to the service of reason to give rise to virtue and because he restrains in a perfect way their sense activity. That is why this man is always in movement toward God by his mind.[20] Even if he experiences at one time everything that can afflict the body, he is not at all moved according to the senses, nor does he mark his soul with any trace of affliction as a substitute for a joyful attitude, for he does not think that physical suffering means a loss of happiness. Indeed there exists but one happiness, a communion of life with the Word, the loss of which is an endless punishment which goes on for all eternity.[21] And that is why by abandoning his body and whatever is the body's he strives intensely toward that communion of life with God, thinking that the only loss—even if he were master of everything on earth—would be in the failure of the deification by grace which he pursues.

Let us therefore purify ourselves from all defilements of the flesh and of the spirit[22] so that we may sanctify God's name by extinguishing lust which indecently flirts with the passions, and let us by reason rein in anger which pleasures incite to a reckless fury. Thus will we welcome the kingdom of God the Father which comes through meekness.

NOTES

[These notes have been emended for this reprinting]

1. Cf. Eph 2:22.
2. Is 66:2 (Sept.).
3. Mt 5:4.
4. Mt 22:30.
5. Mt 25:34.
6. Mt 25:21.
7. 1 Thes 4:15, 16; 1 Cor 15:52.

8. This inflexible habit is the same as the good disposition which is spoken of elsewhere. It underscores the ethical concern of Maximus in the perfecting of the Christian and the primacy of the will in its attainment. Maximus's classic defense of the full integrity and redemptive role of Christ's human will in his more directly dogmatic and polemical writings gives the proper Christological setting to this ascetical truth.

9. Mt 11:29.

10. Gal 3:28. . . .

11. A coat of sheepskin or goatskin. In Origen's tradition, animal skins are the symbol of mortification because they are no longer living. . . .

12. Cf. 2 Kgs 2:11, 12.

13. According to contemporary medicine. . . .

14. A Pauline triad borrowed from the pagan poet (Acts 17:28), which Maximus finds useful.

15. On this point see A. Squire, "The Soul as Virgin and Mother in Maximus the Confessor," *Studia Patristica* 8 (Berlin, 1966): 451–61.

16. Sexual generation, like time and death, is for Maximus a sign of the present fallen condition, which is overcome in the cosmic reconciliation of Christ.

17. In this analysis of expansion and contraction in the understanding of the Trinity, the errors of Greek and Jew respectively, Maximus is indebted to Gregory Nazianzen. . . . The theological precision of what follows is clearly regarded by Maximus as doxological. . . .

18. Utilizing here the distinction logos-tropos.

19. Cf. Col 1:28.

20. Creaturely movement has God as its term, but man's capacity for God, as Maximus showed in his refutation of the Origenist myth, never reaches a term.

21. In spite of this clear language on the eternity of hell, E. Michaud has argued that Maximus held to a universal restoration as did the Origenists; "S. Maxime le Confesseur et l'apocatastase," *Revue internationale de théologie* 10 (1902): 257–72. This has been refuted in an admirable study by Brian Daley, "Apokatastasis and 'honorable silence' in the Eschatology of Maximus the Confessor," *Maximus Confessor* (Fribourg, 1982), 309–39.

22. Cf. 2 Cor 7:1.

THOMAS AQUINAS
THE THIRD PETITION:
"Thy Will Be Done on Earth as It Is in Heaven."*

THE THIRD GIFT which the Holy Spirit works in us is called the gift of knowledge. The Holy Spirit not only gives us the gift of fear and the gift of piety (which is a sweet affection for God, as we have said); but He also makes man wise. It was this for which David prayed: "Teach me goodness and discipline and knowledge."[1] This knowledge which the Holy Spirit teaches us is that whereby man lives justly. Among all that goes to make up knowledge and wisdom in man, the principal wisdom is that man should not depend solely upon his own opinion: "Lean not upon thy own prudence."[2] Those who put all their trust in their own judgment so that they do not trust others, but only themselves, are always found to be stupid and are so adjudged by others: "Hast thou seen a man wise in his own conceit? There shall be more hope of a fool than of him."[3]

The Will of God

Out of humility one does not trust one's own knowledge: "Where humility is there is also wisdom."[4] The proud trust only themselves. Now, the Holy Spirit, through the gift of wisdom, teaches us that we do not our own will but the will of God. It is through this gift that we pray of God that His "will be done on earth as it is in heaven." And in this is seen the gift of knowledge. Thus, one says to God "let Thy will be done," in the same way as one who is sick desires something from the physician; and his

---

**The Catechetical Instructions of St. Thomas Aquinas*, translated by Joseph B. Collins (New York: Joseph F. Wagner, 1939), 149–54. Copyright was not renewed. The Collins translation into English was based on the Mandonnet Latin edition (1927), which was a revision of the Parma edition (1852–73), and with consultation also of the Vivès edition (1871–80).

will is not precisely his own, because it is the will of the physician. Otherwise, if his desire were purely from his own will, he would be indeed foolish. So we ought not to pray other than that in us God's will may be done; that is, that His will be accomplished in us. The heart of man is only right when it is in accord with the will of God. This did Christ: "Because I came down from heaven, not to do My own will but the will of Him that sent me."[5] Christ, as God, has the same will with the Father; but as a Man He has a distinct will from the Father's, and it was according to this that He says He does not do His will but the Father's. Hence, He teaches us to pray and to ask: "Thy will be done."[6]

What Does God Will?

But what is this that is asked? Does not the Psalm say: "Whatsoever the Lord pleased [has willed], He hath done?"[7] Now, if He has done all that He has willed both in heaven and on earth, what then is the meaning of this: "Thy will be done on earth as it is in heaven"? To understand this we must know that God wills of us three things, and we pray that these be accomplished. The first thing that God wills is that we may have eternal life. Whoever makes something for a certain purpose, has a will regarding it which is in accord with the purpose for which he made it. In like manner, God made man, but it was not for no purpose, as it is written: "Remember what my substance is; for hast Thou made all the children of men in vain?"[8]

Hence, God made men for a purpose; but this purpose was not for their mere pleasures, for also the brutes have these, but it was that they might have eternal life. The Lord, therefore, wills that men have eternal life. Now, when that for which a thing is made is accomplished, it is said to be saved; and when this is not accomplished, it is said to be lost. So when man gains eternal life, he is said to be saved, and it is this that the Lord wills: "Now, this is the will of My Father that sent Me, that every one who seeth the Son and believeth in Him may have life everlasting."[9] This will of God is already fulfilled for the Angels and for the Saints in the Fatherland, for they see God and know and enjoy Him. We, however, desire that, as the will of God is done for the blessed who are in heaven, it likewise be done for us who are on earth. For this we pray when we say "Thy will be done" for us who are on earth, as it is for the Saints who are in heaven.

The Commandments: God's Will

In the second place, the will of God for us is that we keep His Commandments. When a person desires something, he not only wills that which he desires, but also everything which will bring that about. Thus, in order to bring about a healthy condition which he desires, a physician also wills to put into effect diet, medicine, and other needs. We arrive at eternal life through observance of the Commandments, and, accordingly, God wills that we observe them: "But if thou wilt enter into life, keep the Commandments."[10] "Your reasonable service . . . that you may prove what is the good and the acceptable and the perfect will of God."[11] That is, good because it is profitable: "I am the Lord thy God that teach thee profitable things,"[12] And acceptable, that is, pleasing: "Light is risen to the just; and joy to the right heart."[13] And perfect, because noble: "Be you therefore perfect, as your Heavenly Father is perfect."[14] When we say "Thy will be done," we pray that we may fulfill the Commandments of God. This will of God is done by the just, but it is not yet done by sinners. "In heaven" here signifies the just; while "on earth" refers to sinners. We, therefore, pray that the will of God may be done "on earth," that is, by sinners, "as it is in heaven," that is, by the just.[15]

Let Thy Will Be Done

It must be noted that the very words used in this petition teach us a lesson. It does not say "Do" or "Let us do," but it says, "[Let] Thy will be done," because two things are necessary for eternal life: the grace of God and the will of man. Although God has made man without man, He cannot save man without his cooperation. Thus, says St. Augustine: "Who created thee without thyself, cannot save thee without thyself,"[16] because God wills that man cooperate with Him or at least put no obstacle in His way: "Turn ye to Me, saith the Lord of hosts, and I will turn to you."[17] "By the grace of God, I am what I am. And His grace in me hath not been void."[18] Do not, therefore, presume on your own strength, but trust in God's grace; and be not negligent, but use the zeal you have. It does not say, therefore, "Let us do," lest it would seem that the grace of God were left out; nor does it say, "Do," lest it would appear that our will and our zeal do not matter. He does say "Let it be done" through the grace of God at the same time using our desire and our own efforts.

Thirdly, the will of God in our regard is that men be restored to that state and dignity in which the first man was created. This was a condition in which the spirit and soul felt no resistance from sensuality and the flesh. As long as the soul was subject to God, the flesh was in such subjection to the spirit that no corruption of death, or weakness, or any of the passions were felt. When, however, the spirit and the soul, which were between God and the flesh, rebelled against God by sin, then the body rebelled against the soul. From that time death and weaknesses began to be felt together with continual rebellion of sensuality against the spirit: "I see another law in my members, fighting against the law of my mind."[19] "The flesh lusteth against the spirit, and the spirit against the flesh."[20]

Thus, there is an endless strife between the flesh and the spirit, and man is continually being brought lower by sin. The will of God, therefore, is that man be restored to his primal state so that no more would the flesh rebel against the spirit: "For this is the will of God, your sanctification."[21] Now, this will of God cannot be fulfilled in this life, but it will be fulfilled in the resurrection of the just, when glorified bodies shall arise incorrupt and most perfect: "It is sown a natural body; it shall rise a spiritual body."[22] In the just the will of God is fulfilled relative to the spirit, which abides in justice and knowledge and perfect life. Therefore, when we say "Thy will be done," let us pray that His will also may be done regarding the flesh. Thus, the sense of "Thy will be done *on earth*" is that it may be done "for our flesh," and "as it is *in heaven*" means in our spirit. Thus, we take "in heaven" for our spirit, and "on earth" as our flesh.[23]

By means of this petition we arrive at the happiness of those who mourn, as it is written: "Blessed are they that mourn; for they shall be comforted."[24] This can be applied to each of the threefold explanations we have given above. According to the first we desire eternal life. And in this very desire we are brought to a mourning of soul: "Woe is me, that my sojourning is prolonged."[25] This desire in the Saints is so vehement that because of it they wish for death, which in itself is something naturally to be avoided: "But we are confident and have a good will to be absent rather from the body and to be present with the lord."[26] Likewise, according to our second explanation—viz., that we will to keep the Commandments—they who do so are in sorrow. For although such be sweet for the soul, it is bitter indeed for the flesh which is continually kept in discipline. "Going, they went and wept," which refers to the flesh, "But coming, they shall come with joyfulness," which pertains to the soul.[27] Again, from our third explanation (that is, concerning the struggle which is ever going on between the flesh and the spirit), we see that this too causes sorrow. For it cannot but happen that the soul be wounded by the venial faults of the flesh; and so in expiating for these the soul is in mourning. "Every night," that is, the darkness of sin, "I will wash my bed [that is, my conscience] with my tears."[28] Those who thus sorrow will arrive at the Fatherland, where may God bring us also!

NOTES

[These notes have been emended for this reprinting]

1. Ps 118:66.
2. Prv 3:5.
3. Prv 26:12.
4. Prv 11:2.
5. Jn 6:38.
6. "Now this is what we implore when we address these words to God: 'Thy will be done.' We have fallen into this state of misery by disobeying and despising the divine will. Now, God deigns to propose to us, as the sole corrective of all our evils, a conformity to His will which by our sins we despised. He commands us to regulate all our thoughts and actions by this standard. And to be able to accomplish this is our aim when we humbly say this prayer to God; 'Thy will be done' " ("Roman Catechism," *Lord's Prayer*, Chapter 12:8).
7. Ps 134:6.
8. Ps 88:48.
9. Jn 6:10.
10. Mt 19:17.
11. Rom 12:1–2.
12. Is 48:17.
13. Ps 96:11.
14. Mt 5:48.
15. "When, therefore, we pray, 'Thy will be done,' we first of all ask our Heavenly Father to enable us to obey His divine commands, and to serve Him all the days of our lives in holiness and justice. Likewise that we do all things in accord with His will and pleasure, that we perform all the duties prescribed for us in the sacred writings, and thus, guided and assisted by Him, so conduct ourselves in all things as becomes those 'who are born, not of the will of the flesh but of God' " ("Roman Cathechism," *Lord's Prayer*, Chapter 12:12).
16. *Super Verbum Apost.*, XV.

17. Zec 1:3.
18. 1 Cor 15:10.
19. Rom 7:23.
20. Gal 5:17.
21. 1 Thes 4:3.
22. 1 Cor 15:44.
23. "When we say, 'Thy will be done,' we expressly detest the works of the flesh, of which the Apostle writes: 'The works of the flesh are manifest, which are fornication, uncleanness, immodesty, lust, etc.' (Gal 5:19); 'if you live according to the flesh you shall die' (Rom 8:13). We also pray God not to permit us to yield to the suggestions of sensual appetite, of our lusts, of our infirmities, but to govern our will by His will" ("Roman Catechism," *Lord's Prayer*, Chapter 12:14).
24. Mt 5:5.
25. Ps 119:5.
26. 2 Cor 5:8.
27. Ps 125:6.
28. Ps 6:7.

ORIGEN

Give Us This Day Our Supersubstantial Bread*

GIVE US THIS DAY OUR SUPERSUBSTANTIAL BREAD—or as Luke has it: *Give us each day our supersubstantial bread.*[1] Since some understand from this that we are commanded to pray for material bread, it will be well to refute their error here, and to establish the truth about the supersubstantial bread. We must ask them how it could be that He who enjoined upon us to ask for great and heavenly favours, should command us to intercede with the Father for what is small and of the earth, as if He had forgotten—so they would have it—what He had taught. For the bread that is given to our flesh is neither heavenly, nor is the request for it a great request.

THE TRUE BREAD

2. We, on our part, following the Master Himself who teaches us about the bread, shall treat of the matter at some length. In the Gospel according to John He says to those who had come to Capharnaum seeking for Him: *Amen, amen, I say to you, you seek [me], not because you have seen miracles, but because you did eat of the loaves and were filled.*[2] He who has eaten of the bread blessed by Jesus and is filled with it, tries all the more to understand the Son of God more perfectly, and hastens to Him. Hence His admirable command: *Labour not for the meat which perisheth, but for that which endureth unto life everlasting, which the Son of man will give you.*[3] And when those who were listening to this asked Him, saying: *What shall we do that we may work the works of God?*

**Origen: Prayer: Exhortation to Martyrdom*, translated and annotated by John J. O'Meara (Westminster, Maryland: Newman Press, 1954), 92–105. This book is volume 19 of the Ancient Christian Writers series. Copyright © Paulist Press. Reprinted with permission of Paulist Press. The English translation was based on the critical Greek text of Paul Koetschau, *Origenes Werke* in *Die griechischen christlichen Schriftseller* (Leipzig: 1899), 2:295–403.

Jesus answered and said to them: This is the work of God, that you believe in Him whom He hath sent.[4] Now God *hath sent His Word, and healed them*—obviously the sick—as it is written in the Psalms.[5] Those who believe in the Word do the works of God which are *meat that endureth unto life everlasting.* And *my Father,* He says, *giveth you the true bread from heaven. For the bread of God is that which cometh down from heaven and giveth life to the world.*[6] The "true bread" is that which nourishes the true man, the *man created* after *the image of God,*[7] and through which he who is nourished by it is made *to the image of Him that created him.* What is more nourishing for the soul than the Word?[8] And what is more precious for the mind of him that understands it than the wisdom of God? And what is in better accord with rational nature than truth?

3. If someone objects at this point, saying that He would not have taught us to ask for the supersubstantial bread while leaving it possible that another kind of bread be understood, let him observe that in the Gospel according to John also He sometimes speaks of bread as being something other than Himself, and sometimes as being Himself. An instance of the former is this: *Moses gave you bread from heaven, not the true bread, but my Father giveth you the true bread from heaven.*[9] But to those who say to Him: *Give us always this bread,* He says regarding Himself: *I am the bread of life. He that cometh to me shall not hunger; and he that believeth in me shall never thirst,*[10] and shortly afterwards: *I am the [living] bread which came down from heaven. If any man eat of this bread, he shall live for ever; and the bread that I will give is my flesh which I will give for the life of the world.*[11]

4. Further, since every form of nourishment is called "bread" in the Scriptures, as is clear from what is written concerning Moses, that for forty days he neither ate "bread" nor drank water;[12] and since the word that nourishes is manifold and varied, for not everyone can receive the solid and strong nourishment of God's teachings: therefore, wishing to give an athlete's nourishment suitable to the more perfect, He says: *The bread that I will give is my flesh, which I will give for the life of the world.*[13] And a little later: *Except you eat the flesh of the Son of man and drink His blood, you shall not have life in you. He that eateth my flesh and drinketh my blood hath everlasting life, and I will raise him up in the last day. For my flesh is meat indeed, and my blood is drink indeed. He that eateth my flesh and drinketh my blood abideth in me, and I in him. As the living Father hath sent me and I*

live by the Father, so he that eateth me, the same also shall live by me.[14] This is the *true meat,* the flesh of Christ, which, being Word became flesh according to what is written: *And the Word was made flesh.* When we [eat and] drink Him, then He *dwells among us.* When He is distributed, then is the text fulfilled, *We saw His glory.*[15] *This is the bread that came down from heaven. Not as your fathers did eat and are dead. He that eateth this bread shall live forever.*[16]

5. Paul, speaking to the Corinthians as *unto little ones* and such as *walked according to man,* says: *I gave you milk to drink, not meat; for you were not able as yet. But neither indeed are you now able; for you are yet carnal.*[17] And in the Epistle to the Hebrews: *And you are become such as have need of milk, and not of strong meat. For everyone that is a partaker of milk is unskillful in the word of justice; for he is a little child. But strong meat is for the perfect, for them who by custom have their senses exercised to the discerning of good and evil.*[18] It is my opinion that the words: *One believeth that he may eat all things, but he that is weak eats herbs,*[19] are not primarily spoken of bodily nourishment, but rather of the words of God which nourish the soul.[20] The true believer and the truly perfect can eat everything, as is shown in the passage, *One believeth that he may eat all things.* But he that is weak and imperfect contents himself with teachings that are simple and not strong enough to make him full of vigour. Paul has him in mind when he says, *But he that is weak eats herbs.*

6. Then, too, what Solomon says in Proverbs teaches, in my opinion, that the man who does not because of his simplicity—and without having erroneous ideas—grasp the more forceful and important doctrines, is in a better position than another who is more apt, quicker, and better at understanding things, but who does not see clearly the pattern of peace and unity in the universe. Here is the text: *It is better to be invited to herbs with love and grace, than to a fatted calf with hatred.*[21] Often we enjoy more a simple and frugal hospitality offered with good conscience by hosts who receive us but cannot offer us more, than a sublime discourse which, however, is raised *against the knowledge of God* with much persuasion, and teaching another doctrine than that of the Father of Our Lord Jesus, who gave us the Law and the Prophets.[22] In order, then, that our soul may not become ill through want of nourishment and that we may not die to God through hunger for the Word of the Lord,[23] let us, while leading in obedience to the teaching of Our Saviour a better life and with greater faith, ask the

Father for the living bread which is the same as the supersubstantial bread.

SUPERSUBSTANTIAL

7. We must now examine the meaning of the word "supersubstantial." First we must note that the term *epiousios* (supersubstantial) is not used by the Greeks: neither does it occur with the scholars, nor does it have a place in the language of the people. It seems to have been invented by the Evangelists.[24] At least, Matthew and Luke, when they introduce it, are in complete agreement in their use of it. The translators of the Hebrew texts have done this same kind of thing with regard to other words also. Thus, what Greek has ever used the terms *enotizou* or *akoutistheti* to signify "receive in your ear" and "make yourself to hear"? A term very similar to *epiousios* is found in the Books of Moses, and is there put in the mouth of God: *You shall be to me a periousios people.*[25] I believe that both words derive from the word *ousia* (substance). The first indicates the bread united with our *ousia*. The second describes the people as abiding with the *ousia* of God and partaking in it.

8. *Ousia*, properly understood, is regarded as incorporeal by the philosophers who insist that the pre-eminent reality is incorporeal.[26] It has, then, for them an unchanging existence which admits neither increase nor decrease. To admit either increase or decrease is the property of corporeal things which, because they are subject to change, need something to sustain and nourish them. If within a given time they acquire more than they lose, they increase; if less, they decrease. Again, it may happen that they receive nothing from outside, in which case they are, so to speak, in a state of pure decrease.

But for those who believe that incorporeal reality is secondary and that corporeal reality is primary, *ousia* can be described as follows.[27] It is the prime matter of all existing things, that from which the things that exist come into being; it is the matter of corporeal things, from which corporeal things come into being; it is the matter of things that have a name, from which these things come into being. It is the first undetermined principle; it is that which is presupposed to things that are; it is that which receives all changes and transformations, while being itself from its very concept unchangeable; it is that which persists through all change and transformation. According to these, *ousia* is from its very concept undetermined and without form. It has no fixed size, and is open to any determination as something made ready. In their terminology they call "determinations" those operations and actions generally, in which movements and dispositions are associated. They hold that *ousia* does not in its own proper concept share in any of these things, but that just the same because of its passivity it is always inseparable from one of them, and prepared to receive all the operations of an agent however that may act on it and transform it. For the force[28] that goes with *ousia* and pervades all things is the cause both of every determination and the operations that concern it. They say that *ousia* is entirely changeable and divisible and that every *ousia* can be fused with any other, but so as to be united with it into one.

9. In conducting our investigation into the meaning of *ousia*, because of the texts speaking of *epiousios* bread and *periousios* people, we have given this explanation of the various significations of the term *ousia*. In what went before we had shown that the bread which we have to ask for is of the spirit. We must therefore think here of *ousia* as being of the same nature as the bread. And just as material bread which is used for the body of him who is being nourished, enters into his substance, *so the living bread* and that *which came down from heaven*,[29] offered to the mind and the soul, gives a share of its own proper power to him who presents himself to be nourished by it. And so this will be the supersubstantial bread which we ask for. And again, as according to the quality of the food it is strong and suitable for athletes, or, on the other hand, is of milk and vegetables,[30] so he who takes food is of varying strength. In the same way it follows that when the Word of God is given as milk to infants, as herbs adapted to the weak, and as meat proper for those engaged in combat, each of those who are nourished will, according as he gives himself up to the Word, be able to do this or that, or become a man of such or such character. One must remember that some so-called food is actually noxious, some is disease-bearing, and some even impossible to take.[31] All this should be taken into account in the analogy with reference to the differences between doctrines that are thought to be nourishing. The supersubstantial bread, then, is that which is most adapted to the rational nature and is akin to its very substance, bringing to the soul health and well-being and strength, and giving to him that eats of it a share of its own immortality. For the Word of God is immortal.

10. This supersubstantial bread, so it seems to me, has another name in Scripture, namely *tree of life*. If a man stretches out his hand and takes of it, he lives forever.[32] This tree is also given a third name, *wisdom of God*, by Solomon when he says: *She is a tree of life to them that lay hold on her, and safe to them that lean on her as on the Lord*.[33] Since the angels also are nourished on the wisdom of God and receive strength to accomplish their own proper works from the contemplation of truth and wisdom, so in the Psalms we find it written that the angels also take food, the men of God, who are called Hebrews, sharing with the angels and, so to speak, becoming table-companions with them. As much is said in the passage, *Man ate the bread of angels*.[34] Our mind must not be so beggarly as to think that the angels forever partake of and nourish themselves on some kind of material bread which, as is told, came down from heaven upon those who went out of Egypt,[35] and that it was this same bread which the Hebrews shared with the angels, the spirits dedicated to the service of God.[36]

11. In our inquiry into the meaning of the supersubstantial bread, and the tree of life, and the wisdom of God, and the nourishment shared by angels and men, it will not be out of place to establish here whether what Genesis tells about the three men who were received by Abraham and who partook of *the three measures of flour which were kneaded into cakes baked upon the hearth*,[37] is merely a figurative account. The saints can sometimes share spiritual and rational food not only with men, but also with the more divine powers. They do so either to help them, or to show what excellent nourishment they have been able to prepare for themselves. The angels rejoice and nourish themselves on such a demonstration, and become the more ready to co-operate in every way and for the future to join their efforts towards a more comprehensive and more profound understanding for him who, provided only with the nourishing doctrines that earlier were his, has brought joy to them and, to put it thus, nourished them. Nor must we wonder that man should give nourishment to the angels. Christ Himself confesses that He *stands at the door and knocks*, that He *may come in to him* who *opens the door to Him, and sup with him*.[38] And then He gives of His own to him who first nourished, as well as he could, the Son of God.

12. He that receives the supersubstantial bread is made strong in his heart and becomes a son of God.[39] But he that shares of the dragon is nothing but a spiritual Ethiopian[40] changing himself into a serpent through the snares of the dragon. Thus, even if he says

that he wishes to be baptized, he hears himself reproved by the Word: *Serpents, ye brood of vipers, who hath showed you to flee from the wrath to come?*[41] And David, speaking of the body of the dragon which is eaten by the Ethiopians, says: *Thou didst crush the heads of the dragons in the water.* [*Thou has broken the head of the dragon*:] *Thou hast given him to be meat for the people of the Ethiopians.*[42] But if, inasmuch as the Son of God exists substantially, as does the Adversary also,[43] there is nothing incongruous in either of them becoming the food of this person or that, why do we hesitate to admit that in the matter of all powers, good and evil, and men, each of us can be nourished by them all? Thus, when Peter was about to join company with the centurion, Cornelius, and those who were with him at Caesarea, and then to share the words of God with the Gentiles also, he saw *a vessel let down by the four corners from heaven wherein were all manner of four-footed creatures and creeping things and beasts of the earth.*[44] And when he was commanded *to rise, to kill and eat,* he declined at first, saying: Thou knowest that *I never eat anything that is common or unclean.*[45] He was then told *to call no man common or unclean*; for that which was cleansed by God must not be called common by Peter. The text says: *That which God hath cleansed, do not thou call common.*[46] Thus the distinction made by the law of Moses in the terminology applied to numerous animals as being clean and unclean food, and that with reference to the varying dispositions of rational beings, teaches us a lesson: namely, that some such beings can serve us as nourishing food, while of others quite the opposite is true, until God purifies them and makes them all nourishing—even those *of every kind.*[47]

13. Since this is the case, and the difference between nourishments is as we have said, the supersubstantial bread is unique—above all those that are mentioned. We must pray to be made worthy of it, and to be nourished by *the Word* of God, which was *in the beginning with God,*[48] so that we may be made divine.

THIS DAY

Someone will say that the term *epiousios* is formed from the verb *epienai*:[49] that is to say, that we are bidden to ask for the bread that properly belongs to the age that is to come. Thus God by anticipation gives it to us now, and in this way what should be given as it were tomorrow is given to us "this day." Here "this day" means the present age and "tomorrow" the age that is to come. But, at least in my opinion, the first meaning given is better, as will become clear if we examine what is meant by the term *semeron* ("this day") which is added by Matthew, and the phrase, *kath hemeran* ("each day"), as is written in Luke.[50]

In many places in Scripture it is customary to use the term "this day" (="to-day") for the entire (present) age;[51] as for example in the text: *He is the father of the Moabites unto this day;*[52] and, *He is the father of the Ammonites unto this day;*[53] and, *This word was spread abroad among the Jews even unto this day;*[54] and in the Psalms, *To-day if you shall hear His voice, harden not your hearts.*[55] And in Josue this is brought out very clearly as follows: *Depart not from the Lord in the days of this day.*[56] And if "this day" stands for the whole of the present age, "yesterday" may stand for the age that is past. I believe that this is so in the Psalms and in Paul's Epistle to the Hebrews. In the Psalms we find: *For a thousand years in Thy sight are as yesterday which is past.*[57] Here, I presume, the famous millennium is in question: it is compared to "yesterday" as distinct from "to-day." And the Apostle writes: *Jesus Christ, yesterday, and to-day, and the same for ever.*[58] It is not surprising at all that all time has the same meaning for God as the interval of one day for us. Indeed I believe that it has less.

14. We must also examine the question as to whether or no the meaning of the feasts and festal assemblies determined by "days" or "months" or "seasons" or "years" is to be explained in terms of *ages*. If the *Law has a shadow of the things to come,*[59] it must be that the many sabbaths are the "shadow" of a great many days, and the new moons will be realized at definite intervals of time. That will come about when the path of a certain moon (I do not know which) will meet with that of a certain sun. And if the first month, and the tenth day until the fourteenth, and the fourteenth to the twenty-first of the feast of Azymes[60] all *have a shadow of the things to come—who is wise*[61] and so much *the friend of God*[62] as to discern the first of many months, its tenth day, and so on? And what need I say of the feast of the seven weeks of days,[63] and the seventh month, of which the first day is called the day of trumpets, and the tenth, the day of atonement?[64] Only God who ordained them knows what they mean. Who is there who has grasped the mind of Christ so well that he knows the meaning of the seventh year of freedom of Hebrew slaves,[65] and the remission of debts, and the intermission of the cultivation of the holy land?[66] Over and above the feast of every seventh year is the feast called the Jubilee.[67]

No one can ever come near divining its precise meaning or the true import of the prescriptions enjoined by it, except Him who knows the Father's will and His disposition for every age according to *His incomprehensible judgments and unsearchable ways.*[68]

15. I have often been puzzled when I put side by side two texts of the Apostle as to how there can be an *end of ages,* in which once and for all *Jesus hath appeared for the destruction of sin,*[69] if after the present age there are to be other succeeding ages. The texts are as follows: in the Epistle to the Hebrews—*But now once at the end of ages He hath appeared for the destruction of sin by the sacrifice of Himself*; and in the Epistle to the Ephesians, . . . *that He might show in the ages to come the abundant riches of His grace, in His bounty towards us.*[70]

My opinion in the face of this difficulty, in which great issues are involved, is that as the completion of the year is achieved in its last month, after which another month begins again, so perhaps many ages, as it were a year of ages, have been completed in the present age, after which certain ages to come will begin and the next age will be their first. It is in these future ages that God will *show the riches of His grace in His bounty.* The man plunged deepest in sin, who has *blasphemed against the Holy Spirit,*[71] will be under the domination of sin during the whole of the present age, and from the beginning to the end of the age to come; after that he will achieve salvation in a way I cannot account for.

16. The man who has grasped these things and considers in his mind a *week* of ages, so that he may have the vision of some holy Sabbath; who has pondered on a *month* of ages, so that he may see God's holy new moon; and a year of ages, that he may contemplate the feasts of the year, when *all the males shall appear before the Lord God;*[72] and the *years* corresponding to these great ages, that he may comprehend the seventh holy year; and the *seven weeks of years* of ages, that he may praise Him who disposed these things so wonderfully: how can he trifle over even the smallest part of an *hour* of a *day* of an age so great? Will he not rather do all he can that by making himself worthy through his preparation in this life to partake of the supersubstantial bread "this day," he may receive it "each day"? The term "each day" has been made clear in what was said above. He who "to-day" prays to God, who is from infinity to infinity, not only for "this day" but also for "each day," will be prepared to receive from Him, who is able to give *more abundantly than we desire or understand,*[73] things greater even—if I may use hyperbole—than the things that *eye hath not seen, greater than ear*

hath not heard, greater than that hath not entered into the heart of man.[74]

17. I have considered it very necessary to raise all these questions in order that the terms "to-day" and "each day" may be understood in our prayer to His Father to give us the supersubstantial bread. Finally, if we consider the term "our" and prefer to consider it as used in the latter Gospel, where there is written not: *Give us this day our supersubstantial bread,* but *Give us each day our supersubstantial bread,*—nevertheless the question arises as to how this bread is "ours." But as the Apostle says that *all things* belong to the saints *whether it be life, or death, or things present, or things to come,*[75] it will not be necessary to say anything about the matter here.

NOTES

[These notes have been emended for this reprinting]

1. Mt 6:11 and Lk 11:3
2. Jn 6:26.
3. Jn 6:27.
4. Jn 6:28 ff.
5. Ps 106:20.
6. Jn 6:32 ff.
7. Cf. Gn 1:26 ff and Col 3:9 ff.
8. Cf. Jn 1:1, 14; 14:6; 17:17; Lk 11:49; 1 Cor 1:24, 30. . . in general, Origen's eucharistic theology is orthodox; but he tends to depreciate a little communion with the Word in the Eucharist in favour of communion with the Word in Scripture.
9. Jn 6:32.
10. Jn 6:34 ff.
11. Jn 6:51 ff; *flesh "which I will give"* is a frequent variant reading.
12. Cf. Dt 9:9 . . . .
13. Jn 6:52.
14. Jn 6:54–57.
15. Jn 1:14.
16. Jn 6:59.
17. 1 Cor 3:1, 3, 2.
18. Heb 5:12–14.
19. Rom 14:2.
20. Cf. Mt 4:4 (Dt 8:3).
21. Prv 15:17 (Sept.).
22. Cf. 2 Cor 10:5; Mt 5:17.

23. Cf. Am 8:11; Rom 14:8.

24. Origen's observation on the rarity of the celebrated word *epiousios* has been completely sustained through the centuries: in addition to its use in the report by Matthew (6:11) and Luke (11:3) of the Lord's Prayer, scholars have been able to point to only one other, and that only probable, occurrence of the word (in a papyrus listing certain expenses, published in 1925). . . .

25. Ex 19:5 . . . . It will be found, I think, that *substance* is throughout this section the least troublesome rendering for *ousia* . . . . As to Origen's derivation of both words [*epiousios* and *periousios*] from *ousia*, this has been advocated also by some modern scholars; but today the etymology is sought more often in a combination of the preposition (for *epiousios*) *epi* + the participle of *einai*; or, more generally, in *epi* + *ienai* in the participial form. The latter was also considered by Origen . . . .

26. For example, the Platonists . . . .

27. For example, the Atomists, Epicureans, and Stoics . . . .

28. *Tonos*, a Stoic term meaning *tension* or *force* . . . .

29. Jn 6:51.

30. Cf. Heb 5:12 ff; Rom 14:2.

31. Cf. 4 Kgs 4:40 . . . .

32. Cf. Gn 2:9; 3:22; Jn 5:24.

33. Prv 3:18 (Sept.).

34. Ps 77:25.

35. Cf. Ex 16:15; Ps 77:24.

36. Cf. Heb 1:14.

37. Cf. Gn 18:2–6.

38. Apoc 3:20 . . . .

39. Cf. Ps 103:15; 1 Thes 3:13; Jas 5:8.

40. Cf. Ps 73:14; Rv 12:3–17; 13:2, 4, 11; 16:13; 20:2.

41. Mt 3:7; Lk 3:7.

42. Ps 73:13 ff.

43. Cf. 2 Thes 2:3 ff; 1 Tm 5:14 . . . .

44. Cf. Acts 10:1, 11 ff, 24, 27; 11:5 ff.

45. Acts 10:14 ff, 11:7 ff.

46. Acts 10:28, 15; 11:9.

47. Cf. Mt 13:47 . . . .

48. Cf. Jn 1:1.

49. That is, *epiousios* means *"of the coming day"* . . . .

50. Origen means that the second meaning of *epiousios "of the coming day,"* when used with either *this day* or *each day* (especially as he understands *day*, namely, as equivalent to *age*) would cause tautology. Cf. the following note.

51. It is clear from the sequel that by *aion* (*age*) Origen means a period of time which recurs—something cyclic. "This day" means, then, *the whole of the present age*, and "each day," *all ages* . . . .

52. Gn 19:37.
53. Gn 19:38.
54. Mt 28:15.
55. Ps 94:8.
56. Cf. Jos 22:29 (Sept.).
57. Ps 89:4.
58. Heb 13:8. . . .
59. Heb 10:1. In his homilies on Numbers (5:1) Origen says that Moses understood all these festal mysteries, but that he did not disclose them.
60. Cf. Ex 12:2–18.
61. Hos 14:10.
62. Jas 2:23.
63. Cf. Dt 16:9 ff.
64. Cf. Lv 16:29 ff; 23:24, 27 ff.
65. Cf. Ex 21:2.
66. Cf. Lv 25:4 ff; Dt 15:1 ff.
67. Cf. Lv 25:8 ff; 27:17 ff.
68. Rom 11:33.
69. Heb 9:26.
70. Eph 2:7.
71. Cf. Mt 12:32; Mk 3:29; Lk 12:10. . . .
72. Dt 16:16.
73. Eph 3:20.
74. 1 Cor 2:9.
75. 1 Cor 3:22.

TERESA OF AVILA

"Forgive Us Our Trespasses as We Forgive Them That Trespass against Us."*

1. OUR KIND MASTER SEES THAT, unless the fault be our own, this heavenly Bread renders all things easy to us and that we are now capable of fulfilling our promise to the Father of allowing His will to be done in us. Therefore, continuing to teach us the prayer He says: "Forgive us our debts, as we forgive our debtors." Notice, daughters, He does not say, "as we *are about* to forgive our debtors," because we are to understand that we must have already done this before we beg for so great a gift [as this Bread] and the surrender of our own will to that of God. Therefore Christ's words are: "as we forgive our debtors." Whoever wishes to be able to say to God in all sincerity: "Thy will be done," must have forgiven others beforehand, at least in intention.

2. Now we see why the saints rejoiced in injuries and persecutions, for thereby they had some payment to offer God when they made this petition. Otherwise, what could such poor sinners as myself do, who have so little to forgive and so much to be forgiven? We ought to think over this very seriously, sisters; it is so grave and so important a matter that God should pardon us miserable creatures our sins which merit eternal fire, that we must pardon all offences committed against us,[1] which are not really affronts nor anything at all. For, how is it possible to wrong, either by word or deed, such a one as I am, who in simple justice deserve to be treated unkindly in this world and tortured by the devils in the next?[2] Thus it is, O my God! that I have no other gift to offer Thee whereby I might

---

*"On the Words 'Forgive us our Trespasses,'" in *The Way of Perfection*, chapter 36, translated from the autograph of Saint Teresa of Jesus by the Benedictines of Stanbrook Abbey in Worcester including all the variants from the Escorial and Valladolid editions, revised with notes and an introduction by Benedict Zimmerman, O.C.D. (London: Thomas Baker, 1925), 217–27.

plead that Thou shouldst remit my debts. Thy Son must forgive me, for no one has done me any real injustice, therefore I have nothing to pardon in return.[3] Accept my wish to pardon others, O my God! for I believe that I could forgive my neighbour anything since Thou dost pardon me, or that I might fulfil Thy will unreservedly—yet, when it comes to the test, if I were unjustly accused, I know not what I might do. But in Thine eyes I am so guilty that all the evil men could say of me would fall far short of the truth, although those who see not all which Thou knowest might think that I had been injured. Therefore, O my Father! Thou must indeed forgive me *freely*, which demands from Thee *mercy*. All praise is due to Thee for bearing patiently with one so poor as I am. When Thy most blessed Son promised Thee this repayment from other men, He left out my name because I am utterly destitute. But, O my God! are there not other souls which, like mine, have never grasped this truth? If there are, I beg them in Thy name to remember it, and to ignore the trifling matters which they call affronts, lest, in their care for points of honour, they resemble children building houses out of straw.

3. Ah, my sisters, would that we realized what such "honour" means, by which true honour is forfeited! I am not speaking about what we are at the present moment: it would indeed be shameful if we did not recognize this. I apply it to myself in the days when I prided myself on my honour, as is the custom of the world, without knowing what the word really meant.[4] Oh! how ashamed I feel at recalling what used to annoy me then, although I was not a person accustomed to stand on ceremony. Still, I did not realize where the essential point of honour lay, for I neither knew nor cared for real honour, which is of some use because it benefits the soul. How truly has some one said: "Honour and profit do not go together"! I do not know whether he applied this meaning to it, still, quoting his words as they stand, the soul's profit and what men call honour can never agree. The perversity of the world is most astonishing: thank God for taking us out of it! May He always keep its spirit as far from this house as it is now! Heaven defend us from monasteries where the inmates are sensitive as to their fancied rights: they will never pay much honour to God there.[5]

4. What can be more absurd than for religious to stand upon their dignity on such petty points that I am absolutely surprised at them! You know nothing about such things, sisters: I will tell you so that you may be on your guard. The devil has not forgotten us—he has invented honours in religious houses—he has settled

the laws by which the dwellers rise and fall in dignity (as men do in the world), and they are jealous of their honour in surprisingly petty matters. Learned men must observe a certain order in their studies which I cannot understand: he who has read theology must not descend to read philosophy. This is a point of honour which consists in advancing and in not retrograding. If obedience obliged any one to do the contrary, he would secretly take it as an affront and would find others to take his part and say that he had been ill-used: the devil would easily find reasons, even from the holy Scriptures, by which he would appear to prove this. Even among nuns, she who has been Prioress must not afterwards fill any lower office: deference must be shown to the first in rank and she takes care we do not forget it; at times this even seems a merit because the Rule enjoins it. The thing is absurd, and enough to make one laugh—or rather *weep*, and with better cause than can be told. I know the Rule does not forbid me to be humble: the regulation is made to maintain order, but I ought not to be so careful of my dignity as to insist on this point's being obeyed as strictly as the rest. And perhaps I keep those injunctions very slackly, while I will give up no jot or tittle of this one. Let others see to what concerns my rank and let me take no notice of it. The fact is, we are bent on rising higher although we shall never mount to heaven by this path, and we will not dream of descending.[6]

5. O my Lord! art Thou not our Pattern and our Master? Indeed Thou art. And in what did Thine honour consist, O ever honoured Master and King? Didst Thou lose it in being humbled even unto death? No, Lord, Thou didst thereby gain it and didst win graces for us all. Therefore, sisters, how far we shall err from the right path if we follow this way, for it leads us wrong from the very beginning. May He grant that no soul may be lost through observing these miserable points of etiquette without realizing in what true honour consists. At last we come to believe that we have done a great thing when we forgive some trifle which was neither an affront nor an injury nor anything of the sort, nor gave us any just cause for resentment. Then afterwards, as if we had done some virtuous action, we petition God to forgive us because we have forgiven others. Give us grace O Lord! to know that we do not understand what we are saying, and that all such souls come to Him as empty-handed as I do myself. Grant this for the sake of Thy loving mercy. Indeed, O Lord! I see nothing that I can offer worthy to obtain from Thee so great a gift, for all earthly things perish, but

hell is eternal: yet I plead to Thee for souls who think that others are always injuring and insulting them.

6. What value God places on our loving and keeping peace with one another! For when once we have given Him our will we have given Him the right to it, and this we cannot do without love. See, sisters, what need there is for us to love and to agree with each other. The good Jesus places it before anything else. He does not mention the many things we gave Him on one single occasion, nor does He offer them in our name to His Father. He might have said: "Forgive us because of our many penances, or prayers, or fasts, or because we have left all for Thee and love Thee fervently, and have suffered for Thee and long to suffer more." He never says: "Because we would lay down our lives for Thee," or recounts the many other things the soul does for God when it loves Him and gives Him its will. He only pleads: "As we forgive our debtors." Perhaps this was because He knew of our attachment to this miserable "honour," so that we will overlook no slight upon it. This being the most difficult thing for us to overcome, our Lord put it in the first place, so that, after having asked such sublime graces for us, He offers this for our repayment.[7]

7.[8] Notice, sisters, that Christ says, "As we have forgiven our debtors," to show that it is a thing we have already done, as I said. Be sure of this—when a soul, after receiving some of the special favours in prayer which I have described and after having been raised to perfect contemplation, does not come away with a firm determination to forgive others, and if occasion offers, does not actually pardon any injury, serious as it may be—unless these fruits are left in the soul, the graces never came from God but were illusions and delight caused by the devil to make such a person think herself holy and therefore worthy of greater honour. I am not speaking of the trifles people call injuries, for these do not affect a soul that God raises to so high a prayer, nor does it care whether it is highly esteemed or no. I am wrong in saying that it does not care, for honour troubles it far more than contempt, and it dislikes rest much more than toil. The good Jesus, knowing that these results remain in the soul that has reached this state of prayer, assures His Father that we forgive our debtors, for when God has really given His kingdom to a person she no longer wishes for any kingdom in this world: she understands that this is the way to reign in a far higher manner, experience having taught her what benefit accrues from it and that the soul makes rapid progress through suffering for God. Only in very exceptional cases does He bestow sublime favours on souls which have not willingly borne many severe trials for His sake, because, as I have already told you in this book, contemplatives have heavy crosses to bear,[9] so our Lord chooses hearts which have been thoroughly tested.

8. You must know, sisters, that such souls, having learnt the worth of all created things, do not pay much heed to any transitory matter—if they experience a first movement of pain at some serious injury or suffering, they have hardly felt it before reason comes to their aid, and, as it were, erects the standard of faith for them and overthrows their pain by the joy of seeing that God has given them an opportunity of gaining, in one day, more graces and lasting rewards than they could have earned for themselves in ten years by any self-sought labours undertaken for Him. From what I have been told by many contemplatives, I believe this is very usual: they prize afflictions as others people prize gold and jewels, knowing that sorrows will make them rich. Such souls have no self-esteem—they are glad that their faults should be known[10] and reveal them to anyone who they know feels esteem for them.[11] It is the same as regards their percentage: they recognize that it will avail them nothing in the eternal kingdom. If they felt any pleasure in being of noble birth, it would only be when it enabled them to render God greater service. If they are not well-born, they are distressed when people over-rate them, and, if they take no pleasure in undeceiving their friends, at any rate they feel no reluctance to doing so. This must be because the souls on whom God has bestowed such great humility and love for Him so entirely forget themselves in all that concerns rendering Him greater service that they cannot believe any one can be troubled by certain annoyances which they themselves do not resent as injuries.

9. These last mentioned effects are proper to persons who have arrived at a high degree of perfection,[12] to whom our Lord often grants the favour of uniting them to Himself by sublime contemplation. But the first degree of this virtue, that is, a firm resolution to bear injuries and the suffering of them although they wound one, is obtained in a very short time by the soul to whom God grants the grace of union. If these effects are not found, and are not greatly increased by this prayer, we must conclude that this was no divine favour but a delusion of the devil sent to increase our self-esteem. The soul may possibly be lacking in this strength when God first bestows these favours on it, but if He continues doing so it will soon gain vigour, if not in the other virtues, at least in this of forgiving injuries.

10. I cannot believe that one who has approached so near to the Source of all mercy, which has shown the soul what it really is and all that God has pardoned it, would not instantly and willingly forgive, and be at peace, and remain well-affected towards any one who has offended her. For the divine kindness and mercy shown her prove the immense love felt for her by the Almighty, and she is overjoyed at having an opportunity of showing love in return.

11. I repeat that I know a number of people on whom our Lord has bestowed supernatural favours, such as the prayer or contemplation I have described, and, although they have other faults and imperfections, yet I never saw one who was unforgiving, nor do I think such a thing possible if these really were divine graces. If any one receives very sublime favours, let her notice whether the right effects increase with them: if these are not found, there is cause for great fear. Let no one fancy that such feelings were graces from God, for He always enriches the souls He visits. This is certain, for although the grace or consolation may pass away quickly, it is detected later on by the benefits it has left in the soul. The good Jesus is well aware of this and therefore deliberately assures His Father that we forgive our debtors.

NOTES

[These notes have been emended for this printing]

1. *Life*, xxi, 12. *Way of Perf.* xii, 8, 9; xiii, 1–4. *Concep.* ii, 15, 16, 32, 33.

2. *Excl.* xiii, 3. *Rel.* i, 28. *Life*, xxxi, 13.

3. Mother Isabel de Jesus, once said to the Saint: "Mother, how can you bear their saying such things about a nun?" (people were speaking very ill about her at the time). She replied: "They have good reason for it. I am surprised at their not flogging me. What do you suppose I care for their words? No music could be sweeter to my ears." (Fuente, vol. VI. 306. Note 7. Deposition of Damiana de Jesus).

4. *Life*, ii, 4.

5. Escorial edition, lxiv. Denounces superfluous honours.

6. So far was the Saint from caring for honors that not only did she wish to leave Avila because she was held there in high esteem, and retire with her dowry to another house of the Order far away where she would be unknown (*Life*, xxxi. 16), but she also wanted to become a lay sister so as to do the meanest and hardest work. She would have executed this design had she not been prevented by authority. (Ribera, bk. IV. xv.)

7. Escorial edition, lxv. Treats of the effects left by perfect prayer.

8. St. Teresa wrote against this paragraph on the margin of the original manuscript: "Effects produced by the good Spirit."

9. *Way of Perf.* xviii, 1.

10. A devout person,while talking to our holy Mother said: "Well, Mother, you may be a saint, but you don't seem one to me." St. Teresa was delighted, and answered: "God reward you for those words. You tell the truth, and you know what I really am." (Deposition of Damiana de Jesus. Fuente, vol. VI. 305. Notes 5, 6.)

11. *Life*, xxxi, 17.

12. *Castle*, M. VI. viii, 5. *Life*, xix, 2.

SIMONE WEIL

"And Forgive Us Our Debts, as We Also Forgive Our Debtors."*

AT THE MOMENT OF SAYING THESE WORDS we must have already remitted everything that is owing to us. This not only includes reparation for any wrongs we think we have suffered, but also gratitude for the good we think we have done, and it applies in a quite general way to all we expect from people and things, to all we consider as our due and without which we should feel ourselves to have been frustrated. All these are the rights that we think the past has given us over the future. First there is the right to a certain permanence. When we have enjoyed something for a long time, we think that it is ours and that we are entitled to expect fate to let us go on enjoying it. Then there is the right to a compensation for every effort whatever its nature, be it work, suffering, or desire. Every time that we put forth some effort and the equivalent of this effort does not come back to us in the form of some visible fruit, we have a sense of false balance and emptiness which makes us think that we have been cheated. The effort of suffering from some offense causes us to expect the punishment or apologies of the offender, the effort of doing good makes us expect the gratitude of the person we have helped, but these are only particular cases of a universal law of the soul. Every time we give anything out we have an absolute need that at least the equivalents should come into us, and because we need this we think we have a right to it. Our debtors comprise all beings and all things; they are the entire universe. We think we have claims everywhere. In every claim we think we possess there is always the idea of an imaginary claim of the past on the future. That is the claim we have to renounce.

---

*Simone Weil, *Waiting for God*, translated by Emma Craufurd (New York: G. P. Putnam's Sons, 1951), 222–25. Reprinted by Harper and Row in paperback in 1973. Originally published as *Attente de Dieu* (Paris: La Colombe, 1950). Reprinted by permission of the Putnam Publishing Group from *Waiting for God* by Simone Weil. Copyright © 1951 by G. P. Putnam's Sons. 1979 Renewed.

To have forgiven our debtors is to have renounced the whole of the past in a lump. It is to accept that the future should still be virgin and intact, strictly united to the past by bonds of which we are ignorant, but quite free from the bonds our imagination thought to impose upon it. It means that we accept the possibility that this will happen, and that it may happen to us in particular; it means that we are prepared for the future to render all our past life sterile and vain.

In renouncing at one stroke all the fruits of the past without exception, we can ask of God that our past sins may not bear their miserable fruits of evil and error. So long as we cling to the past, God himself cannot stop this horrible fruiting. We cannot hold on to the past without retaining our crimes, for we are unaware of what is most essentially bad in us.

The principal claim we think we have on the universe is that our personality should continue. This claim implies all the others. The instinct of self-preservation makes us feel this continuation to be a necessity, and we believe that a necessity is a right. We are like the beggar who said to Talleyrand: "Sir, I must live," and to whom Talleyrand replied, "I do not see the necessity for that." Our personality is entirely dependent on external circumstances which have unlimited power to crush it. But we would rather die than admit this. From our point of view the equilibrium of the world is a combination of circumstances so ordered that our personality remains intact and seems to belong to us. All the circumstances of the past that have wounded our personality appear to us to be disturbances of balance which should infallibly be made up for one day or another by phenomena having a contrary effect. We live on the expectation of these compensations. The near approach of death is horrible chiefly because it forces the knowledge upon us that these compensations will never come.

To remit debts is to renounce our own personality. It means renouncing everything that goes to make up our ego, without any exception. It means knowing that in the ego there is nothing whatever, no psychological element, that external circumstances could not do away with. It means accepting the truth. It means being happy that things should be so.

The words "Thy will be done" imply this acceptance, if we say them with all our soul. That is why we can say a few moments later: "We forgive our debtors."

The forgiveness of debts is spiritual poverty, spiritual nakedness, death. If we accept death completely, we can ask God to make us live again, purified from the evil in us. For to ask him to forgive us our debts is to ask him to wipe out the evil in us. Pardon is purification. God himself has not the power to forgive the evil in us while it remains there. God will have forgiven our debts when he has brought us to the state of perfection.

Until then God forgives our debts partially in the same measure as we forgive our debtors.

AUGUSTINE

Chapter 9 (Matt. 6.13)*

(30) THE SIXTH PETITION IS: "*And bring us not into temptation.*" In place of the word, "*bring,*" many codices have the word, "*lead.*" I regard these words as exactly equivalent; for they are both translated from the same Greek word, which is *eisenégkes*. But in making this application, many persons say: "Suffer us not to be led into temptation." And in this way they clearly show the intended meaning of the word, *lead.*[1] God does not of Himself lead a man into temptation, but He suffers a man to be led into temptation when—through one's just deserts and in accordance with a most hidden disposition—He leaves him bereft of divine aid. Often, for reasons that are quite evident, He adjudges a man deserving of being abandoned and led into temptation. But, to be led into temptation is one thing and to be tempted is another. Without temptation no one can be proved. He cannot be proved to himself, as it is written: "He that has not been tried, what manner of things does he know?";[2] nor can he be proved to another, as the Apostle says: "And your temptation in my flesh, you did not despise."[3] For their steadfastness was proved to him by the fact that they were not turned away from charity by reason of the tribulations which had befallen the Apostle according to the flesh. But, even before we are tried by any temptations, we are known to God, for He knows all things before they come to pass.

(31) Therefore, with regard to the text of Scripture which reads: "The Lord your God tries you, so that He may know whether you love Him," the clause, "So that He may know," is used as the

---

**Saint Augustine: Commentary on the Lord's Sermon on the Mount with Seventeen Related Sermons*, translated by Denis J. Kavanagh, O.S.A. (New York: Fathers of the Church, Inc.: 1951), 138–43. This book is volume 11 of the Fathers of the Church series. Copyright © the Catholic University of America Press. Reprinted with permission of the Catholic University of America Press. The English translation was based on the Third Benedictine Edition of Augustine (Venice: 1807).

equivalent of an expression which means: "So that He may make you know."[4] We ourselves use certain expressions in this way. For instance, we say that a day is joyful because it makes us joyful, and that cold is numb because it makes us numb. Countless expressions of this kind are used in ordinary conversation, in learned discourses, and in the holy Scriptures. But, because the heretics who oppose the Old Testament[5] do not understand this, they think that the brand of ignorance, so to speak, is to be placed on Him of whom it is written: "The Lord your God tries you." As though in the Gospel it were not written of the Lord: "But he said this to try him, for he himself knew what he would do."[6] But, if He knew the heart of the man He was testing, what did He wish to discover by testing? Why, that was done so that the person under trial would become known to himself,[7] so that, when the crowds had been filled with the Lord's bread, he would disapprove his own diffidence in thinking they had had nothing to eat.

(32) Hence, the import of the petition is not that we be not tried, but that we be not brought into temptation. It is as though a man who has to undergo trial by fire would pray, not that he be not touched by the fire, but that he be not consumed by it, for "the furnace tries the potter's vessels, and the trial of tribulation just men."[8] Accordingly, Joseph was tried by the allurement of the adulteress, but he was not brought into temptation;[9] Susanna was tried, but neither was she led into or brought into temptation;[10] and many others of both sexes, particularly Job. When those heretics who impugn the Old Testament wish to deride with sacrilegious lips Job's marvelous trust in the Lord, his God, they especially bandy the taunt that Satan asked to have him in order to submit him to temptation.[11] Since those men are blinded by superstition and wrangling, they cannot discern that God does not occupy a portion of space by bodily mass, and that he is not thus present in one place and absent in another, or at least that He is not partly here and partly elsewhere, but that, being everywhere absolute and not divided into parts, He is everywhere present by His majesty. Having no discernment of all this, they put questions to unskillful men who are entirely unable to understand such things, and ask them how Satan could talk with God. But, if they take a carnal view of the saying, "Heaven is my throne, and the earth my footstool,"[12] (and the Lord Himself bears witness to this passage, when He says: "You shall not swear: neither by heaven, for it is the throne of God; nor by the earth, for it is the footstool of His feet"),[13] what wonder that the Devil was set upon the earth and stood before the feet of God and spoke something in

His presence? When will they understand that God speaks within the conscience of every man who can reason in any manner, even though he be perverse? For, who but God has written the natural law in the hearts of men? This is the law of which the Apostle says: "For when the Gentiles who have no law do by nature what the Law prescribes, these having no law are a law unto themselves. They show the work of the Law written in their hearts, their conscience being their witness even when conflicting thoughts accuse and defend them, on the day when the Lord will judge the hidden secrets of men."[14] Even though some rational souls are blinded by cupidity, every rational soul thinks and reasons. Nevertheless, it is not to the rational soul itself that we ought to attribute whatever is true in its reasoning; we must attribute it to the very light of the truth by which it is enlightened, even though feebly in proportion to its capacity, in order that it may be able to perceive some truth in its reasoning. Therefore, although the soul of the Devil is perverse by depraved desire, what wonder that it is represented as having heard by the voice of God—which is the voice of Truth—whatever was true in his thought with regard to a just man whom he desired to tempt? On the other hand, it is to his own cupidity that we must attribute whatever untruth there was in his thought—the cupidity that has earned for him the name of the Devil.[15] Furthermore, as the Lord and Ruler of all things and as the universal Dispenser of merit, God has spoken to both the good and the bad, even though it was generally done through a bodily and visible creature. In this way, He has spoken through angels who appeared in human form, and He has spoken through the Prophets who used to say: "Thus speaks the Lord." And so, what wonder that God is said to have spoken to the Devil, even though He may not have spoken through the mere medium of thought, but through some creature adapted for such an operation?

(33) And let them not think that the fact of God's having talked with the Devil is any reward of the Devil's merit or righteousness of a sort, for God was speaking to an angelic spirit—a fatuous and covetous spirit, to be sure—just as He would speak to a fatuous and covetous human soul. Now, let these same men tell us how God spoke to the rich man whose foolish cupidity He would reprove, saying: "Thou fool, this night is thy soul demanded of thee: those things thou hast provided, whose will they be?"[16] The Lord Himself says this in the Gospel, to which even the heretics bow their heads whether they like it or not. If they are disturbed by the fact that Satan asked God for a righteous man in order to test

his righteousness, I am not explaining why it happened, but I am compelling them to explain why it is that in the Gospel the Lord Himself said to His disciples: "Behold, Satan has asked to have you, that he may sift you as wheat,"[17] and why He said to Peter: "But I have prayed that thy faith fail not."[18] When they have explained this to me, they will have given themselves the explanation they are demanding of me. If they are unable to explain it, then let them not dare brazenly censure in any book the very thing about which they make no objection when they read it in the Gospel.

(34) Temptations, therefore, occur through Satan, but they occur through God's permission and not by virtue of Satan's power. And they occur for the purpose either of punishing men for their sins or of proving and exercising them in accordance with the mercy of the Lord. As to the kind of temptation any man falls into—that is a matter of supreme importance. For Judas, the betrayer of his Master, did not fall into the same kind of temptation as Peter, the terrified denier of the Master. There are also, I believe, temptations that arise from human nature; for, in keeping with human frailty, every well-disposed man falls short of some one or other of the counsels. For instance, through eagerness to correct a brother, he may become slightly more impatient than Christian forbearance allows, and thus become angry with that brother. It is of such temptations that the Apostle speaks when he says: "May no temptation take hold of you but such as is human,"[19] for the same Apostle says: "God is faithful, Who will not suffer you to be tempted beyond what you are able to bear, but with the temptation will effect a means of escape, that you may be able to bear it."[20] In that pronouncement, he clearly shows that we ought not to pray to be free from temptation, but that we ought to pray not to be led into temptation, for we are led into temptation if we encounter such temptations as we are unable to bear. But, even though dangerous temptations—into which it would be dangerous to be brought or led—may arise from either prosperity or adversity in temporal affairs, no one is overcome by the trials of misfortune unless he is dazzled by the delights of prosperity.

NOTES

[These notes have been emended for this reprinting]

1. "Hence, many persons word the petition in this way, and it reads this way in many codices, and blessed Cyprian [Cf. *De Oratione Dominica*,

25] has written it this way, namely, 'Suffer us not to be led into temptation'" (De Dono Perseverentiae, 6:12).

2. Eccl 34:11.

3. Gal 4:13.

4. Dt 13:3. An instance of Augustine's anticipating the Vulgate. The Vulgate reads: "That it may appear," instead of "That He may know."

5. The Manichaeans.

6. Jn 6:6.

7. "God is said to learn when He makes us learn."

8. Eccl 27:6.

9. Gn 39:17ff.

10. Dn 13:20ff.

11. Jb 1:11.

12. Is 66:1.

13. Mt 5:34.

14. Rom 2:14.

15. The name is derived from the Greek word, "*diábolos*," which means *slanderer*.

16. Lk 12:20.

17. Lk 22:31.

18. Lk 22:32.

19. 1 Cor 10:13.

20. Ibid.

ALFRED DELP

Lead Us Not into Temptation*

WE OUGHT TO OFFER THIS PRAYER VERY SERIOUSLY. Our Lord knew what it was to be tempted and what bitter struggles temptation may entail. Who can be sure of himself? When things are going well we let these words pass over us negligently, thinking very little about them as if they really did not apply to us at all. And then all of a sudden the sky becomes overcast—a storm arises, and with the wind blowing from all directions at once we do not know which way to turn. Take this journey of mine up the perilous face of my cliff. How many hours of weakness and despair have had to be endured in making that climb, hours of sheer helplessness, of doubt, not knowing which was the best course. How is it that conditions suddenly get distorted, their balance disturbed and their threads twisted and entangled producing a pattern far from our intention and quite beyond our power to unravel? No one can escape the hour of temptation. It is only in that hour that man begins to sense his weakness and to have a faint inkling of the vital decisions he is expected to make. If only I can manage to keep a hold on this perilous perch and not faint and let go.

I have committed my soul to God and I rely on the help of my friends.

Temptation assails us from within and without. Compulsion, force, pain, humiliation, one's own cowardice, God's silence, complete inability to cope with an external situation, all these call for painful decisions. And added to all these there is fear, that creeping worm that eats its way into a man's very substance. The devil within may break loose—indignation, doubt, the overwhelming wish to live which cannot be suppressed. All these can cause

---

*Alfred Delp, *The Prison Meditations of Father Alfred Delp*, translator unknown (New York: Herder and Herder, 1963), 134–37. Copyright © Crossroad Publishing Company. Reprinted by permission of the Crossroad Publishing Company. This work, entitled *Im Angesicht des Todes*, was originally published in 1956.

many hours of bitter struggle and when it dies down the world no longer seems the same place. One's skin is turned to leather, criss-crossed with scars and wounds.

We have only God to fall back on in such a moment. This, and the knowledge that we have not brought the temptations upon ourselves voluntarily are our only hope. God bids us pray that we may be spared such trials. I advise everyone to take this admonition seriously to heart. What a witches' cauldron my own experience has been. How it will end, what still awaits me sitting here on the brink of the precipice, and how long I shall have to stay here before I must take the plunge, I have no idea. Nor do I know for certain that the gnawing worm within may not become active again. We must guard against every kind of false security—only then will we find access to God's great peace and omnipotence. How very different my feelings were during those hours in court. Then, although I knew from the start that I was doomed, I had no real sense of defeat. That was thanks to divine strength. And life from that moment took on a new meaning. It was clear and unmistakable that life is worth living and worth dying for. If this is true it applies in the fullest measure to moments of temptation when man cannot depend on his own strength alone.

Deliver us from evil

This part of the prayer again applies to man involved in temptation. Resistance is not only a manifestation but a thing that weighs the outcome in the balance. We are under a strain and begin to doubt whether we shall find salvation. In temptation it is a question of deciding for or against God and the essence of temptation is that it robs our judgment of its clear-cut certainty in making decisions. No one can escape deciding for God but the danger of making the wrong decision is a thing a man must pray to be spared. And incidentally this prayer requires far more humility and honesty than are usual nowadays.

The evil from which we pray to be delivered is not that which is most oppressive in life, such as poverty, worries, hardship, burdens, sacrifices, pain, injustice, tyranny and so on; it is the chain of circumstance that leads us into temptation, disturbing the balance, pushing life off-centre distorting the perspective. It will be seen at once that the so-called "good things" of life are just as liable to cause such disturbance as the painful and hard realities. These things all possess the potential power to lead or force us into temptation and by that I mean all the things that can possibly come between us and God.

Life is a contest, and this is emphasized by the words "deliver us from evil." The passage is even more eloquent than the one preceding it. In the natural course of existence we are again and again brought up against both the agony in the Garden and the temptation of the wilderness. There, too, genuine temptation had to be met, because our Lord was weak with hunger and because the devil found him vulnerable. The devil. Yes there is not only evil in this world, there is also the evil one; not only a principle of negation but also a tough and formidable anti-Christ. Man should give thought to the fact that he must distinguish between the spirits. And to the fact that wherever self is stressed, as in strength that glories in its own might, power that idolizes itself, life that aims at "fulfilling itself" in its own way and by its own resources, in all these, not the truth, but the negation of truth may be suspected. And there is only one thing a man can really do about it—fall down on his knees and pray. Only after ten long years—ten years too late—do I fully realize this.

LEONARDO BOFF

Save Us From the Evil One*

> The SS hanged two Jewish men and a youth in front of the whole camp. The men died quickly, but the death throes of the youth lasted for half an hour. "Where is God? Where is he?" someone asked behind me.
>
> As the youth still hung in torment in the noose after a long time, I heard the man call again, "Where is God now?"
>
> And I heard a voice in myself answer: "Where is he? He is here. He is hanging there on the gallows..."
>
> *The Crucified God* (New York: Harper and Row, 1974) pp. 273–74, citing Elie Wiesel in *Night*

If the petition "and do not bring us to the test" contains an element of anxiety, the final petition of the Lord's Prayer culminates in a paroxysm, as we cry out to our Father: "but save us from the evil one!" There is now nothing left to ask; it has all been said. To be saved from evil and from the evil one means being ready to enjoy the freedom of the sons of God in the Father's kingdom. When evil has been conquered, the kingdom may come, and the new heavens and the new earth may be inaugurated, where God's name is hallowed and his will is fully done. But evil will have to be conquered, because it is still a persistent part of history and is continually threatening humanity, "like a roaring lion prowling around looking for someone to devour" (1 Pt 5:8).

---

*Leonardo Boff, *The Lord's Prayer: The Prayer of Integral Liberation*, translated by Theodore Morrow (Maryknoll, N.Y.: Orbis Books, 1983), 109–20. Copyright © Orbis Books. Reprinted by permission of Orbis Books, Satprakashan Sanchar Kendra, Indore, India, Collins Dove, Australia, and Claretian Publications, Philippines. This book, entitled *O Pai-nosso*, was originally published in Brazil in 1979.

Evil As Situation

It is important that we do not minimize our awareness of evil. It is not just some static in the airwaves, some detour of human activity that causes us to arrive late at the goal toward which we strive. It is much more; it is a dynamic thing, a direction taken by history, a design for our lives. Evil, in this sense, has the characteristics of a structure, and this structure organizes a system of transformations that confer unity, consistency, totality, and self-regulation to all the processes that are maintained within the confines of the system.[1]

This structure creates its own scenarios of sin and wickedness; the scenario is made up entirely of elements contained in a backdrop that characterizes a given moment in history. Evil deeds are expressions of predetermined structures and scenarios. We may appropriate these structures and scenarios, may internalize them in our lives, may make them actual life goals, and thus may move into iniquitous, sinful practices. For example, the Puebla conference denounced the capitalist system as a system of sin (no. 92). Due for the most part to this system, "sinful structures" have taken shape on the Latin American continent and give rise to "a grave structural conflict": the increasing wealth of a few running parallel to the growing poverty of the masses (no. 1209).

This system creates its conflict-ridden economic and political scenarios: political repression and labor-union repression, "national security" governments, social crises, and so forth. The political events appearing in the daily newspapers are embodiments of this backdrop. Concrete persons incorporate into their social life this system, which in essence is an exclusivist one, involving the accumulation of wealth and privileges in the hands of a few who bear little social responsibility and become the agents who maintain the system and participate in its injustice.[2] A whole cycle of evil is thus established.

Evil exists in history because there is temptation. And persons fall into temptation; they sin, they betray the promptings of conscience, they disobey the voice of God, which is usually articulated by the signs of the times.[3] This sin creates its own history and its own mechanisms of production. It achieves a relative autonomy; it exercises power over each one of us, to the point that we feel enslaved: "I am the purchased slave of sin. . . . The good which I want to do, I fail to do; but what I do is the wrong which is against my will. . . . I perceive that there is in my bodily members a different law . . . making me . . . a prisoner under the law that is in my members, the law of sin" (Rom 7:14, 19, 23).

We live in the "sin situation" that St. John calls the sin of the world (Jn 1:29). It needs to be explained that "the sin of the world" does not mean that the world itself is sin. The world is primarily the good creation of God, for the sake of which the Father sent his beloved Son (Jn 1:9, 10, 3:16; 2 Cor 5:19; 1 Tm 1:15). Creation, however, has been polluted by humankind's historical wrongdoing. "Sin entered into the world" (Rom 5:12) and, although not completely corrupting the world, it has left deep marks on it (Jas 1:27). Thus the world as we experience it at present is "enmity to God" (Jas 4:4), is the source of unhappiness (2 Cor 7:10) and has not recognized Jesus Christ (Jn 1:10). Thus "the world" is not to be understood here in a metaphysical but in a historical sense; this world is the symbol of those who are capable of "stifling the truth in their wickedness" (Rom 1:18), of "spilling the blood of the prophets since the foundation of the world" (Lk 11:50) and of giving support to every sort of hypocrisy and sin (Mt 23:29–36).

The seriousness of sin lies in the fact that it constitutes a situation or structure. Every situation possesses its degree of independence and objectivity; sin is not just a personal matter, it has an important social and historical dimension. By a situation we mean "that combination of circumstances in which we find ourselves at a given moment; the situation completely envelops us, involves us, makes us a part of the world around us."[4] This situation was not humankind's original destiny, but it has become so. Its destiny was created by the sins of human beings across the whole sweep of history.

These sins did not die with the persons who committed them but have been perpetuated by actions that survived their perpetrators in the form of institutions, prejudices, moral and legal standards, and social customs. A large number of them represent a perpetuation of vices, racial and moral discrimination, injustice, against groups of persons and social classes; just because someone was born black or poor subjected him or her to a social stigma. This historically created situation becomes a matter of destiny for those born into it: they become victims of the processes by which traditional norms are socialized and internalized—those norms that are so often the bearers of wrongdoing and sin. The person in question has already been categorized, quite apart from his or her own will in the matter or his or her own decisions.

Such persons participate in this process because of the sin of the world; to the extent that they appropriate and accept the situation, the sin of the world grows as their own personal sins are contributed to it. Thus on the one hand they are victims of the sin of the world (because already situated within it), while on the other hand they become agents to reproduce the sin of the world through their own personal sins (by helping to maintain and reanimate the situation).

There is a kind of sinister solidarity in the evil that rankles humankind, throughout history (Rom 5:12–14, 16). But we must not lose our perspective here: if there is considerable solidarity with the old Adam, there is much more with the new Adam, because "where sin was multiplied, grace immeasurably exceeded it" (Rom 5:20), and "death established its reign . . . but life shall reign all the more" (Rom 5:17). But there is no need to emphasize the power of evil; we know that it was so strong that it could do away with the Son of God when he appeared incarnate in human history (Jn 1:11). And it continues to do away with the other sons of God to this very day.[5]

Embodiments of Evil

Who is behind all this evil? Who really causes wrongdoing? The Scriptures are quite clear on this. There is a spiritual being who is by definition "the tempter" (Mt 4:3), the "enemy" (Mt 13:39; Lk 10:19), the great dragon (Rv 12:9, 20:2), the serpent (2 Cor 11:3), the one who was a murderer and liar from the beginning (Jn 8:44; 1 Jn 3:8), the evil one (Mt 13:39; Lk 8:12; Acts 10:38), Satan (Mk 3:23, 26, 4:15; Lk 13:16), Beelzebub (Mt 12:24, 27; Mk 3:22; Lk 11:15, 18, 19), the prince of this world (Jn 12:31; 2 Cor 4:4; Eph 2:2). Simply stated, he is the evil one, the author of lies, of hatred, of sickness, and of death (Mk 3:23–30; Lk 13:16; Acts 10:38; Heb 2:14). Human beings who do not deal justly or love their brothers or sisters (1 Jn 3:10) are seen to be offspring of the devil, as was Cain (1 Jn 3:12) and Judas Iscariot (Jn 6:70, 13:2, 27). The tares of Jesus' parable are the children of the evil one, who are opposed to the children of the kingdom (Mt 13:38)—who *are* the kingdom of God.

How are we to understand this malevolent spiritual being? Is this a being who was created good by God but who, while undergoing a period of testing, fell into rebellion against God, becoming the Evil One by antonomasia? Or is this a literary device, a metaphorical personification representing our experience of being held captive by a widespread evil historically generated by the apostasies of humankind itself? It is an important question in connection with this last petition of the Lord's Prayer. Is "evil" to be understood as the evil one or as "evil" in the abstract? Are we to be delivered from evil (sin, despair, sickness, death) or from the evil one (the devil, Satan)?

There is still some difference among biblical scholars on this point, because there is no satisfactory way of resolving the question on the basis of language analysis.[6] But the great majority understand "evil" as the evil one (Satan, the devil). This final petition intensifies the one immediately preceding it: "do not bring us to the test"—and *especially* (singling out the worst example)—"save us from the evil one."

The context of the Lord's Prayer, as we have mentioned several times already, is apocalyptic and eschatological. At the end of history there will be a great confrontation between Christ and the antichrist, between the children of the kingdom and the children of the evil one (Mt 13:37–40). Christ and the antichrist will deploy all their forces. Human beings, historically weak and sinful, will run a most serious risk; they will be able to apostatize and fall into the snares of the devil. In this context, believers will pray from the depth of their being and with great anxiety: "Father, save me from the evil one, when he appears!" Paul well said: God the Father "has rescued us from the domain of darkness and brought us away into the kingdom of his dear Son" (Col 1:13).

If the exegetes choose to interpret "evil" as "the evil one," this does not mean that the problem as to the existence of the evil one (Satan, the devil) has been theologically settled. It is not enough to establish that the evil one is clearly mentioned in the Scriptures. One has to inquire as to the theological content of this expression. Does it have to do with a spiritual being or with a literary embodiment of the prevalence of evil? On this point, more than a serious exegesis is required; there needs to be reflection at the epistemological and theological levels.

We know that the question of demons has been the subject of heated discussion among theologians.[7] Not a few theologians tend to grant only a symbolic existence to the demons. It is good for us to ponder the words of the respected Catholic exegete, Rudolph Schnackenburg:

> There is a new relevance to the question of whether it is necessary to understand Satan (having eliminated mythological

and "humanized" conceptions of him) as a personal spiritual power or merely as the incarnation of evil, inasmuch as this evil is present in history and dominates it through human activities. Today we would not defend the first option with the same certainty as in the past. The demythologization debate counsels caution. The problem of how far one may and should interpret, in line with our present state of knowledge, the affirmations of the New Testament, being bound as they are to a worldview no longer held, is very difficult and cannot be answered by just one exegete. And this has relevance also to the discussion that has now been rekindled concerning angels and demons. The diversity of statements, the stylistic forms previously fashioned, the multiple sources of our ideas concerning Satan, the demons, and the "powers," all converge to indicate that in all this we are not dealing with modes of expression that should not be interpreted literally, as though they had no real substance.[8]

This position gives evidence of intellectual honesty in the face of investigations by exegetical science, and at the same time an awareness of the difficulty of resolving the problem by recourse to this science alone. We do not expect to decide the question here.[9] We only want to call attention to the fact that it is characteristic of religious thought the world over not to find the expression of evil in abstract principles but in living forces, whether benevolent or malevolent, which take on an objective metaphysical reality.[10] Evil has never been experienced in a vague, abstract form, nor have grace and goodness. We are always dealing with concrete situations, whether favorable or unfavorable, with the destructive or constructive historical forces of human relationships, of decent, comradely relationships, with ideologies of power and domination, or with those of cooperation and participation, with concrete bearers in the form of groups or of persons who embody these ideologies in their practical social life. Evil has a definite physiognomy, even though it may be concealed behind masks and disguises.

In the Old Testament, for example, there are incarnations of political powers that rise up against God and his holy people: Gog and Magog (Ez 38) or the "little horn" and the fourth beast of the Book of Daniel (7:7, 8),which probably represents the Syrian empire of Antiochus Epiphanes (175–164 B.C.) under whom the people of Israel were cruelly oppressed (Dn 7:25). The apocalyptic environment has given us a "theology of the tyrant of the end times" as the last great adversary of God. The New Testament projects the figure of the antichrist (2 Thes 2:1–12; Rv 13:1–11; 1 Jn 2:18, 19, 4:3; 2 Jn 7). He experiences a *parousia* similar to that of Christ and is surrounded by a community of evildoers (2 Thes 2:9–11; Rv 13:8). Christ incarnates the mystery of piety (1 Tm 3:16); the antichrist embodies the mystery of iniquity (2 Thes 2:7).[11]

Religious metaphysics, with its tendency to concretization, hypostatizes these realities within a supernatural framework. This is its vocabulary and the grammar of the expression of its workings. Theological understanding, for its part, seeks to get beyond the pictures and, so far as possible, to identify the realities and the ideas pertaining to them. Although seeming to desacralize them, it seeks to understand them as intrahistorical realities, manifestations of human wickedness that become embodied in collective forces and representations, against whom mere individuals find it difficult to protect themselves. The evil one would then simply be the organization of injustice, or humankind's departure from its essential calling, the aberration that becomes historically stratified and is forever opposed to the spirit of God, of justice, or goodness—in a word, to the realities of the kingdom.

We may assume that psycho-social development does not move inexorably in the direction of a growth in truth, concord, community, and the participation of everyone in the whole of life, but toward the exasperation that comes from contradictions. In this type of representation, the end of the world will signify an immense process of catharsis, a purifying crisis, at the end of which God will triumph and will lead history on to a transhistorical stage. *Et tunc erit finis*—and then it will be over. That is, the end will then come, and with it a new beginning: there will be an end to this dialectical type of history, and a new phase of history will be inaugurated, a movement toward God for which human beings have anxiously hoped. The Christian faith expresses this truth in its symbolic vocabulary: "The Lord Jesus will destroy the lawless one with the breath of his mouth, and annihilate by the radiance of his coming" (2 Thes 2:8).

Jesus and the Victory Over Evil

There is a profound and solid conviction in the New Testament to the effect that Jesus is the great deliverer from the power of Satan.[12] According to the mythology of that day, all diseases and infirmities are manifestations of the power of Satan. He holds humanity captive, so that it is subject to every sort of tribulation. But now one who is stronger has arisen to conquer the "strong man" (Mk 3:27).

Jesus accepts the religious metaphysics of the time. He understands Satan as a force in history (the *dynamis* of Lk 10:19) with an organization like that of an army of soldiers (Mk 5:9; Mt 10:25). He himself is aware that the end of Satan's power is at hand: "If it is by the finger of God that I drive out the devils, then be sure the kingdom of God has already come upon you" (Lk 11:20).

The kingdom of God is being built in opposition to the kingdom of this world, and it inflicts damage on the evil one (Mk 1:23–25, 39, 4:39; Lk 13:16).[13] Each time demons are driven out, one more degree of victory over him has been achieved, in anticipation of his final destruction. This victorious power is conferred upon the disciples (Mk 6:7; Mt 10:8; Lk 10:19). When the seventy-two disciples came back jubilant from their mission, saying: "In your name, Lord, even the devils submit to us," Jesus entered into their joy and said: "I watched how Satan fell, like lightning, out of the sky" (Lk 10:17–18). Jesus had a vision; in the annihilation of Satan's power he saw the state of paradise emerging, where humankind is to be reconciled with nature, for "nothing will ever harm you" (Lk 10:19).

As important as this perspective is in the gospels, we must not allow it to get out of focus. For Jesus, this focus is not so much the victory over the evil one as the proclamation of the good news of God's plan of salvation, especially for the defenseless, the poor, the lowly. It is the healings more than the victories over the diabolical dimension of life that manifest the presence of the kingdom, of the new order that God desires, and the inauguration of the new age. Thus the apostles are blessed in that they see what many prophets and kings desired to see and did not (Lk 10:23–24; Mt 13:16–17).

As a consequence, Jesus' followers do not begin by requiring renunciation of the devil, as the Essenes of Qumran did, but what he asks of them is adherence to the kingdom. In his exhortation he does not warn them to beware of uncontrollable and diabolical forces, but to beware of the yearnings of their own hearts, for these are what corrupt a person's life (Mk 7:15). What keeps someone from entering the kingdom and experiencing the transcendent meaning of life is not so much the devil as wealth (Lk 6:24–25, 12:13, 21, 16:13), excessive worries (Mt 6:19–34), a self-centered attitude (Mk 9:43–48), passing judgment on others (Mt 7:1–5), lusting for power, honor, and glory (Mk 10:35–45), an exaggerated, sterile piety (Mk 11:15–19), gullibility (Mk 13:5–7), and the temptation to abuse the good faith of others (Mk 9:42; Mt 18:6; Lk 17:1–3).[14]

The principal cause of the world's ills is to be found in our insensitivity, our lack of solidarity, and the failure of love. It is this that Jesus criticizes in the Pharisees (Mt 23:23). These are the real demons that we must exorcise from our lives. When this is accomplished, the grace of God is seen to be victorious in the world. To follow Jesus, which is the central theme of the gospels, calls for creating this new mentality, a truly liberated attitude. "If God is on our side, who is against us?" (Rom 8:31).

The Final Cry of the Human Heart: Save Us, Father!

The Greek term used in the Lord's Prayer for "save" is *rysai.* It original sense differs from that of the Latin *liberare* or the English "liberate." The common meaning of "liberation" presupposes an experience of captivity, of being in chains and oppressed. This meaning could be verified here, inasmuch as the presence of sin and the evil one imposes slavery on human life. And God has been revealed as a liberator (Ps 18:2, 40:17, 70:5, 144:2; Dn 6:27). His liberating action has been conveyed in St. Jerome's Vulgate by the term *liberare* (about two hundred times).[15] For instance, a truthful witness *saves* lives (Prv 14:25); the Israelites are *liberated* from Egyptian captivity (Ex 3:8, 14:30, 18:10).

But the original meaning of the Greek *ruesthai* is that of snatching a person away from the brink of an abyss, protecting someone from the vicissitudes of a journey, protecting someone from the traps that lie in the path. As we read in the Psalms: "Keep me from the trap which they have set for me. . . . Let the wicked fall into their own nets, while I pass in safety" (Ps 141:9–10); "let no flood carry me away, no abyss swallow me up" (Ps 69:15); "he himself will snatch you away from fowler's snare or raging tempest" (Ps 91:3).

The underlying experience is that of life as a pilgrimage, as a covenant with God to walk in his paths. Along this path we experience dangers of every kind; there are yawning abysses, there are traps laid by enemies, and we can be attacked. Within the framework of this figurative language, what does the evil one do? His task is to tempt us, to draw us away from the good path, to give us wrong directions. And what does God do? God protects us from the dangers, pulls us away from the ambushes, and shows us the right direction to travel. God said to Jacob: "I will be with you, and I will protect you wherever you go and will bring you back to this land; for I will not leave you until I have done all that I promised" (Gn 28:15). In Isaiah, he says: "Thus says the Lord, your ransomer. . . I lead you in the way you must go" (Is 48:17). And the same prophet asks God in a rather complaining tone: "Thou, Lord, art our father. . . our Ransomer from of old. . . . Why, Lord, dost thou let us wander from thy ways?" (Is 63:16–17).

What are these ways or paths of God? They are the ways or paths that lead us toward justice, truth, and fellowship, overcoming the forces of selfishness and oppressive power. As may be seen from the above texts, "saving," "liberation," or "deliverance" is found in the context of a "pilgrimage," a "journey," and of the dangers that go with it, a trek that leads either toward the realization of human desires or toward their frustration.

Each generation has its own "evil one" against which it must particularly protect itself and because of which it must implore divine protection. This evil being embodies the widespread wickedness that permeates humanity. In our own time, the evil one who offends God and debases human persons appears in the form of a collective selfishness embodied in an elitist, exclusivist social system that has no solidarity with the great multitudes of the poor. He has a name; he is the Capitalism of private property and the Capitalism of the state. In the name of money, privileges, and the reinforcement of governmental structure he holds men and women in terror. Many of them are imprisoned, tortured, and killed. Two-thirds of the population are held prisoner under the yoke of a legion of demons: hunger, sickness, disintegration of the family, and a shortage of housing, schools, and hospitals. This evil one has his ways of tempting; he slyly creeps into our minds and makes the heart insensitive to those structural inequities that he has created.

In the context of apocalyptic eschatology the evil one directly named in this petition of the Lord's Prayer assumes that humanity is drawing close to its final destination. Emerging all along this final leg of the journey are the many obstacles, the many gaping abysses, and the danger of defection from the undertaking that is about to achieve its goal. In the midst of this distressing situation the believer and the believing community cry out: "Father, save us from the evil one and from all evil! As you have not allowed us to fall into temptation, now snatch us away from the maneuverings of the evil one!" But the danger does not beckon only at the end of history; it is part of the structuring of the present; it lurks in every corner and seeks to destroy us. And so we cry out to the Father: "Save us from evil! Protect us from moving away from the dimension of goodness. Father, do not let us forsake you!"

If we have prayed from the depths of our hearts, then our confidence can be restored, because it is Jesus who has given us his guarantee: "If you ask anything in my name, I will do it" (Jn 14:14); "courage! The victory is mine; I have conquered the world" (Jn 16:33); "stand upright and hold your heads high, because your liberation is near" (Lk 21:28).

NOTES

[These notes have been emended for this reprinting]

1. See Jean Piaget, *Le Structuralisme* (Paris: Presses Universitaires de France, 1968), pp. 5–16. See also *Structuralism*, trans. Cheminah Maschler (New York: Basic Books, 1970).

2. See E. Tamez, S. Trinidad, et al., *Capitalismo: violencia y antivida*, 2 vols. (San Jose, Costa Rica: DEI, 1978).

3. See Clodovis Boff, *Os sinais dos tempos: Pautas de leitura* (Sao Paulo, 1979), which is a very important work on this theme.

4. Piet Schoonenberg, "O pecado do mundo," *Mysterium Salutis* II/3 (Petropolis: Vozes, 1972), p. 306

5. Boff, "O pecado original," pp. 109–33.

6. See L. Sabourin, *Il Vangelo di Matteo: Teologia e Esegesi* (Rome: 1976), pp. 448–50; J. Schmid, *Das Evangelium nach Mattaus*, Regensburger Neues Testament, vol. 1 (Regensburg, 1965), pp. 133–35; Ernst Lohmeyer, *The Lord's Prayer*, trans. John Bowden (New York: Harper and Row, 1965), pp. 209–17. In Greek, the phrase is *apo tou ponerou*; the noun (*ponerou*) is in genitive case; we do not know morphologically whether the nominative is neuter (*poneron*) or masculine (*poneros*). In the first case it would signify iniquity or evil; in the second, the evil one. Probably the masculine (*poneros*) is intended, because of the definite article (*tou*) that precedes it. The neuter normally appears without the article. Luke omits this petition; it is in Matthew's version. The Greek fathers, sensitive to the nuances of their language, interpret this in the sense of the evil one (masculine). The Latin fathers, on the contrary—because in Latin the article does not exist—take it in the sense of iniquity, evil (neuter)—*libera nos a malo*.

7. On this question, see the two basic positions: Christian Duquoc, "Satan—symbole ou realite," *Lumiere et Vie* 78 (1966), 99–105; Herbert Haag, *El diablo, un fantasma* (Barcelona: Herder, 1973), and Joseph

Ratzinger, "Abschied vom Teufel?" in *Dogma und Verkundigung* (Munich, 1973), pp. 225–34.

8. Rudolf Schackenburg, "Der Sinn der Versuchung Jesu bei den Synoptikern," in *Schriften zum Neuen Testament* (Munich, 1971), p. 127.

9. See the fundamental work of Herbert Haag in collaboration with other exegetes and theologians, *El Diablo: Su existencia como problema* (Barcelona: Herder, 1978).

10. See G. Van der Leeuw, *Religion in Essence and Manifestation*, trans. J. E. Turner (New York: Harper and Row, 1963), vol. 1, chaps. 15, 16, and 19.

11. See J. Ernst, *Die eschatologischen Gegenspieler in den Schriften des Neuen Testaments* (Regensburg, 1967), pp. 221–40.

12. A systematic and rigorously exegetical treatment of this can be found in Haag, "Jesus y la realidad del mal," *El diablo: Su existencia*, pp. 199–246.

13. Joachim Jeremias, "Overcoming the Rule of Satan," in *New Testament Theology* (New York: Scribner, 1971), pp. 85–96.

14. See Haag, *El diablo: Su existencia*, p. 244.

15. See *Reallexikon fur Antike und Christentum*, vol. 8 (1972), p. 303, s.v. "Freiheit."

PART FOUR

In Conclusion

THE LORD'S PRAYER IN THE LITURGY

THE PATERNOSTER FROM VERY EARLY TIMES in the church was prayed in both the sacrament of baptism and in the eucharist. In the fourth century Cyril of Jerusalem mentions the Lord's Prayer as part of the eucharistic celebration, and there is reason to believe its use was widespread and dates from earlier times. In the West, Gregory the Great indicates in his liturgical writing that the Pater was said before the communion in the mass. Jungmann in his monumental history of the mass of the Roman rite calls the Lord's Prayer the "center" of the communion preparation.[1] He points out a certain fittingness that the Lord's Prayer is situated at the ending of the eucharistic prayer and the beginning of the communion. The thou-petitions give an echo of the eucharistic prayer. Thus, "hallowed be thy name" repeats the sanctus; "thy kingdom come" corresponds to the epiclesis, the calling down of the Holy Spirit upon the gifts of bread and wine; "thy will be done" reflects the sacrifice of Calvary re-presented in the Lord's supper. The we-petitions look the other direction and anticipate the communion rite. Thus, "give us this day our daily bread" refers to the eucharistic bread soon to be received; "forgive us our sins as we forgive others" is the requirement of unity and love within the community that would gather at one table in the sign of peace to eat the one bread of the Lord; and finally, "deliver us from evil," and the embolism or amplification that follows it, yearns for that condition of peace and absence of evil that would make the best conditions for maximizing the eucharistic communion in one's life and that of the entire human community.

The Lord's Prayer was the first Christian prayer given to the catechumen. It was given back in public recitation after the baptismal immersion and before the reception of his or her first eucharistic communion. Both the Lord's Prayer and the Apostles' creed were the sacred Christian texts given with solemnity to the catechumen at an appropriate time for their study and memorization. Neither the creed nor the Pater were to be profaned by their recitation outside of liturgical ceremony. If recited in private devotion, it was to be quietly and to oneself. They were not even to be written down, but to be taken to heart and committed to memory. These mysteries were for Christians only. At the moment of baptism the catechumens profess their faith by the recitation of the creed by heart and out loud before the assembly of the faithful. Immediately afterwards, they recited the Lord's Prayer publicly in preparation for the receiving of first communion and full communion within the Christian eucharistic body. Thus, communion in the Roman eucharistic liturgy is prepared for by the recitation of the Pater. Communion of the sick also is preceded by the recitation of the Lord's Prayer. The Good Friday liturgy, sometimes called the mass of the presanctified, does not recite the eucharistic prayer. After the long petitionary prayers for the universal church the communion service is initiated with the solemn recitation of the Paternoster.

The Lord's Prayer in the liturgy is surrounded with some supplementary words to introduce and to conclude the gospel text itself. Just as the eucharistic prayer begins with a preface (Holy, holy, holy) that worships the thrice holy God of hosts before presuming to address the Lord of heaven, so the Lord's Prayer is introduced with a brief preface that acknowledges the transcendence of the Father and our bold daring to say "Our Father," even though commanded to do so by Jesus who is Lord and only Son of the Father. Subsequently, the embolism of the Lord's Prayer was a liturgical addition that allowed a more ample petition for deliverance from every evil of the human condition. The familiar doxology, "for thine is the kingdom and the power and glory now and forever" and the Amen were additions that fit the liturgical role of the Lord's Prayer. The doxology concludes the Lord's Prayer, just as the doxology, "Through him, with him, and in him" concludes the "Great Prayer," that is, the eucharistic prayer or the canon of the mass. When recited in the community, the Pater fittingly concludes with Amen. In baptism, the Amen ratifies the Lord's Prayer as recited by the newly baptized. Then as today the Lord's Prayer is itself the preparation for eucharistic holy communion in the body of Christ.

Some manuscripts of the gospel of Matthew add either or both the Amen and the doxology. The Vulgate includes the Amen,[2] and the King James, or authorized version (1611), includes the doxology. A doxology was commonly added as a conclusion of the Lord's Prayer.[3] Neither of these additions to the Lord's Prayer are found in the earliest and best manuscripts of the gospel, and almost no one today maintains that they were originally in the gospel text. Their inclusion comes from scribes copying manuscripts after these prayerful additions were commonly used in the liturgy. So to speak, they hummed along with the tune they knew by heart and added what was so familiar from liturgical practice. The Revised Standard version no longer includes either the Amen or the doxology as part of the gospel.

I

The Book of Revelation ends with these lines: "'Yes, I am coming soon.' Amen! Come, Lord Jesus! The grace of the Lord Jesus be with all" (22:20–21). Amen is a Semitic word that means "thus" or "it is true." In the gospels Jesus introduces many of his more solemn sayings with that phrase: "Amen, amen I say to you." Amen is rooted in the verb *'mn*, which is related to various Hebrew words indicating truth, faith, and trust. In saying Amen one is saying "yes" to all of life in God's providence, who is sovereign Lord of all that comes about. Karl Barth writes that the Amen is the "certainty of God's response." And Paul concludes: "For the Son of God, Jesus Christ, who was proclaimed to you by us, Silvanus and Timothy and me, was not 'yes' and 'no,' but 'yes' has been in him. For however many are the promises of God, their Yes is in him; therefore the Amen from us also goes through him to God for glory" (2 Cor 1:19).

At the end of prayer spoken in community by a leader of the assembly, the whole congregation ratifies that prayer with the Amen. It is their signature to the substance of the prayer they have just heard and to which they join their hearts signed over in this one-word exclamation. "So be it" in English captures something of the content of Amen. The word is so ancient and venerable in Jewish and Christian prayer that it defies adequate translation. The Amen demands participation of the people of God. They must validate the prayer of their community leader, who collects in a public prayer the many prayers of each individual's soul. Without that ratification, the congregation remains only audience. With a wholehearted and sincere Amen, the person who has listened has truly spoken in the silence of their heart the very same prayerful words and with the identical purpose to reach God. Cyril of Jerusalem writes: "After completing the prayer [the Pater] you say 'Amen,' sealing it with that Amen, that is to say, may the whole of this prayer taught by God be efficacious."[4]

II

After the recitation of the Lord's Prayer in the eucharistic celebration, a short prayer, called the embolism, follows. It echoes the last line "deliver us from evil" and amplifies what that deliverance entails. The evils that we might fear here and now are detailed, and the full implication of the prayer for freedom from evil is contemplated. The embolism is something of an encore that repeats the theme of the previous music, but gives it a different and more ornate arrangement. The word embole means a bulge, and in medical terms we speak of a pocket swelling in a blood vessel as an embolism. Since it was never clear in the Greek word for evil, *ponērou*, whether evil in general or the evil one, that is, Satan, was intended, there was an opening neatly provided for some commentary upon the text. The embolism functions like a marginal gloss, an explanation of the last line of the Pater, and an unfolding of its many implications.

The embolism in the *Sacramentary* used in the Catholic liturgy reads as follows:

> Deliver us, Lord, from every evil, and grant us peace in our day. In your mercy keep us free from sin and protect us from all anxiety as we wait in joyful hope for the coming of our Savior, Jesus Christ.

This elaboration of the final petition of the Lord's Prayer is recited immediately after it. The Amen is not said in the eucharistic celebration. This particular embolism is one of many composed through the ages in different places and in different ways. For example, the embolism in the St. James liturgy reads:

> Lord, lead us not into temptation, Lord of hosts! for thou dost know our frailty; but deliver us from the wicked one, from all his works, from all his assaults and his craftiness; through thy holy name, which we call upon to guard us in our lowliness. For thine is the kingdom and the power and the glory, belonging to Father, Son and Holy Spirit, now and forever and in all eternity. Amen.[5]

In the eastern liturgies this supplement regularly accentuates not only the last petition, to deliver us from evil, as is typical of western liturgies, but the last two petitions, "sometimes by just repeating the words, sometimes by a marked expansion."[6]

An analysis of the embolism in the Roman liturgy shows a certain parallel with the we-petitions in the Lord's Prayer. Accordingly, "deliver us from every evil, and grant us peace in our day" is seen as the ideal condition in the community for the reception of the "daily bread" of the Lord's eucharistic table. "In your mercy keep us free from sin" dovetails well with "forgive us our sins as we forgive the sins of each other." And finally, "protect us from all anxiety as we wait in joyful hope for the coming of our Savior, Jesus Christ" would seem to be the desideratum of the petition "do not bring us to the test (lead us not temptation) but deliver us from evil."

The wording of the embolism "protect us from *all anxiety*" provides an especially poignant commentary on the Our Father as a whole. The innumerable bidding prayers of the faithful stem from the insecurity of the human condition, where we need so much for happiness and can control so little. Hence life is filled with anxiety that we will not have enough with which to live and be happy. Not only are we poor in body, but we are impoverished in soul. Not only do we hunger for bread for body, but also for truth and love for our souls. The Paternoster collects all these petitions and sums them up in the simple and inclusive petitions of the Lord's Prayer. Accordingly, the embolism provides a sequel, a rerun of the same theme, that we are needful but God's resources are bountiful. The flesh is vulnerable to a thousand tragedies, and we are all dying whatever our blessings, and yet the truth is that as children of the Father in heaven we are "free from all anxiety." And, "as we wait in joyful hope for the coming of our Savior Jesus Christ," we may be reminded of the words of Paul: "Who will separate us from the love of Christ?" (Rom. 8:35).

III

The doxology is commonly held today to be an early liturgical addition to the Lord's Prayer, patterned on the Jewish doxologies that were common at the end of petitionary prayer. Most Jewish prayers ended with a formula of praise and worship, which might be freely chosen by the one praying. In the very early liturgical text of the Lord's Prayer found in the *Didache*, which dates from the late first century and perhaps from within the community of Matthew, the doxology is somewhat abbreviated: "For Thine is the power and the glory for evermore."[7] The text of the Pater in the *Didache* shows some minor differences with the established text of Matthew, and it is not surprising that the doxology would also be subject to local rendition. The doxology became popular in liturgical celebration, and it made its way into gospel manuscripts later on as an interpolation. The best and the oldest manuscripts of the gospels do not have a doxology.[8]

In the Roman Sacramentary the doxology follows the embolism. We read: "For the kingdom, the power, and the glory are yours, now and for ever." The derivation of that text is generally ascribed to 1 Chronicles 29:11. At the very end of the account of David's life, we read these words that recapitulate his whole kingdom:

> Thine, O Lord, is the greatness, and the power, and the glory, and the victory, and the majesty; for all that is in the heavens and in the earth is thine; thine is the kingdom, O Lord, and thou art exalted as head above all.

One is easily reminded of the Magnificat of Mary, whose soul magnified the Lord who did great things in her. In the last book of the Bible there are many passages that exalt the coming victory of God over the forces of evil in the world: "Worthy art thou, our Lord and God, to receive glory and honor and power" (Rv 4:11). Of such sentiments is the doxology that follows the Lord's Prayer.

Finally, one might ask to what does the doxology refer in the Lord's Prayer itself? Does this concluding praise refer to all of the Lord's Prayer? Does it refer to just the last petition to "deliver us from evil"? Karl Barth writes that the reason why we ask to be delivered from the Evil One is "because the Kingdom, the power, and the glory belong to God, and not the Devil, sin, death or hell."[9] The doxology would also appear to echo the thou-petitions in the first part of the Pater. Thus, "thine is the glory" is reminiscent of "hallowed be thy name"; "thine is the kingdom" repeats "thy kingdom come"; and "thine is the power" corresponds to "thy will be done." Indeed one might argue that the doxology refers to the whole Paternoster.[10]

TWO READINGS: THE ESCHATOLOGICAL AND THE EVERYDAY

THE LORD'S PRAYER SEEMS straightforward and simple, but upon examination it showed a remarkable compression of rich meanings. Every line of the prayer offered alternative readings. Throughout the commentary I have tried to point these out in the appropriate places. The task before us now is to make some kind of summary statement about the various readings of the Lord's Prayer. The interpretations of each article branch into two large and imprecise alternatives based upon what emphasis is given to the prayer. If one chooses the more eschatological reading then a whole line of wordings will follow. If one chooses the more temporal and this-world reading, another whole line of wordings will follow. Both readings are important, and both are found in the Lord's Prayer in Matthew and in Luke.

The eschatological reading fits the nature of God as the Almighty, the infinite and sovereign One whose providence reigns supreme. History is in God, not God in history. Matthew's version fits well the eschatological, without precluding that Matthew has another side as well. His Lord's Prayer stresses the importance of worship, while not denying the value of human behavior. It centers upon the saving work of God, while not denying the moral work of humankind. The temporal-secular reading fits the nature of God as the *incarnate* one, the human being enfleshed in the created Many of space and time, where providence reigns supreme within history as well as in eternity. Luke's version fits well the temporal-secular, without precluding that Luke has another side as well. His Lord's Prayer stresses the importance of daily behavior, which expresses the commitment of faith. While not denying the value of mystery and worship, nor denigrating the grace of God, it calls attention to the ongoing moral effort of the individual believer. Matthew's text lends itself to an end-time and spiritual reading of the Lord's Prayer, and Luke's to a more literal and daily life orientation.

Let us compare these two approaches with each article of the Lord's Prayer. "Our Father who art in heaven" could also be rendered *our heavenly Father*. The first wording might better fit the eschatological reading, which emphasizes the sovereignty of God. The second wording would fit the temporal-secular well, since the emphasis falls more explicitly on the word Father, which implicates God in the world.

"Hallowed be thy name." The eschatological approach might see this petition as mainly a doxology, in parallel with the traditional Trinitarian doxology: "Glory be to the Father, etc." The temporal-secular viewpoint might be more comfortable with an interpretation that sees this phrase as a petition for the name of God to be made holy in believers, whose moral life should correspond in reality with the holy name taken upon their lips.

"Thy Kingdom come." The eschatological approach will read the word Kingdom with upper case emphasis, thinking of the entire range of God's presence in the fulfillment of creation. This fullness of the Kingdom culminates in communion with the transcendent God in the final coming. The temporal-secular viewpoint will see the kingdom of God as first of all the reign of God in our hearts, the conformity of our wills and moral behavior here and now with the will of the heavenly king, whose kingdom then will be one of justice and peace and even in this world.

"Thy will be done." The eschatological approach will be more comfortable with the will of God as the universal providential care for the common good of all creation, a will that needs to be ever done on earth just as it is in heaven. The temporal-secular viewpoint will see the will of God more in terms of the ethical demands of being a follower of Christ and a son and daughter of the Father, whose will should be done on earth as it is now being done by the blessed in heaven. The angels and saints in heaven are our spiritual models to urge us on to holiness even on earth. The eschatological viewpoint might read the will of God in heaven as a given and perfect victory (on earth as it is already done in heaven). The temporal-secular approach might read the will of God in heaven as also a work of wisdom and grace. May God's will be done both on earth and in heaven, for even heaven falls under divine providence and needs to be sustained by God.

"Give us this day our daily bread." The eschatological version will be more comfortable with a translation such as *supersubstantial* bread. Daily bread is the bread of the eschatological banquet, which includes the scriptures as the nourishing word of God, and the eucharist as the spiritual bread of life. The temporal-secular version will find more fitting the quotidian bread, the bread of the poor, the daily bread of everyday life, the needs of the body as well as the soul, and yet all because of the spirit. Both readings are important. Bread should represent the many created gifts of God, physical and spiritual, that are the means to our union with the infinite God now and in eternity.

"Forgive us our trespasses." The eschatological approach will prefer the translation *debts*, the more generic word that refers to all that we owe to one another. In short, forgive us all the evils of the human condition that make human life indebted while awaiting the fullness of the Kingdom. The temporal-secular viewpoint will find the word *sins* more instructive, for it calls to mind that we must change our lives from immoral disgrace to holy grace. Prayer to God that does not embody itself in true moral virtue risks being empty prayer.

The eschatological approach might prefer "as we forgive" to mean *just as we forgive*, we who have received your grace enabling us to forgive others in the pattern of your forgiveness of us. The temporal-secular viewpoint would prefer to emphasize that we will be forgiven only to the extent that we have given forgiveness, not so much because the divine love waits for our love to earn God's response, but because we can only know we have received God's love when we find ourselves in turn receptive to our brothers and sisters. To act with a gracious heart is the proof of having accepted the forgiveness of God, the only sign of which resides in our own graciousness of heart in our conduct with others. Love of neighbor, even love of enemies, is the evidence of one's love from God and of God.

"Lead us not into temptation." The eschatological reading will prefer the translation that reads the *time of trial* or the *test*. Save us from the time of trial. Put us not to the test. This evil is the grand temptation, in which all temptations are resolved and once and for all overcome: light versus darkness, right versus wrong, God versus Satan. Nothing but the grace of God will avail in this eschatological and universal struggle between good and evil. The temporal-secular reading will see temptation(s) as the everyday moral struggles that prepare and temper the soul for the great temptation (test) that is one's death and entry into eternal life.

"But deliver us from evil." The eschatological reading will prefer the text to read the *evil one*. It sees all evil focused in the adversary of God and humankind, the figure of Satan. The war between

God and the Devil is the historical and apocalyptic struggle between good and evil. The temporal-secular reading prefers to see a correspondence between temptations and evil in the abstract. Free us from temptations and all other evils as well. Deliver us from every evil. Not only the devil is the source of temptation, but all of this world can be an obstacle to human beings who should seek their creator through the creation. The daily human condition tends to both point to the creator and to distract one from the creator. Evil need not always be personal, therefore, but is often situational.

As we have seen, the petitions in the Lord's Prayer can be read with two different emphases: the eternal or the temporal, the eschatological and the everyday, the infinite and the finite, the Matthean perspective and the Lucan, in heaven as on earth, Christ as Lord and Jesus as man, the all in the One, and the One in the all, the One and the Many.

An eschatological reading of the petitions in the Lord's Prayer.[11]

Even *now* we live in eternity.

The saving and glorious deeds our God has done.

0. The Father is the almighty Father of our Lord Jesus Christ.

1. The hallowed name is the ineffable name of the transcendent God.

2. The Kingdom has come in Jesus Christ who is Lord.

3. The will of God to be done on earth is the paschal mystery of death and resurrection to which every human being is called for their salvation.

4. The daily bread is the banquet in heaven which we taste in anticipation in word and sacrament on earth. The real presence of Jesus in the eucharist is a prime example of realized eschatology.

5. Forgiveness of sins lies in the mystery of the love that Jesus embodies on the cross. In baptism one receives the Holy Spirit, all personal sins are forgiven, and a new and forgiving heart of flesh is created. We are forgiven, therefore we are forgiving. That total forgiveness received and given is also an example of realized eschatology.

6. Evil is the loss of God for all eternity. The enemy is the evil one, the prince of this world, and to be lost is to fail the *test* of faith and trust in God. One prays to be delivered from the great trial of the godly to come in the last days. "But fear not, I have overcome the world."

An everyday reading of the petitions in the Lord's Prayer.

Now we live in time that is grace, and *then* in eternity.

The cost of discipleship and what we now must do.

0. The Father is the pantocrator who is now ever-providing for the created world and who is Father of Jesus Christ our Lord.

1. The hallowed name is spoken in our daily prayer today.

2. The Kingdom has come within us, in our midst, in the community, and in the history of the world.

3. The will of God is our holiness in this life, and the indwelling of the divine life even here on earth.

4. Our daily bread is primarily the soul food that we receive in scripture and sacrament for the long journey of everyday living. The eternal is now present in the temporal, and yet to be fulfilled in union to come.

5. The forgiveness of sins is a life of mercy always. Seventy times seven we forgive our brother and sister. Our forgiving is how we know we have been forgiven. The eternal is now present in the temporal, and yet salvation fully is yet to come.

6. The evil we would be delivered from is the overall systemic evil that plagues our world, where everyone is sinned against and often *tempted* to sin in return.

As we have seen all along, the eschatological reading of the Pater Noster does seem particularly to fit the Matthean Lord's Prayer. Indeed, the whole gospel of Matthew has a pronounced sympathy with the eschatological viewpoint. The gospel so read might revive our eschatological yearning for the return of Christ. "The Pater Noster, said as a fervent maranatha, would not be an inappropriate welcome."[12] Nonetheless, the Lucan Lord's Prayer, which is less eschatological, remains valuable, and perhaps the more so when the eschatological perspective dominates our reading of the prayer. "Already in the Lucan form of the PN . . . the intensity of the eschatological aspiration has begun to yield to the hard facts of daily Christian living. It is a sign of the genius of this prayer, taught by the divine Master, that it could serve to express such different aspirations."[13] We need Matthew and Luke. We know the kingdom of God is now (imminent) and yet to come (transcendent). We cannot isolate one side of the mystery of the One and the Many, either making God everything and creation nothing, or making creation something and God not everything. The mystery of God is One and Many; the mystery of the kingdom of God has come and is to come, is today and then. The Lord's Prayer is Matthew and Luke.

FINAL WORDS

THE LORD'S PRAYER IS A *COLLECT* PRAYER. The total impact of the Our Father is not only the sum of the three thou-petitions and the three we-petitions. The whole is more than the sum of its parts. The Pater is a prayer that sums up or "collects" all other prayers. The liturgical practice of inviting prayer requests and then having the presider lift up all the petitions of the assembly in the prayer called the "collect" captures the essence of the Our Father. It collects the various prayers of the human family and presents them succinctly. In morning and in evening prayer in the liturgy, the prayers of petition are summed up with the Lord's Prayer as the final collect. Just as many grains of wheat are united in the one bread, many prayers are brought together in this one prayer. The one Father in heaven knows all that we need. The one bread of life is the remedy for all the tribalisms and provincial outlooks that divide the nations and the peoples of the world. We are brothers and sisters of the one Father-God, and the concerns of any one of us should be the concerns of all of us.

The Lord's Prayer is a *recognition* prayer. Its petitions state the way things are. The words of the Pater present the simple truth. This is who God is; this is what we must have. There is no unknown God addressed whose goodwill must be cajoled with many formula words and sacrifices. The God who is called upon already loves humankind and knows our predicament. Indeed our prayer is not even our own initiative but a response to the prior and hidden invitation in our hearts to call upon our Father in heaven in faith. God has heard our prayers before we have asked them, and as Barth says, therefore we are commanded to pray. God's will is sovereign. The Lord's Prayer assumes God's initiative in the very praying of the prayer as well as the eventual outcome of its petition. The Lord's Prayer seeks only to root us in the truth, and to bring us to dwell in the ways of God. "Lord, teach us to pray" means teach us to enter the mystery of God. In the words of the Paternoster we enter the mystery of the sisterhood of man and the fatherhood of

God. We know who God is, and we know now who we are. We know how to pray, and what to pray for. We live even now in grace always, and eternity is ours when we pray, "Our Father." Lohmeyer concludes: "All struggle has become acceptance and all duty grace, and in grace we live as long as we are still in this today, and look for the tomorrow."[14]

The Lord's Prayer is a *mystical* prayer. The text of the Pater is a school for the spiritual life. The eastern fathers and the western teachers of spirituality saw in these few words a concise guide to the development of the Christian life of holiness and union with God. The Lord's Prayer was the gateway to a mystical life with the Trinity. The Pater can only be said and understood by the light of the indwelling Holy Spirit in the soul of the believer. The Our Father calls for an obedient soul, an availability before the Lord that is the essence of the spiritual life. We are to listen to God with all our being. The Lord's Prayer invites thanksgiving that we are already gifted by God with our daily bread, the forgiveness of our sins, and deliverance from every evil. Therefore Christians always and everywhere give thanks to you almighty Father for your Son Jesus Christ whom we know through the gift of the Holy Spirit in our hearts.

In the mystical tradition, when we pray for bread we acknowledge that all we receive is a gift from God. There is no such thing as a mere thing. Bread in all its wonder is sacrament; it carries to us the love of God as gift contained in all that God has created out of a profound love. And hallowed is God's name. In the mystical tradition, when we pray for forgiveness from God and from each other we acknowledge that all persons are mysteries. Even our sins are distortions of that God-given restlessness that can find no peace in this world without God. Every person is a parable of God's infinitely resourceful courtship of their freedom to love in return for love received in the beginning. Our life is a story and the ending has yet to be known. The providence of God remains sovereign over all our history, and no one is beyond receiving perpetual forgiveness as did the good thief: "this day will you be with me in paradise." And so we pray, Thy Kingdom come. In the mystical tradition, when we pray for deliverance from evil we acknowledge that all words to describe the fullness of being that is God or the emptiness of being that is evil remain symbols only. Word are metaphors that try to capture what words cannot contain. Evil is a black void without meaning. God is an avalanche of inaccessible light. The mystery of the One and the Many and created human freedom escapes all our words.

We finally stammer. We ultimately must adore the sovereign Lord who has shared the infinite mystery of God with flesh and blood.

The Lord's Prayer is a prayer of *perpetual mercy*. Believers in the Father's love can afford unlimited mercy because they are rich in God's mercy. We have been given so much, forgiven altogether, and therefore we love much. As you have received mercy so give mercy. Forgiving love is all that we can bring to one another. We cannot create from nothing; we cannot give eternal life. Those are God's gifts, but they are ours to share. Therefore because we are rich in God's forgiving love we can be accepting of one another. "Watch and pray" Jesus counseled his disciples. There was nothing they could do to spare his life. The cross is our vocation. Moreover, we burden each other with our daily sins. But we can do this. We can ever thoroughly give; we can *for*give one another. Pray the Lord's Prayer and forgive each other. Pray and Love. Forgiving love: "Neither do I condemn you. Go, and sin no more."

The Lord's Prayer is an *eschatological* prayer, a resurrection prayer. This is the day the Lord has made. This is a new day of creation, like the first day that knew no past. All human history is indebted. We sin against each other every day. All human future is temptation and becomes a test. All human experience is led astray so easily. Yet Paul says, "I know in whom I have believed." Unless the Lord lives we are in despair. Death seems to overcome the world. But, thanks be to God, Christ is risen; Christ will come again. Therefore pray and dance before God. Therefore accept and receive in order to give back and to forgive. When we forgive altogether there is no more to give. A forgiving love of others is the infallible sign that one has embraced the unconditional, gratituitous, resourceful love of the Father for each and every human being who calls upon God's most hidden name made flesh and manifest in Jesus Christ who is Lord.

The Lord's Prayer is a *doxological* prayer. "Hallowed be thy name" praises the Father for the *gesta Dei*, the work of creation and providence in which we are brought into this life and enabled to know God. "Thy Kingdom come" praises God for the *gesta Christi*, the work of redemption in the incarnation of the Son of God. God's wisdom and plan of salvation are praised and thanks are given. The kingdom is the work of God's wisdom and eternal providence which from the beginning gave to us the only begotten Son, our Lord Jesus Christ. "Thy will be done" speaks of the praise due to God for the completion of the work of sanctification, the *gesta Spiriti*, the outpouring of the Holy Spirit. We will be given the wherewithal to receive the gift of God. "Thy will be done" is a judgment, where judgment is the revelation that the sovereign will of God will finish what God has begun, that the world will be fulfilled and completed. Union in heaven with God has been achieved on earth transfigured by the grace of the Holy Spirit. "Come, Lord Jesus!"

Petitions to God about God's own cause sound like declarations about God's resourcefulness. "Thy kingdom come" trails off into a outburst of praise, a doxology of the one and almighty God. May God be God! Prayer to God about the things of God quickly becomes worship, praise and glory given to God, thanksgiving. "Glory be to God." Its setting within community makes for liturgy, the public and solemn worship of the divinity of God who is gracious in our regard. The doxological element in the thou-petitions is more readily seen when the whole Pater is prayed from the eschatological perspective rather than the temporal-secular. The compression of events into an eternal moment that intersects time seems to invite contemplation of the mystery of God, who is everywhere and always. Petition becomes doxology as the Many is enfolded in the One.

The Lord's Prayer is a *repetitious* prayer. It is so not only because we repeat its words so many times in a lifetime, but also because it says only one thing. Let the Father be Abba; may God be God. We have seen how receiving forgiveness from God is true for us and good in us only in our giving of forgiveness. Forgiveness is not two separate motions. We can receive it or we can give it. Forgiveness is like a two-sided coin. It is never so thin that there is no other side. To the extent that I have received forgiveness I find myself giving it. And similarly with all of the petitions of the Paternoster. When the Father's name is hallowed, it is we who have grown eyes to see the awesome God. When the kingdom comes, it is we who rejoice to be its members. When the divine will is done on earth, it is our heart that has been converted to appreciate what God has done in us. We receive our daily bread as gift from God only to the extent that we are giving our days as the gift of ourselves to feed others. When God delivers us from evil, we find that we have already begun to deliver ourselves and those in our care from the evil that we deplore.

The Lord's Prayer is a *simple* prayer. We pray to *our* Father for *our* daily bread. The reason why we cannot love everyone at the same time is because we can be in only one body, and at one place at one time. I cannot be responsible for the welfare of *every*body, but only some*body*. My spirit wants to love everyone, but my flesh can embrace only someone. It is in Jesus who is Lord and in the Abba prayer, which is the prayer of Jesus, that we human beings can stand before God who loves us all and gives to all without diminution of anyone of us. God can love us all, and God can be in all places and at all times. When we pray for our daily bread and then receive the eucharistic body of Jesus who is Lord, we hold a piece of earthly bread and at the same time the mystical body of the Lord that enfolds each one of us. In this sacrament I give myself to everyone, and everyone in Jesus gives themselves to me. Only in God is the Many One. And hence we pray to our Father for the one bread of the one faith in the one prayer to the one Lord. How simple and how poignant. Only God is unconditional love. Thus there is only one prayer and only one petition. May God be God. "Abba, Father."

APPENDIX

GREEK

Matthew 6:9–13

italics = not in Luke

Pater *hēmōn ho en tois ouranois*
Father our who art in the heavens

hagiasthētō to onoma sou
hallowed the name thy

elthetō hē basileia sou
be come the Kingdom thy

genēthētō to thēlema sou
be done the Will thy

> *hos en ouranō kai epi ges*
> as in heaven so on earth

ton arton hēmōn ton epiousion dos hēmin sēmeron
the bread our the "daily" give us this day

kai aphes hēmin ta opheilēmata hēmōn
and forgive us the debts our

> hōs kai hēmeis aphēkamen tois opheiletais hēmon
> just as we forgive those debtors our

kai mē eisenenkēs hēmas eis peirasmon
and not lead us to temptation

alla rhusai hēmas apo tou ponērou
but deliver us from the evil

GREEK

Luke 11:2–4

italics = not in Matthew

Pater
Father

hagiasthētō to onoma sou
hallowed the name thy

elthetō hē Basileia sou
be come the Kingdom thy

ton arton hēmōn ton epiousion *didou* hēmin *to kath hēmeran*
the bread our the "daily" give us the each day

kai aphes hēmin tas *hamartias* hēmōn
and forgive us the sins our

> *kai gar autoi aphiomen panti opheilonti hēmin*
> even as ourselves forgive all offending us

kai mē eisenenkēs hēmas eis peirasmon
and not lead us to temptation

The Differences between Matthew and Luke from an Analysis of the Greek Text

Luke uses the present tense, "*give* (didou) us this day our daily bread," and Matthew a Greek past tense, the aorist (dos). In effect the Lucan text says keep on giving us now and in the future to come our daily bread. The Matthean text suggests give us once and for all, now and forever, this bread. Luke writes "give us *day by day* (kath hemeran) our daily bread," whereas Matthew writes more immediately "give us *this day* or *today*" (sēmeron).

Luke asks that the Father "forgive us our *sins* (hamartias)," and Matthew "forgive us our *debts* or *trespasses* (opheilēmata)," which is a somewhat broader word for any burdening or offending against God or neighbor. Luke's wording of "*as* we forgive those who trespass against us" could be rendered *even as* we too (kai gar in Luke and hos kai in Matthew), thereby suggesting a temporal sequence more than a causal one: forgive us even as we too continue now to forgive. Matthew writes "as *we* forgive *those* who trespass against us." In Luke, the wording is explicitly broad and ample: "as we *ourselves* [autoi is added] forgive *everyone* [panti is added]." Luke writes "As we forgive those *offending* (opheilonti) against us." Luke uses the present participle of the verb, which suggests offenses that are ongoing and an expected part of daily life, whereas Matthew uses a noun, "as we forgive our *debtors* or *offenders* (ophiletais)."

In general, Luke's use of the present tense suggests ongoing giving and forgiving day by day, whereas the Matthean text with the aorist tense and the more economical phrasing lends itself readily to an eschatological reading. In effect the Lucan text prays to keep on giving and forgiving now and in the future to come, whereas the Matthean text suggests once and for all, the now that is forever.

LATIN

Pater noster, qui es in coelis.
Sanctificetur nomen tuum.
Adveniat regnum tuum.
Fiat voluntas tua,
  sicut in coelo et in terra.
Panem nostrum quotidianum da nobis hodie,
et dimitte nobis debita nostra,
  sicut et nos dimittimus debitoribus nostris.
Et ne nos inducas in tentationem,
sed libera nos a malo.

This is the liturgical translation of the Paternoster found in the Roman missal. The Lord's Prayer was translated into Latin for the liturgy before the Vulgate of Jerome. The Greek word for "daily" bread is *epiousion*, found in both Matthew and Luke, and nowhere else in the Bible. The Old Latin versions prior to Jerome translated the Greek in various ways: *quotidianum* (in English quotidian, or daily) is most frequent, and it remained the word employed in liturgical Latin for the Pater through the centuries. There were other Latin translations that did not perdure, such as *victum nostrum alimentarium*. The Paternoster used in litugy and devotional prayer is taken from Matthew's version of the Lord's Prayer. Jerome in the Vulgate translation of Matthew chose to render the Greek *epiousion* as *supersubstantialem* (supersubstantial), and the same word in Luke he rendered *quotidianum* (daily). Consequently, some of the early English translations of the Pater from the Vulgate, such as Wycliffe's in 1380 and the Rheims version in 1580, follow Jerome and write "give us this day our *supersubstantial bread*." The reader is directed to the complex discussion of *epiousion* in the commentary itself.

ANGLO-SAXON[1]

Fader uren thu arth in heofnum
Sie gehalgud noma thin
To cymeth ric thin
Sie willo thin suaels in heofne & in eortho
Hlaf[2] usenne ofer wistlic[3] sel us todaeg
& forgef us scylda[4] usna suae uae forgeofon scyldgum usum
& ne inlaed usih in costnunge[5] uh gefrig usich from yfle

Versions of the Paternoster from the earliest Anglo-Saxon of Caedmon and the Venerable Bede to Wycliffe's fourteenth-century English were translated from the Latin Vulgate. Wycliffe accomplished the first comprehensive translation of the Bible from Latin to English. Prior to him, significant passages had been rendered in the vernacular tongue, and Latin manuscripts were often glossed with interlinear translation.

1. *The English Hexapla* (London: Samuel Bagster and Sons, Paternoster Row, 1805), 3. The *Hexapla* includes Wiclif (1380); Tyndale (1534); Cranmer (1539); Geneva (1557); Anglo-Rhemish (1582); and the Authorized or King James (1611). The Anglo-Saxon text is taken from the *Durham Book*.

2. Note the world for bread is the word "hlaf," or loaf, as in loaf of bread. Bread was then a more generic word for food, and what we now call bread was called a loaf.

3. "wistlic": the adjective is related to Old Englsih "wist," meaning provision or sustenance. "Ofer wistlic" might be rendered over-substantial, or supersubstantial.

4. I have not found a derivation for "scylda," which is a translation of the Latin *debita*.

5. "costnunge" is an obscure word for temptation or trial, possibly a derivative of an Icelandic word.

EARLY MIDDLE ENGLISH—12TH CENTURY[1]

Ure Fadyr in heaven rich,
Thy name be halyed ever lich,
Thou bring us thy michell bliss,[2]
Als hit in heaven y-do,
Euar in yearth beene it also.
That holy bread that lasteth ay
Thou sent it us this ilke day.
Forgive ous all that we haue don,
As we forgiveth uch other mon.
Ne let ous fall into no founding,[3]
Ac shield ous fro the fowle thing.[4]

Pope Adrian, who was English, sent this translation from Rome to England about 1156.

1. *The Lord's Prayer in the Principal Languages, Dialects and Versions of the World* (Chicago: G. F. Bergholtz, 1884), 56. Hereinafter cited as *The Lord's Prayer in the Principal Languages.*

2. "michell" is a variant of much; "bliss" means joy and is related to the word bless. Here "much bliss" refers to the kingdom (of God).

3. "founding" is an interesting translation of the Latin *tentationem.* Lead us not into temptation or put us not to the test. As one speaks of a ship foundering in a storm, the prayer asks protection from foundering.

4. "the fowle thing" or foul thing is the evil one. Thus, deliver us from evil or the evil one.

ENGLISH, LATTER PART OF THE 12TH CENTURY[1]

Ure Fadir that hart in hevene,
Halged be thi name with giftes sevene,[2]
Samin cume thi kingdom,
Thi wille in herthe als in hevene be don.
Ure bred that lastes ai[3]
Gyve it hus this hilke dai,
And ure misdedis[4] thu forgyve hus
Als we forgyve tham that misdon hus.
And leod us in tol na fandinge,[5]
Bot frels us fra alle ivele thinge.

1. *The Lord's Prayer in the Principal Languages*, 57 [from the Cotton Ms. Cleopatra].

2. "giftes sevene" are the sevenfold gifts of the Holy Spirit. See our discussion above of the Marcion interpolation on page 42.

3. "that lastes ai," renders that lasts aye, is an interesting translation of *epiousios*, customarily rendered in English as daily, that is, sustaining bread.

4. "misdedis" or misdeeds.

5. "fandinge" is a variant of "founding" from to founder.

JOHN WYCLIFFE[1]
(1380)

Oure fadir that art in heuenes
halowid be thi name,
thi kyngdom come to,
be thi wille don in erthe as in heuene,
geue to us this day oure breed ouir other substaunce,[2]
forgeue to us oure dettis,
as we forgeuen to oure dettouris,
lede us not in to temptaciouen:
but delyeur us from yuel amen.[3]

John Wycliffe (1330–1384), also written Wiclif, Wicliffe, Wickliffe, came from Wiclif in Yorkshire. He lived during the time of Chaucer and the divided papacy of the Avignon captivity. Wycliffe is considered a forerunner of the Protestant reformation. He published two English versions of the Bible from the Latin, one closer to the Vulgate and the other anglicized by John Purvey.

1. The version used here is from a manuscript critically edited for *The English Hexapla.* See also the Rawlinson Ms. 259 in the Bodlein, Oxford, which is the revision by John Purvey. It is reprinted in facsimile by International Bible Publications (Portland, Oregon, 1986). See also *The Lord's Prayer in the Principal Languages,* 61.

2. The Greek *epiousios* is here translated "ouir other sustaunce" or, our other substance. Our bread once eaten becomes, of course, our substance. In the *Oratio Dominica, Polyglottos, Polymorphos* (Londini, prostant apud D. Brown, 1713), the Wycliffe text reads "our breede our daily substance."

3. Note also that with Wycliffe we have already most of the familiar wording of the text of the later King James version of the Lord's Prayer.

The Liturgical English Translation of the Lord's Prayer

The Our Father known to most English-speaking Christians in their prayers and in liturgical use in church services stems from the first English translation by William Tyndale of the original Greek. He published a vernacular New Testament, which was printed in Germany in 1525–26. Martin Luther had just published his printed German vernacular translation in 1522. The critical edition of the Greek New Testament (1522) by Desiderius Erasmus with the accompanying Latin translation was readily available to Tyndale. As a private citizen and a protesting believer and because of his own enthusiasm for a Bible accessible to the laity, Tyndale undertook this task without assistance from church or state. It is estimated that three-quarters of the Tyndale New Testament can be substantially found in the King James (1611), the long prevailing authorized version of the Bible in English. In the Lord's Prayer Tyndale's use of the word "trespasses," which is translated as "debts" in the King James, has perdured through the centuries, even though no biblical translation today uses that word in the Lord's Prayer. The British revised version of 1881, the American Standard version (the revision of 1901), and the joint venture of the Revised Standard Version (1950s) maintain the word "debts" in the Matthean Lord's Prayer. Both Roman Catholics and Anglo Catholics, however, in their private and public prayer have stood by the Tyndale translation, which has been traditional for so long. Tyndale was to the English translation of the New Testament what Jerome was to the Latin translation. They were both first to be widely accepted and to become familiar in the liturgy. Moreover, they were both masters of cadenced prose.

The standardization of the Our Father, largely using Tyndale's translation, came from the efforts of King Henry VIII and the newly founded Church of England to establish a common text for liturgical prayer. The Great Bible of 1539 was the first authorized translation, but there were to be several authorized versions during those early decades of the English vernacular Bible. Standardization was urgent for common prayer because hardly any two translations into English found in early manuscripts or early printed books agreed in spelling and wording. Prior to the introduction of the vernacular the Pater and Ave were said in Latin learned by rote. The *Book of Common Prayer* grew out of these efforts to compile a "book of ordinary prayers in English." By royal decree English Catholics were now to learn their catechism (the Pater, the Ave, the Decalogue, and the Creed) in English. And in order to pray uniformly in community, Englishmen should adopt a standard version. The royal Primer of Henry VIII (1545) provided some unification. Notice that it changed the Tyndale translation of "thy will be fulfilled" in the Lord's Prayer to "thy will be dooen." Subsequently, the First Prayer Book of Edward VI (1549) changed the "let us not be led into temptation" of the Primer of Henry VIII to "lead us not into temptation." At this point the Lord's Prayer reads as we know it to this day. In summary, the standard Our Father derives its phrases largely from the translation of William Tyndale, who in turn borrowed pre-Reformation translations of the Vulgate. Even Mary Tudor in her efforts at undoing the English Reformation did not change the Our Father then in use, since by this time it had become familiar to the devotion of so many people. Apart from differences in spelling and punctuation, the text of the Our Father has remained the same in common use in the English-speaking churches, Catholic and Protestant, from the mid-sixteenth century to this day.

One might note that the problem of standardization of the Lord's Prayer was similar to the problem of authorization in a vernacular translation of the Bible. The resistance to an English translation that was not made from the Latin Vulgate came in part from the familiarity of that text through liturgical custom, ancient commentaries, and essential church doctrines. People in their devotions grew accustomed to the old Bible in its familiar phrasing. Even if a better source text in the Greek manuscripts was suggested, it was resisted. Similarly, any new translation of the Lord's Prayer in English ran up against the familiar wording that people cherished from their childhood. Eventually the authorized English translation of the Bible would be just as entrenched as the authorized Latin (Vulgate) translation had been. At the time of the Reformation, however, the very first English translation from the Greek enjoyed an enormous opportunity. New wording could be introduced because the Greek text provided a biblical authority independent of the Roman church tradition. Part of the objection against the Tyndale unauthorized translation of the New Testament was that it concealed a Reformation theology in its particular wording and in the abundant marginal notes that set up the Greek text in opposition to some of the traditional readings of the Vulgate. The Roman Catholic position always maintained that the Bible is a church book, established as a canon of texts by the church community and read authoritatively only in the church community. Hence its translation and reproduction belong also to the church community's authorization. In many places Tyndale's choice of words is revealing. Where one expected church, one reads congregation, for priest one reads elder, for charity one reads love, for grace one reads favor, for penance one reads repentance. The English translation was thus seen by many as a biblical warrant for Reformation theology. Interestingly, the King James version goes back in many instances to the more Catholic wording before Tyndale, and its wide acceptance may be in part due to its sensitivity in this regard.[1]

---

1. Herbert Thurston, "The Our Father in English," *Familiar Prayers* (London: Burns & Oates, 1953), 22–37. See pages 31–32 in particular.

WILLIAM TYNDALE[1]
(1525/26)

O oure father which arte in heven, halowed be thy name.
Let thy kyngdom come.
Thy wyll be fulfilled,[2] as well in erth as hit ys in heven.
Geve vs this daye oure dayly breade.
And forgeve vs oure treaspases, even as we forgeve them which treaspas vs.
Leede vs not into temptacion, but delyvre vs from yvell.
For thyne is the kyngedom and the power, and the glorye for ever. Amen.[3]

The versions from Tyndale to the King James were all translated from the Hebrew and the Greek. The Catholic Rheims version, however, was translated from the Latin Vulgate with consultation of the original languages. It was not until the middle of the twentieth century that Catholic vernacular translations were taken entirely from the original biblical languages. The *Bible de Jerusalem* was among the first, and that translation into French was subsequently translated into English as the *Jerusalem Bible.* See also *The New Jerusalem Bible* (1985).

1. James W. Thirtle, *The Lord's Prayer: An Interpretation Critical and Expository* (London: Morgan and Scott, 1915), 214. Hereinafter cited as Thirtle.

2. "fulfilled" is an earlier version of "thy will be *done.*"

3. The doxology is included. It was found in some of the later Greek gospel manuscripts but not in the Latin Vulgate. It is now commonly thought to be a liturgical interpolation.

THE GREAT BIBLE[1]
(1539)

Oure father which art in heauen, halowed be thy name.
Let thy kingdome come.
Thy will be fulfilled, as well in erth, as it is in heuen.
Geue vs this daye oure dayly bred.
And forgeue vs oure dettes, as we forgeue oure detters.
And leade vs not into temptation: but delyuer vs from euyll.
For thyne is the kyngdom and the power, and the glorye for euer. Amen.

The so-called "Great Bible" is also called the Cranmer Bible, for Thomas, the archbishop of Canterbury, collaborated in its translation under the patronage of Thomas Cromwell. It might be called the first authorized version in English since it enjoyed the cooperation of both church and state in its production.

1. Text taken from Thirtle, 215. See also *The English Hexapla*.

PRIMER OF HENRY VIII[1]
(1545)

Our father whiche art in heauen, halowed be thy name.
Thy kyngdome come.
Thy will be dooen in[2] yearth, as it is in heauen.
Geue vs this dai our daily breade.
And forgeue vs our trespaces,[3] as we forgeue them that trespace against vs.
And let vs not bee led[4] into temptacion, But deliuer vs from euill. Amen.

A primer is a small introductory book, either a grammar book for reading and writing, or a prayer book for beginners or layfolk. Although there were some earlier editions of a primer, this Royal Primer might well be considered the first attempt at a standardization of English church prayers, the equivalent of the *Book of Common Prayer*.

1. Text taken from Thirtle, 216.

2. Note the use of "in" earth, which is also found in the King James.

3. Note the "trespaces" from the Tyndale translation, itself beholden to the Wycliffe in Mt 6:14.

4. "Let us not bee led" is more accurate rendition than "lead us not." God leads no one into temptation, but protects us from being lead into temptation.

FIRST PRAYER BOOK OF EDWARD VI[1] (1549)

Oure father whiche arte in heauen, hallowed be thy name.
Thy kyngdom come.
Thy wyll be done in earth as it is in heauen.
Geue vs this daye oure dayly bread.
And forgeue vs oure trespasses, as we forgeue them that trespasse agaynst vs.
And leade vs not into temptacion.
But deliuer vs from euell. Amen.[2]

1. Text taken from Thirtle, 216.

2. Except for particulars of orthography and punctuation, this text has been perpetuated to our day in *The Book of Common Prayer.*

RHEIMS VERSION[1]
(1582)

Our Father which art in heauen,
Sanctified be thy name.
Let thy Kingdom come.
Thy wil be done, as in heauen, in earth also.
Giue vs this day our supersubstantial bread.
And forgive vs our dettes, as we also have forgiven our dettors.
And leade us not into tentation, but deliuer vs from euil.

During the reign of Elizabeth I, English Catholic scholars took refuge in Rheims, where a Catholic English translation of the New Testament was published in 1582. Some years later both testaments of the Bible together were published in Douay as the so-called Douay Bible. During the reign of the Catholic Mary Tudor, Protestant scholars took refuge in Geneva where a Protestant English translation of the Bible was published in 1560. The Rheims version, however, was taken from the Vulgate, as were all Catholic translations until the middle of the twentieth century. The critical Vulgate edition of Clement VIII did not appear until 1592. The Rheims version does use the Greek as an aid when the Latin text is obscure, but the English stays close to the Latin and English latinate words are preferred whenever possible.

1. Text taken from Thirtle, 217. See also *The English Hexapla.*

KING JAMES OR THE AUTHORIZED VERSION[1] (1611)

Our father which art in heauen, hallowed by thy Name.
Thy kingdome come.
Thy will be done, in earth, as it is in heauen.
Giue vs this day our dayly bread.
And forgiue vs our debts, as we forgiue our debters.
And lead vs not into temptation, but deliuer vs from euill:
For thine is the kingdome, and the power, and the glory, for euer. Amen.[2]

No other version has so affected the English language and literature as the King James, which to this day is still read. The Revised Standard Version(s) try to conserve as much of the language of the King James as is compatible with contemporary textual scholarship.

1. Text taken from *The English Hexapla*. See also Thirtle, 217.

2. The *Amen* is also found in the Latin Vulgate, but the doxology is not.

REVISED (AUTHORIZED) VERSION[1]
(1881)

Our Father which art in heaven,
Hallowed be thy name.
Thy kingdom come.
Thy will be done, as in heaven so on earth.
Give us this day our daily bread[2]
And forgive us our debts, as we also have forgiven our debtors.
And bring us not into temptation, but deliver us from the evil one.[3]

The Revised Version (1881) is the British revision of the King James. The American revision (1901) was called the American Standard Version. Both of these revisions and as much as could be conserved of the King James were combined in the Revised Standard Version currently in use in both countries.

1. Text taken from Thirtle, 217.

2. In the margin: "Gr. our bread for the coming day."

3. In the margin: "or, evil." The doxology is given in the margin only.

CONTEMPORARY VERSIONS OF THE LORD'S PRAYER

Living Bible[1]

MATTHEW

Our Father in heaven, we honor your holy name.
We ask that your kingdom will come now.
May your will be done here on earth, just as it is in heaven.
Give us our food again today,[2] as usual, and forgive us our sins, just as we have forgiven those who have sinned against us.
Don't bring us into temptation, but deliver us from the Evil One.

LUKE

Father, may your name be honored for its holiness; send your Kingdom soon.
Give us our food day by day.
And forgive our sins—for we have forgiven those who sinned against us.
And don't allow us to be tempted.

1. *The Six Version Parallel New Testament* (Wheaton, Ill.: Christian Life Publications, 1974), 14–15 and 180–181. Hereinafter cited as *Six Version Parallel.*

2. In these contemporary versions the reader is invited to notice the rendition of pivotal phrases of the Lord's prayer such as: "daily bread," "forgive us our trespasses / debts / sins," "lead us not into temptation / put us not to the test," and "from evil / the evil one."

Revised Standard Version[1]

MATTHEW

Our Father who art in heaven,
Hallowed be thy name.
Thy kingdom come,
Thy will be done,
  On earth as it is in heaven.
Give us this day our daily bread;
And forgive us our debts,
  As we also have forgiven our debtors;
And lead us not into temptation,[2]
  But deliver us from evil.[3]

LUKE

Father, hallowed be thy name.
Thy kingdom come.
Give us each day our daily bread; and forgive us our sins,
  for we ourselves forgive every one who is indebted to us;
  and lead us not into temptation.[2]

The RSV took the King James, the Revised (1881) and the American Standard (1901) plus contemporary scholarship and, while preserving the old, made a new version. It is generally considered a literal translation, especially the Old Testament. The footnotes to the RSV text are quite helpful.

1. Text taken from the *Six Version Parallel*, 14–15 and 180–181.

2. The New RSV (1989) reads: "And do not bring us to the time of trial." A footnote gives an alternate reading: "And do not bring us into temptation."

3. The New RSV reads: "But rescue us from the evil one."

New English Bible[1]

MATTHEW

Our Father in heaven,
thy name be hallowed;
thy kingdom come,
thy will be done,
on earth as in heaven.
Give us today our daily bread.
Forgive us the wrong we have done,
as we have forgiven those who have wronged us.
And do not bring us to the test,[2]
but save us from the evil one.

LUKE

Father, thy name be hallowed;
thy kingdom come.
Give us each day our daily bread.
And forgive us our sins,
for we too forgive all who have done us wrong.
And do not bring us to the test.[2]

The NEB uses contemporary British usage, and it is a somewhat more free translation than the RSV.

1. *Six Version Parallel*, 14–15 and 180–181.

2. The *Revised English Bible* (1989) reads: "And do not put us to the test."

Phillips Modern English[1]

MATTHEW

Our Heavenly Father, may your name be honoured;
May your kingdom come, and your will be done on earth as it is in Heaven.
Give us each day the bread we need for the day,
Forgive us what we owe to you,
as we have also forgiven those who owe anything to us.
Keep us clear of temptation, and save us from evil.

LUKE

Father, may your name be honoured—may your kingdom come.
Give us the bread we need for each day, and forgive us our failures,
for we forgive everyone who fails us;
and keep us clear of temptation.

1. *Six Version Parallel,* 14–15 and 180–181.

Jerusalem Bible[1]

MATTHEW

Our Father in heaven,
may your name be held holy,
your kingdom come,
your will be done,
on earth as in heaven.
Give us today our daily bread.
And forgive us our debts,
as we have forgiven those who are in debt to us.
And do not put us to the test,
but save us from the evil one.[2]

LUKE

Father, may your name be held holy,
Your kingdom come;
give us each day our daily bread,
and forgive us our sins,
for we ourselves forgive each one who is in debt to us,
And do not put us to the test.

The French *Bible de Jerusalem* was the first Catholic Bible translated directly from the Hebrew and Greek since Jerome did so with the Vulgate in Latin. The English *Jerusalem Bible* is in turn a translation of the French, with consultation by the translators of the Hebrew and Greek.

1. *Six Version Parallel*, 14–15 and 180–181.

2. The *New Jerusalem Bible* (1985) reads: "Evil One" with capital letters.

New American Bible[1]

MATTHEW

Our Father in heaven,
hallowed by your name,
your kingdom come,
your will be done,
on earth as in heaven.
Give us today our daily bread; and forgive us our debts,
as we forgive our debtors;
and do not subject us to the final test,
but deliver us from the evil one.

LUKE

Father, hallowed be your name,
your kingdom come.
Give us each day our daily bread and forgive us our sins
for we ourselves forgive everyone in debt to us,
and do not subject us to the final test.

This revision attempts to eliminate unwarranted sexist language. The footnotes to the entire NAB text are quite helpful.

1. New York: Catholic Book Pub. Co., revised edition of the New Testament, 1986.

INTERNATIONAL CONSULTATION ON ENGLISH TEXTS[1]

1. Our Father in heaven,
2. hallowed be your Name,
3. your kingdom come,
4. your will be done,
5. on earth as in heaven.
6. Give us today our daily bread.
7. Forgive us our sins
8. as we forgive those who sin against us.
9. Save us from the time of trial
10. and deliver us from evil.
11. For the kingdom, the power, and the glory are yours now and for ever.

This is a translation offered for general contemporary liturgical use, and it is accompanied by ample notes that give the justification of the ecumenical commission that drew us this particular wording of the Lord's Prayer.

1. ICET. *Prayers We Have in Common*, 2nd rev. ed. (Philadelphia: Fortress Press, 1975).

INTERNATIONAL COMMISSION ON ENGLISH IN THE LITURGY

Our Father who art in heaven,
Hallowed by thy name.
Thy kingdom come.
Thy will be done on earth as it is in heaven.
Give us this day our daily bread;
and forgive us our trespasses
As we forgive those who trespass against us
And lead us not into temptation
but deliver us from evil.

This is the translation used in the *Sacramentary* and in contemporary Catholic liturgical service.

THE LORD'S PRAYER IN MATTHEW

Heavenly Father,
Hallowed be thy name.
Thy kingdom come
Thy will be done, on earth and in heaven.
Give us this day our journey bread.
And forgive us all what we owe even as we forgive one another.
Save us from the time of trial,
And deliver us from all evil.

THE LORD'S PRAYER IN LUKE

Father,
Hallowed be your name.
Your kingdom come.
Give us this day our journey bread.
And forgive us our sins, even as we ourselves forgive everyone sinning.
And lead us to enter not into temptation.

Author's translation

NEW TESTAMENT ANALOGUES

The Lord's Prayer as such is found only in Matthew and Luke. The substance of that prayer, however, has been pointed out in Mark in a passage of a few words, and in John in the elaborate sacerdotal prayer of the seventeenth chapter. Paul's awareness in his epistles of the importance of "Abba, Father" has also been noted. Finally, the First Epistle of Peter is thought to be a succinct summary of the gospel message. The Lord's Prayer has often been seen as a short form of the "articles of faith," just as the creed is seen as a summary of the gospel good news. See John S. Dunne, "The Metamorphoses of Faith," *The Review of Politics* 29 (1967): 291–302.

Mark 11:25

> "When you stand to pray, forgive anyone against whom you have a grievance, so that your heavenly Father may in turn forgive you your transgressions."

Mark's gospel does not contain a version of the Lord's Prayer, but various commentators have pointed to this passage as evidence of the evangelist's awareness of its substance. The verse that follows in some Bibles, "But if you do not forgive, neither will your heavenly Father forgive your transgressions," is not found in the earliest and the best manuscripts. The *New American Bible* places 11:26 in a footnote with the explanation that this text is probably a scribal interpolation echoing a parallel verse taken from Matthew 6:15.

John 17[1]

The Sacerdotal Prayer of Jesus

Our Father who art in heaven:
"Father": see John 17:1, 5, 21, 24
"Holy Father": see John 17:11
"Righteous Father": see John 17:25
Hallowed be thy name:
"Name": see John 17:6, 11, 12, 26
Thy Kingdom come:
"Give glory to your son": see John 17:1–2
Thy will be done on earth as it is in heaven:
"So that they may be one just as we are": see John 17:4–5, 11, 21
Give us this day our daily bread:
"I pray for them": see John 17:9. See also John 6 passim.
Forgive us our trespasses:
"So that they may all be one": see John 17:20–23
Lead us not into temptation:
"I guarded them": see John 17:12
Deliver us from evil:
"Keep them from the evil one": see John 17:15

1. Frederick Chase raises a thoughtful discussion whether "it is possible to disconnect the prayer which the Lord taught as the typical Christian prayer from the prayer which he Himself prayed? Is not the one the best guide to a true understanding of the other? And indeed, however great the difference as to surroundings and form of expression, there are striking points of contact between the two prayers. The same great spiritual realities lie at the root of both." See *The Lord's Prayer in the Early Church* (Nendeln, Liechtenstein: Kraus reprint, 1967), 110–111. See also William O. Walker, Jr., "The Lord's Prayer in Matthew and in John," *New Testament Studies* 28 (1982): 237–256. Also George J. Brooke, "The Lord's Prayer Interpreted Through John and Paul," *Downside Review* 98 (1980): 298–311.

The Epistles of Saint Paul[1]

Our Father who art in heaven:
"Abba! Father!": see Gal 4:6
Hallowed be thy name:
"Your name is above every name": see Phil 2:9
Thy Kingdom come:
"Let all things be subject to you that you may be everything to everyone": see 1 Cor 15:28
Thy will be done on earth as it is in heaven:
"Let us prove what is your will, what is good and acceptable and perfect": see Rom. 12:2
Give us this day our daily bread:
"Give us the one bread, for we who are many are one body
for we all partake of the one bread": see 1 Cor 10:17
Forgive us our trespasses:
"And as you reckon us righteous apart from works,
so let us owe no one anything, except to love one another":
see Rom 4:6–7 and Rom 13:8
Lead us not into temptation, but deliver us from evil:
"And do not let us be tempted beyond our strength; and with the temptation provide the way of escape, so that we can endure it": see 1 Cor 10:13

1. Text taken from George J. Brooke, "The Lord's Prayer Interpreted Through John and Paul," *Downside Review* 98 (1980): 306.

I Peter[1]

The First Epistle of Peter is read in the Office of Readings during Easter week following the baptism of the catechumens. It has long been seen as a triumphant compendium of the faith.

Our Father who art in heaven:
"Father": see I Peter 1:3, 14, 17, 23; 2:2
"in heaven": see I Peter 1:4

Hallowed be thy name:
"Blessed be the God and Father of our Lord Jesus Christ": see I Peter 1:3–5, 15, 16; 3:15

Thy Kingdom come:
"A chosen race, a royal priesthood, a holy nation, a people of his own": See I Peter 1:6ff; 2:9

Thy will be done on earth as it is in heaven:
"Be holy because I [am] holy": see I Peter 1:14–16
"will of God": see I Peter 2:15; 3:17; 4:2, 19

Give us this day our daily bread:
"You have tasted that the Lord is good": see I Peter 2:2
"Cast all your worries upon him because he cares for you": see I Peter 5:7

Forgive us our trespasses:
"All of you, be of one mind": see I Peter 3:8–9
"Love covers a multitude of sins": see I Peter 4:8

Lead us not into temptation:
"trial by fire": see I Peter 4:12

Deliver us from evil:
"Your opponent the devil is prowling": see I Peter 5:9

1. Text taken from James W. Thirtle, *The Lord's Prayer: An Interpretation Critical and Expository* (London: Morgan and Scott, 1915), 185–186. Thirtle makes reference to John Albert Bengel's *Gnomon of the New Testament* as a source used for the verse analogues.

NOTES

Introduction

1. Ernst Lohmeyer, *The Lord's Prayer*, trans. John Bowden (London: Colins, 1965), 297.

2. Henry Schurmann, *Praying with Christ: The "Our Father" for Today*, trans. William Michael Ducey and Alphonse Simon (New York: Herder, 1964), 3–4.

3. George H. Palmer, *The Lord's Prayer* (Chicago: Pilgrim Press, 1932), 8.

4. Martin Marty, *The Hidden Discipline* (St. Louis: Concordia, 1962), 83.

5. Jean Carmignac, *A L'Ecoute du Notre Pere* (Paris: Letouzey Editions, 1971), 91.

6. Joachim Jeremias, *The Lord's Prayer*, trans. John Reumann (Philadelphia: Fortress, 1969), 9.

7. Eugene La Verdiere, *When We Pray: Meditations on the Lord's Prayer* (Notre Dame, Ind.: Ave Maria Press, 1983), 65.

8. James W. Thirtle, *The Lord's Prayer: An Interpretation Critical and Expository* (London: Morgan and Scott, 1915), 3.

9. Peter Chrysologus, Sermon 70, *Fathers of the Church*, vol. 17. For Patristic authors cited throughout this work, see the Patristic bibliography, which lists the English editions readily available to the reader.

10. Augustine, "Letter to Lady Proba," Epistle 130, *Fathers of the Church*, vol. 18.

11. John Ruskin, *The Lord's Prayer and the Church*, in *The Complete Works of John Ruskin*, vol. 34, Library Edition (London: George Allen, 1908), 195.

12. Gregory of Nyssa, "Commentary on the Lord's Prayer," *Ancient Christian Writers*, vol. 18.

13. T. W. Mason, "The Lord's Prayer," *Bulletin of John Rylands Library* 38 (1955): 448.

14. Joachim Jeremias, *The Prayers of Jesus* (Naperville, Ill.: Alec R. Allenson, 1967), 108–115.

15. Frederick H. Chase, *The Lord's Prayer in the Early Church* (Cam-

bridge: Cambridge University Press, 1891; reprint, Nendeln, Liechtenstein: Kraus, 1967), 53.

16. All biblical quotations from the New Testament are taken from the revised edition of the *New American Bible* (NABRNT). All biblical quotations from the Old Testament are taken from the *Revised Standard Version* (RSV).

17. Peter Edmonds, "The Lucan Our Father: A Summary of Luke's Teaching on Prayer?" *Expository Times* 91 (1980): 141.

18. Joseph Blenkinsopp, "Notes and Comments Apropos of the Lord's Prayer," *Heythrop Journal* 3 (1962): 51–60.

19. Raymond Brown, "The Pater Noster as an Eschatological Prayer," *Theological Studies* 22 (1961): 208.

Part One

1. Cyprian of Carthage, *Fathers of the Church*, vol. 36.

2. In my remarks here and elsewhere I am indebted to Origen's commentary on the Lord's Prayer. His treatise on prayer influenced many of the subsequent Patristic writings on this subject, and to this day it remains an outstanding commentary on the Our Father. *Ancient Christian Writers*, vol. 19.

3. See Phyllis Trible, *God and the Rhetoric of Sexuality* (Philadelphia: Fortress, 1978).

4. Gregory of Nyssa, *Ancient Christian Writers*, vol. 18.

5. Ruskin, *Lord's Prayer and the Church*, 196–197.

6. Dante Alighieri, Canto 11: 1–3, *Purgatorio*, trans. John Ciardi (New York: Mentor, 1957), 120.

7. John Henry Newman, *The Idea of a University* (London: Longmans & Green, 1896; reprint, Notre Dame, Ind.: University of Notre Dame Press, 1982), 46–47.

8. Schurmann, *Praying with Christ*, 18–28.

9. See Willem F. Bakker, *The Greek Imperative: An Investigation into the Aspectual Differences between the Present and Aorist Imperatives in Greek Prayer from Homer up to the Present Day* (Amsterdam: A. M. Hakkert, 1966).

10. Cyprian of Carthage, *Fathers of the Church*, vol. 36.

11. Origen's commentary on the Lord's Prayer is most helpful in the linguistic analysis of the petitions. Overall, his remarks remain the single most valuable early Patristic text. *Ancient Christian Writers*, vol. 19.

12. Marty, *The Hidden Discipline*.

13. Cyril of Jerusalem, "Mystagogical Catechetics," *Fathers of the Church*, vol. 64.

14. Krister Stendhal, "Notes for Bible Study," *International Review of Mission*, vol. 69 (Geneva: World Council of Churches, 1980), 302.

15. In his commentary on the Lord's Prayer Tertullian places "thy will be done" before "thy kingdom come," which is itself worded "thy Spirit come." See *Fathers of the Church*, vol. 40.

16. Cyril of Jerusalem, "Mystagogical Catechetics," *Fathers of the Church*, vol. 64.

17. Richard J. Dillon, "On the Christian Obedience of Prayer (Matthew 6:5–13)," *Worship* 59 (1985): 413–426.

18. Marty, *The Hidden Discipline*, 73–74.

19. Cyril of Jerusalem, "Mystagogical Catechetics," *Fathers of the Church*, vol. 64.

20. Origen, *Ancient Christian Writers*, vol. 19.

21. Augustine, "Commentary on the Sermon on the Mount," *Fathers of the Church*, vol. 11.

22. Cyprian of Carthage, *Fathers of the Church*, vol. 36.

23. Origen, *Ancient Christian Writers*, vol. 19.

24. *The Roman Catechism*, Part IV, Chapter X, Question III (references are to the Latin edition). The *Roman Catechism*, following the Council of Trent, gives a long theological and pastoral commentary on the Lord's Prayer in part IV.

25. George Thompson, "Thy Will be Done in Earth, as it is in Heaven: Matthew 6:11; A Suggested Re-interpretation," *Expository Times* 70 (1959): 379–381.

26. *Selected Writings of Maximus Confessor*, trans. George Berthold (New York: Paulist, 1985).

Part Two

1. In the Orient rice is the staple food, and no doubt had Jesus been born in the far East he would have spoken of rice as the staff of life. Separating the essence of Christianity from its embodiment in western culture remains an issue requiring sensitivity and the lived experience of Christians in the far East.

2. Alfred Delp, *The Prison Meditations of Father Alfred Delp* (New York: Herder and Herder, 1963), 132.

3. Monika K. Hellwig, *The Eucharist and the Hunger of the World* (New York: Paulist, 1976), 50.

4. See Macrina Wiederkehr, *A Tree Full of Angels* (San Francisco: Harper and Row, 1988), 76–77.

5. See the exhaustive discussion in Gerhard Kittel, ed., *Theological Dictionary of the New Testament*, vol. 2, trans. Geoffrey Bromiley (Grand Rapids, Mich.: Eerdmans, 1964), s.v. *epiousios* by Werner Foerster.

6. Sebastian Falcone, "The Kind of Bread We Pray for in the Lord's Prayer," in *Essays in Honor of Joseph P. Brennan*, ed. Robert F. McNamara (Rochester: St. Bernard's Seminary, 1976), 36–59.

7. Bruce M. Metzger, "How Many Times does *Epiousios* Occur outside the Lord's Prayer?" *Expository Times* 69 (1957): 52–54.

8. George Arthur Buttrick, ed., *The Interpreter's Dictionary of the Bible*, vol. 3 (New York: Abingdon, 1962), s.v. "Lord's prayer" by C. W. F. Smith.

9. The Falcone article is a recent and comprehensive review of the entire *epiousios* discussion. Falcone claims a bibliography of over one hundred scholars who have investigated this one word. See also Dikran Hadidian, "The Meaning of *Epiousios* and the Codices Sergii Armenian Mss; Matthew 6:11; Luke 11:3," *New Testament Studies* 5 (1958–59): 75–81.

10. Migne, *PL* 26:43 reads "reperi MAHAR, quod dicitur crastinum." Note the footnote there which argues MAHAR reflects the Aramaic vernacular. See also Emile Bonnard, ed. and trans., *Sources Chretiennes*, vol. 242, *Commentariorum in Evangelium Matthei Libri Quatuor*, vol. 242 (Paris: Editions du Cerf, 1977), 130–133. The pertinent text reads: "In euangelio quod appellatur secundum Hebraeos pro supersubstantiali pane maar repperi, quod dicitur crastinum, ut sit sensus: *Panem nostrum* crastinum, id est futurum, *da nobis hodie.*"

11. One might also note that several Coptic versions of the Lord's Prayer render the Latin word *crastinum*, or morrow. See the chart of the many ancient non-Greek versions of the Lord's Prayer: Falcone, 44.

12. Colin Hemer, "Epiousios," *Journal for the Study of the New Testament* 22 (1984): 91. See also Henri Bourgoin, "Epiousios Expliqué par la Notion de Préfixe Vide," *Biblica* 60 (1979): 91–96. Bourgoin speaks of "pain essentiel" or "pain de vie."

13. Yamauchi, who holds that the bread is physical with spiritual overtones, says of Jeremias who argues for both the spiritual and physical dimension that he "would have his bread and eat it too." See Edwin M. Yamauchi, "The 'Daily Bread' Motif in Antiquity," *Westminster Theological Journal* 28 (1966): 145–156.

14. Joachim Jeremias, Ernst Lohmeyer, Leonardo Boff, and Raymond Brown all concur that the text refers to a spiritual bread, but with overtones of a common and physical bread.

15. Along with Stendhal and Lohmeyer I would also hold that the bread must be construed as both eschatological and everyday, both eucharist and agape meal, patterned on the one eucharistic meal as in 1 Cor 11:17–23, both love of God and love of neighbor as in Mt 25:31–46, both soul and body, both eternity and time, both the One and the Many. Lohmeyer writes: "future bread in that of today, and today's bread in that which is to come." See Lohmeyer, *The Lord's Prayer*, 155.

16. In the Orient it was not customary to have a daily eucharist, and hence daily bread might well refer to spiritual communion rather than primarily to a sacramental communion.

17. Stendhal, "Notes for Bible Study," 320.

18. Various Bible translations:

Twelfth-century ms.	"bred that lastes" "that holy bread that lasteth ay"
Thirteenth-century ms.	"bread . . . we craven"
John Wycliffe (1380)	"ouer othir substaunce"
William Tyndale (1525)	"dayly breade"
Rheims version (1582)	"supersubstantial bread"
Living Bible	"our food again today, as usual"
Phillips	"the bread we need for the day"
Good News Bible margin	"the food for today/tomorrow"
Jerusalem Bible margin	"necessary for subsistence" or "for tomorrow"
Revised Version margin	"our bread for the coming day"
Revised Standard Version margin	"our bread for the morrow"
New American Bible margin	"daily" or "future"
New English Bible margin	"our bread for the morrow"
New Swedish Bible	"the bread of the day to come"

19. In the West, Tertullian also prefers "spiritual bread," and Ambrose, following Origen, reads "the bread of eternal life."

20. Many contemporary commentators make mention of a bread that is spiritual, a bread of tomorrow's kingdom of God given to us even today.

21. Origen, *Ancient Christian Writers*, vol. 19.

22. See Caroline Walker Bynum, *Holy Feast and Holy Fast: The Religious Significance of Food to Medieval Women* (Berkeley: University of California, 1987).

23. The contemporary movie, "Babette's Feast," gives an outstanding depiction of the depth of sacramental involvement and transformation embodied in the preparation of a meal.

24. Ruskin, *The Lord's Prayer and the Church*, 206.

25.

Versions	Matthew's Lord's Prayer	Matthean Commentary (6:14)
12th-century ms.	misdedis / that misdon us	
William Tyndale	trespass / trespass	trespass
King James	debts / debtors	trespasses
Revised Standard	debts / debtors	trespasses
New English Bible	wrong done / wronged us	wrongs
Phillips	what we owe / owe to us	failures
Jerusalem	debts / in debt	failings
	Luke's Lord's Prayer	
William Tyndale	sins / treaspasseth us	
King James	sins/ indebted	
Revised Standard	sins / indebted	
New English Bible	sins / done us wrong	
Phillips	failures / fails us	
Jerusalem	sins / in debt to us	

26. Excerpt taken from "That Night When Joy Began," *Collected Shorter Poems 1927–57* (New York: Random House, 1937), 47.

27. Simone Weil, *Waiting for God*, quoted without page reference in an unpublished essay on the Lord's Prayer by Helen Luke of Apple Farm Community in Three Rivers, Michigan. See Simone Weil, *Waiting for God*, trans. Emma Craufurd (New York: G. P. Putnam's Sons, 1951), 223.

28. Helen Luke, unpublished manuscript.

29. This text in Luke is not found in the earliest and best manuscripts. See the footnote to this passage in the New American Bible.

30. Manson, "The Lord's Prayer," 109.

31. Sebastian Moore, *The Crucified Jesus is No Stranger* (New York: Seabury, 1981), 88.

32. C. F. D. Moule in "'. . . as we forgive . . .': A Note on the Distinction between Deserts and Capacity in the Understanding of Forgiveness," in *Donum Gentilicium: New Testament Studies in Honour of David Daube*, ed. E. Bammel, C. K. Barrett, and W. D. Davies (Oxford: Clarendon Press, 1978), 74. See also *Évangile selon Saint Luc*, translation and commentary by Albert Valensin and Joseph Huby, in *Verbum Salutis*, III (Paris: Beauchesne and Sons, 1952), 144–151.

33. Max Zerwick and Mary Grosvenor, *A Grammatical Analysis of the New Testament* (Rome: Biblical Institute Press, 1981), 203, and *Biblical Greek*, trans. Joseph Smith (Rome: Scripta Pontifici Instituti Biblici, 1963), 145.

34. Phillip Van Linden, *The Gospel of Luke and Acts* (Wilmington, Del.: Glazier, 1986), 109 and 126.

35. Thirtle, *The Lord's Prayer*, 259. See also pp. 132–144, especially 136–139, and 256–261.

36. Samuel T. Lachs, "On Matthew 6:12," *Novum Testamentum* 17 (1975): 6–8.

37. Karl Barth, *Prayer*, 2nd ed., trans. Sara Terrien (Philadelphia: Westminster, 1985), 77.

38. Origen, *Ancient Christian Writers*, vol. 19.

39. Carmignac, *A L'Écoute du Notre Père*, 58–86. See also Geoffrey Willis, "Lead us Not into Temptation," *Downside Review* 93 (1975): 281–288. The Greek verb, *eistherein*, (lead us) is cast in the aorist tense, subjunctive mood, with a negative. It is considered the equivalent, however, of a positive imperative: do not lead us. Jean Carmignac in his study of Qumran texts points out that the syntax of verb negatives in Hebrew and Aramaic permits the *not* to modify *into temptation* rather than the verb *lead*. Thus the sentence might read: "lead us (to enter) not into temptation." Carmignac offers this translation into French: "Garde-nous de consentir à latentation," which might be translated: keep us from consenting to temptation. The Spanish of the Lord's Prayer captures something of this wording: "Y no nos dexes caer en la tempta-

cion," which might be translated, "do not allow us to fall into temptation."

40. G. E. Duffield, ed., *The Work of William Tyndale* (Philadelphia: Fortress, 1965), 262. The text is taken from Tyndale's "Commentary on the Gospel of Matthew."

41. See the footnote to this passage in the *New American Bible.*

42. The *New English Bible* translates *peirasmos* in both Matthew and Luke: "Do not bring us to the test." The *New Jerusalem Bible* and the *Revised English Bible* translate *peirasmos* in both Matthew and Luke "Do not put us to the test." The *New American Bible* translates *peirasmos* in both Matthew and Luke: "Do not subject us to the final test." The *New Revised Standard Version* has "And do not bring us to the time of trial."

43. Stendhal, "Notes for Bible Study," 337.

44. A good explanation of this matter is found in Leonardo Boff, *The Lord's Prayer: The Prayer of Integral Liberation,* trans. Theodore Morrow (Maryknoll, N.Y.: Orbis, 1983), 132, footnote 113. In English evil is not related to the (d)evil, as French *mal* (evil) is related to *malin* (the evil one). The derivation of evil stems from Anglo-Saxon roots surrounding the preposition *up* or *over,* with the sense of trespassing or transgressing. The word *devil* is derived from the Latin *diabolus,* which in turn comes from two Greek words, *dia* and *ballein,* which can be translated literally *to throw across.* Interestingly, the meaning of to trespass and the meaning of to throw across would seem to share some common ground.

45. Barth, *Prayer,* 84.

46. See the Patristic bibliography for references to the Greek Patristic commentaries on the Lord's Prayer. These are all brief works, and the reader will have no difficulty locating the relevant passage.

47. Peter Chrysologus, Sermon 70, *Fathers of the Church,* vol. 17.

48. Chase, *The Lord's Prayer in the Early Church,* 166–167.

49. Boff, *The Lord's Prayer,* 112–113.

50. Delp, *Prison Meditations,* 137.

51. Helen Luke, an unpublished essay.

52. Barth, *Prayer,* 82.

53. Martin Luther, *The Small Catechism* (St. Louis: Concordia Press, 1943), 159.

54. Augustine, *Confessions,* Bk. 10.

55. Peter Chrysologus, Sermon 70, *Fathers of the Church,* vol. 17.

56. John Chrysostum, Homily on Matthew 6:9–13, cited in Adalbert Hamman, ed., *Le Pater Expliqué par les Pères* (Paris: Editions Franciscaines, 1961), 111.

57. Augustine, Sermon 58, cited in Hamman, *Le Pater Expliqué,* 152–153.

58. Hamman, *Le Pater Expliqué,* 15–17.

59. See also Jean Magne, "Répétitions de Mots and Exégèse Dans Quelques Psaumes and Le Pater," *Biblica* 39 (1958): 177–197.

60. Weil, *Waiting for God,* 226–227.

Part Four

1. Joseph Jungmann, *The Mass of the Roman Rite* (New York: Benziger, 1959), 461–470.

2. The eucharistic liturgical Latin text of the Pater, which antedates the Vulgate, does not include the Amen, which first appears in Alcuin's recension of the sacramentary in the early ninth century. See Jungmann, *Mass of the Roman Rite,* 469.

3. "Didache," 8:2–3, *Ancient Christian Writers,* no. 6.

4. Cyril of Jerusalem, "Mystagogical Catechetics," *Fathers of the Church,* vol. 64.

5. Karl Becker and Marie Peter, editors and compilers, *Our Father: A Handbook for Meditation,* trans. Ruth Mary Bethell (Chicago: Regnery, 1956), 83. The rite of St. James is an early Coptic liturgy.

6. Jungmann, *Mass of the Roman Rite,* 466.

7. "Didache," 8:2.

8. Raymond Brown, "The Pater Noster as an Eschatological Prayer," *Theological Studies* 22 (1961): 208, footnote 134.

9. Karl Barth, *Prayer According to the Catechisms of the Reformation,* adapted by A. Roulin, trans. Sara Terrien (Philadelphia: Westminster Press, 1952), 77.

10. See Jan Milic Lochman, *The Theology of Praise* (Atlanta: John Knox Press, 1982). This book is devoted to the doxology of the Lord's Prayer.

11. The eschatological reading of Matthew is favored by many commentators, such as Raymond Brown, Ernst Lohmeyer, and Leonardo Boff. I mention these scholars particularly because they represent a wide spectrum of theological endeavor.

12. Brown, "Pater Noster as an Eschatological Prayer," 208.

13. Ibid.

14. Lohmeyer, *Lord's Prayer,* 284.

BIBLIOGRAPHY OF PATRISTIC COMMENTARY IN ENGLISH ON THE LORD'S PRAYER

In this short bibliography I have listed the major works of the Greek and Latin Fathers that are readily available in English. Le Breton claimed that Patristic commentary on the Lord's Prayer was the topic earliest and most frequently taken up by these authors. For those who read French, *Le Pater Expliqué par les Pères*, edited by Adalbert Hamman (Paris: Editions Franciscaines, 1961), remains the best single-volume collection of Patristic materials devoted to the Lord's Prayer. In addition to the authors listed below, Hamman includes commentary from John Chrysostum, Theodore Mopsuestia, Ambrose of Milan, John Cassian, and others.

Three other collections of Patristic authors deserve mention. (1) *Ancient Christian Writers* [abbreviated ACW] (Westminster, Md., and New York: Newman Press). (2) *Fathers of the Church* [abbreviated FC] (New York: Fathers of the Church, Inc., and Washington: Catholic University Press). (3) *Classics of Western Spirituality* [abbreviated CWS] (Mahwah, N.J.: Paulist Press). Each of these series gives English translations and informative introductions and explanatory notes. With rare exception, one volume is dedicated to one author. Given the appropriate volume number, the treatise on the Lord's Prayer is easily found. None of these commentaries on the Lord's Prayer is lengthy. Within the treatise itself, divisions follow the several petitions of the Lord's Prayer. This arrangement allows the reader to find the relevant passage without a detailed reference.

AUTHOR	OPUS	SOURCE
GREEK PATRISTIC AUTHORS:		
Cyril of Jerusalem	"Mystagogical Catechetics"	FC 64; Hamman
Origen	"Prayer and the Lord's Prayer"	ACW 19; Hamman; CWS
Gregory of Nyssa	"The Lord's Prayer"	ACW 18; Hamman
Maximus the Confessor	"Commentary on the Our Father"	CWS

LATIN PATRISTIC AUTHORS:

Tertullian	"Prayer"	FC 40; Hamman
Cyprian of Carthage	"The Lord's Prayer"	FC 36; Hamman
Augustine	"The Sermon on the Mount"	FC 11; ACW 5; Hamman
Augustine	"Letter to Lady Proba" #130	FC 18
Peter Chrysologus	Sermons #67–72	FC 17; Hamman
Caesarius of Arles	Sermons	FC 31 & 47

BIBLIOGRAPHY OF BOOKS IN ENGLISH SINCE 1850 DEVOTED TO THE LORD'S PRAYER

The complete Paternoster book bibliography would be enormous. If articles were included they would make up yet another book. The comprehensive bibliography by Jean Carmignac in *Récherches sur le Notre Père* (Paris: Editions Letouzey, 1969) is the single most complete resource. With regard to medieval commentary on the Lord's Prayer, references in Carmignac can be found to the following authors: Alcuin, Bernard of Clairvaux, Peter Abelard, Bonaventure, Albert the Great, Thomas Aquinas, Hugh of St. Victor, Anselm of Canterbury, Alexander of Hales, Meister Eckhart, Aimon d'Auxerre, Pierre d'Ailly, Dionysius the Carthusian, Nicholas of Cusa, and Cajetan. Somewhat later commentators on the Lord's Prayer, such as William Tyndale, Martin Luther, John Calvin, Desiderius Erasmus, and the *Roman Catechism* of the Council of Trent are also referenced in Carmignac. Comprehensive Paternoster bibliography is also conveniently gathered in *Vaterunser: Bibliographie*, compiled by Monica Dorneich (Freiburg: Herder, 1982). Both Carmignac and Dorneich include titles in English. However, the English titles are only a limited selection, and the bibliographies in many of the English book commentaries on the Lord's Prayer remain useful. *Our Father: A Handbook for Meditation*, edited by Karl Becker and Marie Peter, is an ample anthology of Paternoster commentary through the centuries. To a reader of my bibliography I would recommend the following authors as the most helpful overall: Leonardo Boff, Frederick Chase, Joachim Jeremias, Ernst Lohmeyer, Henry Schurmann, Ernest Scott, James Thirtle, and Eugene LaVerdiere.

Barclay, William. *The Beatitudes and the Lord's Prayer for Every Man.* New York: Harper and Row, 1968.

———. *The Plain Man Looks at the Lord's Prayer*. Glasgow: Collins, 1964.

Barth, Karl. *Prayer*. Translated by Sara Terrien. Philadelphia: Westminster, 1985.

Becker Karl and Marie Peter, eds. *Our Father: A Handbook for Meditation.* Translated by Ruth Mary Bethell. Chicago: Regnery, 1956.

Berrigan, Daniel. *The Words Our Savior Gave Us*. Springfield, Ill.: Templegate, 1978.

Boff, Leonardo. *The Lord's Prayer: The Prayer of Integral Liberation*. Translated by Theodore Morrow. Maryknoll, N.Y.: Orbis, 1983.

Brocke, Michael and Jakob Petuchowski, eds. *The Lord's Prayer and Jewish Liturgy*. New York: Seabury, 1978.

Burney, C. F. *The Poetry of Our Lord: An Examination of the Formal Elements of Hebrew Poetry in the Discourses of Jesus Christ*. Oxford: Clarendon, 1925.

Cartwright, Colbert S. *The Lord's Prayer Comes Alive*. St. Louis: Bethany Press, 1973.

Chase, Frederick H. *The Lord's Prayer in the Early Church*. Cambridge: Cambridge University Press, 1891; reprint, Nendeln, Liechtenstein: Kraus, 1967.

Clark, Glenn. *I Will Lift Up Mine Eyes*. San Francisco: Harper and Row, 1984.

Claudel, Paul. *Lord, Teach Us to Pray*. Translated by Ruth Bethell. New York: Longmans & Green, 1948.

Crosby, Michael. *Thy Will be Done: Praying the Our Father as Subversive Activity*. Maryknoll, N.Y.: Orbis, 1977.

Dalman, Gustaf. *The Words of Jesus Considered in the Light of Post-Biblical Jewish Writings and the Aramaic Language*. Translated by D. M. Kay. Edinburgh: T. & T. Clark, 1902.

Davidson, John A. *The Lord's Prayer*. New York: World Publishing, 1970.

Delp, Alfred. *The Prison Meditations of Father Alfred Delp*. New York: Herder and Heder, 1963.

Dods, Marcus. *The Prayer that Teaches to Pray*. New Canaan, Conn.: Keats Publishing, 1980.

Ebeling, Gerhard. *The Lord's Prayer in Today's World*. Translated by James W. Leitch. London: S.C.M. Press, 1966.

Evely, Louis. *We Dare to Say Our Father*. Translated by James Langdale. New York: Herder & Herder, 1965.

Farrar, Frederic. *The Lord's Prayer: Sermons Preached in Westminster Abbey*. New York: Thomas Whittaker, 1893.

Foley, Leonard. *Slowing Down the Our Father*. Cincinnati: St. Anthony Messenger Press, 1986.

Foote, Henry W. *Thy Kingdom Come: Ten Sermons on the Lord's Prayer, Preached in King's Chapel, Boston*. Boston: Roberts Bros., 1891.

Gladden, Washington. *The Lord's Prayer: Seven Homilies*. Boston: Houghton Mifflin, 1880.

Guardini, Romano. *The Lord's Prayer*. Translated by Isabel McHugh. New York: Pantheon, 1958.

Hamman, Adalbert. *Prayer: The New Testament*. Translated by Paul Oligny. Chicago: Franciscan Herald Press, 1971.

Harner, Philip. *Understanding the Lord's Prayer*. Philadelphia: Fortress, 1975.

Hinde, Thomas. *Our Father*. New York: G. Braziller, 1976.

Hodgson, Leonard. *The Lord's Prayer: Six Sermons Preached in the Cathedral Church of Winchester during Advent and Christmastide, 1933.* New York: Longmans & Green, 1934.

Hoffmann, Oswald C. *The Lord's Prayer*. San Francisco: Harper & Row, 1982.

Jeremias, Joachim. *The Lord's Prayer*. Translated by John Reumann. Philadelphia: Fortress, 1964.

———. *Abba: The Prayers of Jesus*. Translated by John Bowden and Christoph Burchard. Philaelphia: Fortress, 1978.

Keller, Weldon Phillip. *A Layman Looks at the Lord's Prayer*. Chicago: Moody Press, 1976.

LaVerdiere, Eugene. *When We Pray: Meditations on the Lord's Prayer*. Notre Dame, Ind.: Ave Maria Press, 1983.

Laymon, Charles M. *The Lord's Prayer in its Biblical Setting*. Nashville: Abingdon, 1968.

Lochman, Jan Milic. *The Theology of Praise*. Atlanta: John Knox Press, 1982.

Lohmeyer, Ernst. *The Lord's Prayer*. Translated by John Bowden. London: Collins, 1965.

Lowe, John. *The Lord's Prayer*. Oxford: Clarendon, 1962.

Lustiger, Jean Marie. *The Lord's Prayer*. Translated by Rebecca Howell Balinski. Huntington, Ind.: Our Sunday Visitor Press, 1988.

Mangan, Celine. *Can We Still Call God "Father"? A Woman Looks at the Lord's Prayer Today*. Wilmington, Del.: Michael Glazier, 1984.

Maritain, Raïssa. *Notes on the Lord's Prayer*. Translated by Raïssa Maritain. New York: P. J. Kenedy, 1964.

Marty, Martin. *The Hidden Discipline*. Saint Louis: Concordia, 1962.

Maurice, Frederick D. *The Lord's Prayer: Nine Sermons Preached in the Chapel of Lincoln's Inn . . . 1848*. Cambridge: Macmillan, 1851.

McNabb, Vincent. *The Craft of Prayer*. Westminster, Md.: Newman Press, 1951.

McNeile, A. H. *"After This Manner Pray Ye": Studies in the Lord's Prayer*. New York: Longmans, 1917.

Palmer, George Herbert. *The Lord's Prayer*. Chicago: Pilgrim Press, 1932.

Rommel, Kurt. *Our Father Who Art in Heaven*. Philadelphia: Fortress, 1981.

Ruskin, John. *The Lord's Prayer and the Church*. In *The Complete Works of John Ruskin*. Vol. 34. Library Edition. London: George Allen, 1908.

Saphir, Adolph. *Our Lord's Pattern for Prayer*. London: J. Nisbet, 1872; reprint, Grand Rapids, Mich.: Kregel Publications 1984.

Schurmann, Henry. *Praying with Christ: The Our Father for Today*. Translated by William Ducey and Alphonse Simon. New York: Herder & Herder, 1964.

Scott, Ernest F. *The Lord's Prayer: Its Character, Purpose, and Interpretation*. New York: Scribner, 1951.

Sheed, Francis. *The Lord's Prayer: The Prayer of Jesus*. New York: Seabury, 1975.

Shriver, Donald W. *The Lord's Prayer: A Way of Life*. Atlanta: John Knox Press, 1983.

Slattery, Charles. *How to Pray: A Study of the Lord's Prayer*. New York: Macmillan, 1920.

Steuart, Robert. *The Our Father*. London: Blackfriars, 1955.

Thielicke, Helmut. *Our Heavenly Father: Sermons on the Lord's Prayer*. Translated by John Doberstein. New York: Harper & Row, 1960.

Thirtle, James. *The Lord's Prayer: An Interpretation Critical and Expository*. London: Morgan & Scott, 1915.

Tittle, Ernest. *The Lord's Prayer*. Nashville: Abingdon-Cokesbury, 1942.

Torrey, Charles. *Our Translated Gospels: Some of the Evidence*. New York: Harper, 1936.

Toth, Tihamer. *The Our Father: A Course of Sermons*. Edited by Newton Thompson. Tanslated by V. G. Agotai. St. Louis: Herder, 1943.

Trueblood, Elton. *The Lord's Prayers*. New York: Harper & Row, 1965.

Underhill, Evelyn. *Abba: Meditations Based on the Lord's Prayer*. London: Longmans, Green, 1940.

van den Bussche, Henri. *Understanding the Lord's Prayer*. Translated by Charles Schaldenbrand. New York: Sheed & Ward, 1963.

Veith, Johann Emanuel. *The Our Father: Being Illustrations of the Several Petitions of the Lord's Prayer*. Translated by Edward Cox. Boston: Patrick Donahoe, 1871.

von Harnack, Adolph. *New Testament Studies II: The Sayings of Jesus, the Second Source of St. Matthew and St. Luke*. Translated by J. R. Wilkinson. New York: Putnam, 1908.

Ward, Joseph Neville. *The Personal Faith of Jesus*. Minneapolis: Winston, 1981.

Watson, Thomas. *The Lord's Prayer*. Contained in *A Body of Practical Divinity*. Edinburgh: n.p., 1692. Revised edition, 1890; reprint, London: Banner of Truth Trust, 1965.

Weil, Simone. *Waiting for God*. Translated by Emma Craufurd. New York: Putnam, 1951.

Wilke, Richard. *Our Father*. Nashville: Abingdon, 1978.

LOURDES LIBRARY
GWYNEDD-MERCY COLLEGE
GWYNEDD VALLEY, PA 19437